GREAT DESSERTS

GREAT DESSERTS

Christian Teubner · Sybil Gräfin Schönfeldt

HAMLYN

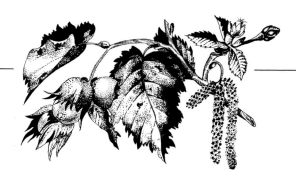

This edition published in 1983 by
Hamlyn Publishing
Astronaut House, Feltham, Middlesex, England
© Copyright Hamlyn Publishing 1983, a division of
The Hamlyn Publishing Group Limited
Third impression 1984

First published under the title
Das Grosse Buch der Desserts
© Copyright by Teubner Edition 1981

ISBN 0 600 32330 7

Set in 9½ on 10½ Monophoto Times by
Tameside Filmsetting Limited, Lancashire

Printed and bound by Graficromo s.a., Cordoba, Spain

Translated from the German by Richard and Ruth Heppel

Contents

INTRODUCTION

For many centuries now fine desserts have been one of our favourite luxuries. Although they cannot in themselves be counted among life's essentials they do play their part in our cultural history – and a fascinating and varied one at that. The first desserts were no doubt simply bowls of honey and fruit. Then, over the centuries, the arts of cooking and eating developed as an integral part of man's culture and traditions. If the other arts, whether music, drama or painting, and great traditions such as those concerned with annual feasts and celebrations, are the very stuff of a civilised society, then so also must be the creation of fine and sophisticated food.

All the familiar classic desserts, whether international or regional specialities, from cream caramel and chocolate mousse to Austrian strudel and English Christmas pudding, are here in all their variety. But this book is intended to be a collection of delicious desserts *and* a work of reference which will teach and inform in the clearest possible way. Thus you will find in each chapter a number of master recipes with step-by-step photographs showing the various stages of their preparation. These recipes at the same time provide the basis for variations, imaginative derivatives and entirely new creations. Quantities are geared to household use, but they can easily be halved or doubled if need be – except of course in the case of dishes that have to fit specific jelly, pudding and soufflé moulds.

Great Desserts has been designed to provide a solid foundation
of basic recipes and techniques as well as to inspire the reader to attempt
more creative cooking. A number of the recipes will of course demand
patience and prove more difficult to prepare than others, but this should not
be a deterrent. Rather, we should be encouraged to master them by the
inherent interest and variety of their ingredients – the exotic fruits and strange
spices and the infinite possibilities of a myriad different liqueurs and
flavourings. And then, the reward of our perseverance will be the
discovery that a fine dessert truly is the richest experience
gastronomy has to offer.

SUGAR

In the opinion of our more distant forebears, sweet foods were the prerogatives of the gods and the blessed, and to this day nectar and ambrosia epitomise the highest bliss. The first sweet dish that might just qualify as a dessert, however rudimentary its form, was probably honey gathered from wild bees. The Greeks so loved and esteemed it that they associated it with Pan and his songs, and later the bee keepers and gingerbread makers of the Middle Ages grew rich, fat and respected on it. Rendered fruit pulp was sweet too, likewise the essence of fruits preserved in wine or other forms of alcohol, as well as the soft flesh of dried grapes, figs, dates and other fruit from the sun-warmed south. For those who lived in more northern climes, sweetness cost money for transportation was a long and expensive business. Before the age of railways, this involved long and hazardous journeys by road, sailing ship and river barge, in constant danger from robbers and pirates, over land and by sea. But what a marvellous moment it must have been when a traveller returned home and unwrapped a curious spice, a jar of sweet and exotic substance or a plant which, he swore, would bear the strangest fruit.

The history of sugar really began with the crusades, since it was then that Europeans first tasted cane sugar, *Saccharum officinarum,* which had already existed in many parts of the world for thousands of years. Originally it was a native of what is now called New Guinea, where it evolved between 15000 and 8000 BC into the prime-yielding sugar cane we now know; it found its own way northwards to India, then westwards to Persia (now Iran) and eastwards across various South Sea Islands – without help or planning of any kind on the part of man. 'Reed honey' as it was called did not become familiar to European cooks until the King of Jerusalem and the Knights of Saint John and the Teutonic Order ordered sugar plantations to be laid out in the conquered Holy Land. With other hitherto unknown delicacies such as figs and pumpkins, melons, lemons, dates and oranges, cane sugar was shipped northwards by way of Venice. But, although the Arabs had improved manufacturing techniques, medieval sugar must often have had a bitter aftertaste, for the refiner's art was still in its infancy and so-called purified sugar still contained several substances that impaired its sweetness. Nor was it improved by long journeys in ships, on the backs of mules and in waggons. But it did nonetheless become more expensive owing to the many customs' tariffs imposed on it, of which the ultimate consumer naturally had to bear his share. In short, honey tasted better in comparison, everyone was used to it and it was cheaper, so sugar came to be regarded either as a medicine (for stomach ache, flatulence and obstructions of the intestinal tract), as a status symbol or as an investment.

When North America was discovered, a city such as Cologne imported 9 tons of sugar a year, and anyone who had a sugar loaf in his store cupboard was considered a man of substance. Sugar had already become what it was destined to be again and again in the course of its history: a commodity to speculate in. In the sixteenth and seventeenth centuries the price of sugar was extremely sensitive to wars, to shifts in the relationships between states, to changes in the areas of its cultivation and in trade routes. It fell so low in the period of poverty and want during and after the Thirty Years War that the sugar industry only began to yield sizeable profits as the result of scientific methods of cultivation introduced in the Dutch and French West Indies in the seventeenth and eighteenth centuries.

It was then that the craft of confectioner, or 'sugar baker' came into being. In Prussia, sugar refineries were established by the Great Elector, but in the neighbouring states smuggling was rife and the Hapsburg Emperor Charles VI was obliged to revoke privileges he had already bestowed on his Netherlands dominions because England and Holland would otherwise have objected and thus probably prevented Maria Theresa from becoming heir to his throne. But gradually all the states and free cities set up their own sugar refineries and the well-dried sugar loaf, wrapped in blue paper, had its place in every properly furnished pantry. But the raw material still came from the 'sugar islands' and,

In North America the Indians tapped the maple tree to obtain sugar from the sap, the best-known exponents of this being the Iroquois. The sap ran at the onset of spring, and with it the Indians hailed the awakening of nature. To this day in the United States and Canada life would not be sweet without maple syrup.

when the celebrated slave rebellion in Santo Domingo forced up prices and shortly afterwards Napoleon I's continental system caused sugar to become scarce again, people began to experiment with sugar production in Europe itself. New attempts were made to grow sugar cane, and ways of obtaining sugar from the maple tree or the corncob after the methods of the Red Indians were eagerly investigated. But the great breakthrough came with the experiments of a Berlin pharmacist called Markgraf. He discovered the sweetening power of the beet, boiled its sap down to a syrup, and from this obtained a 'salt' that was indistinguishable from cane sugar. He reported his discovery in 1747 to the Berlin Academy but was apparently not interested in its practical application and Frederick the Great seems to have been otherwise preoccupied at the time. So it was another Berlin chemist, Franz Karl Achard and another Prussian king, Frederick William III, who eventually started up the sugar beet industry which today is responsible for half the world's total sugar production.

Sugar Cane and Sugar Beet

You cannot identify by taste which plant produced the sugar you use for sweetening coffee or making desserts: the sugar cane or the sugar beet. In either case it is saccharose, identical in chemistry and to the palate. Each, moreover, has roughly a half share of the world market, with cane marginally ahead of beet. Cultivation and processing are very largely mechanised, at any rate in those countries in which sugar is produced from beet. In the case of sugar, grown mostly in the developing countries, methods of cultivation and harvesting are certainly still found which correspond with those described in the colonial days: sharpening the machete and wielding it by hand on the sugar canes, one at a time. An expert can harvest up to 3 tons a day, depending on whether the ground is level or hilly, and the canes are then bundled and carried on muleback in loads of up to 200 kg/420 lb to the nearest track that will take a tractor. It is hard work, especially in the humid heat of these tropical territories.

Sugar: White, Dark Brown and Those in Between

The simple distinction we make between brown and white sugar ignores a whole series of intermediate varieties. Not all of these are important for making desserts, but some of the dark ones in particular can be used to impart a special flavour. Sugar crystals are naturally colourless even though through refraction they appear white to us. When sugar is extracted from the cane or the beet other vegetable matter passes into the juice and this is to a large extent filtered out. But, although partially purified, the juice still contains components which are only separated from it through the thickening of the juice itself, which causes the sugar to crystallise. Nevertheless, the syrupy residue (molasses) cannot be completely removed by centrifugal force but clings in some measure to the crystals. At this stage it is raw sugar or brown sugar and its colour and taste are characterised by the greater or lesser amount of this clinging residue. Further washing and refining turn this raw sugar into the familiar 'refined sugar' which is the kind most used in the making of desserts. Moist, brown sugar used to be shunned as an inferior product by all except the gingerbread makers and tea drinkers, who liked its very typical flavour (in sugar candy form). Nowadays these richly flavoured sugars have been rediscovered and are used, not only in Irish Coffee but also to add their particular depth of sweetness to sauces and creams.

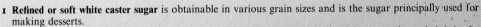

1 **Refined or soft white caster sugar** is obtainable in various grain sizes and is the sugar principally used for making desserts.
  Icing sugar is caster sugar ground very fine and is used when a quick-dissolving sugar is needed; it is also ideal for icing and decorating.
2 **White lump sugar** is made by pressing caster sugar. It is rubbed over the zest of citrus fruits to extract their aromatic oil for a sweet sauce.
3 **Brown lump sugar** is made by pressing brown sugar and is popular in England and France as a coffee sweetener.
4 **Sugarloaf.** This traditional shape comes from crystallising refined sugar, but today is used only for making claret cup.
5 **White sugar candy** is obtained by slow crystallisation from a pure sugar solution and can be bought in various sizes.
6 **Brown sugar candy** takes its colour from the brown sugar out of which it is made, but it can be found in various shades.
7 **Brown sugar** is raw sugar which, especially in this country, comes in various shades of brown.
8 **Demerara sugar** is one of the many kinds of brown sugar with relatively large granules.
9 **Preserving sugar** is, as its name suggests, ideal for making preserves and jams. Its crystals dissolve readily and give the clearest possible results.

From a Light Syrup to a Caramel

Although sugar is chiefly used in the form of crystals, such as white caster or icing sugar, for dessert recipes, many of these call for a liquid form. Sugar syrup (clarified sugar) has a great variety of uses in sauces, fruit ices, sorbets and many other recipes, and it therefore pays to have some in stock; the pastry cook always keeps it handy. 'Clarified sugar' is an obsolete term dating back to the time when refined sugar was unknown and the syrup had to be 'cleared' or clarified with egg white – an unnecessary process nowadays, but the name still persists.

Sugar Boiling

The refined sugar must first be mixed with water, the quantity depending on the intensity desired. This mixture is then brought to the boil in a copper pan with occasional stirring so that the sugar dissolves evenly. Once the solution has boiled it must not be stirred any more, otherwise it may crystallise or, as the experts would have it, 'die'. The whole process depends on forestalling this, and hence the sugar crystals forming around the edge of the pan must be constantly removed with a wet brush. When cooking with gas – which is recommended because it is easy to regulate – the flame should not be turned up so high that it appears around the sides of the pan.

The thickness of the syrup, that is the proportion of sugar to water, is dictated by the purpose for which it is to be used. To avoid unnecessary boiling, only the prescribed amount of water should be used. The table opposite tells you what this is, and also shows the temperature appropriate to each kind of syrup. Except in the case of clarified sugar, the simplest way to measure the density is with a thermometer – indirectly, that is, by way of the temperature. If no sugar thermometer is available, old-fashioned testing methods can be used, but these are not very accurate, nor are they particularly easy or hygienic to use.

Sugar Syrup

This is the most important kind of boiled sugar for dessert making. The density of sugar syrup or clarified sugar cannot be accurately measured by the temperature and accordingly a saccharometer (Araometer) is used for this, showing the degree of concentration on the Baumé scale. But it must be remembered that this instrument gives lower readings at high temperature than when the syrup is cold. However, if a saccharometer is not available, syrup can also be boiled in accordance with the following instructions which are certain to produce the correct result, provided that the directions given are strictly followed.

Light syrup
Boil 500 g/18 oz sugar with 1 litre/1¾ pints water for 1 minute. This makes about 1.2 litres/2¼ pints syrup measuring 17° Baumé when hot. When cooled it would register about 20° Baumé.

Medium syrup
Boil 500 g/18 oz sugar with 750 ml/1¼ pints water for 1 minute. This makes about 1 litre/1¾ pints syrup measuring 21° Baumé when hot, 24° Baumé when cold.

The sugar syrup recipe in the table opposite makes a concentrated syrup which is ideal for the store cupboard and with its heavy consistency and density of 30–32° Baumé corresponds to the clarified sugar of old. It can also be thinned with water when the recipe calls for a less concentrated syrup, but the density will then need to be checked with the saccharometer.

Finally, a word about sugar colouring, the concluding stage of the boiling process. It is now caramel, having been heated to over 180 C/350 F, that is to say, burnt. Hot water is then added and it is brought to the boil again. This dark brown syrup, which incidentally no longer has a sweet taste, is used to give colour to custards and similar desserts.

It is essential to keep the rim of the pan clean. Splashes of syrup cling firmly to it and crystallise, and this process would be transferred to the liquid, thereby adversely affecting the consistency of the resulting syrup. They must therefore be loosened and washed off with a damp brush and this should be repeated every few minutes until the syrup has reached the desired temperature.

Glucose syrup is a viscid starch-sugar, not to be confused with glucose (grape sugar). It does help a little to prevent the sugar from crystallising (dying) while being boiled. Should you feel the need, add about 25 g/1 oz to 500 g/18 oz sugar. The only problem is that glucose is almost impossible to buy retail, but should you know a fine baker or confectioner one or the other might well be able and willing to help out.

Sugar syrup/Clarified sugar Boil 500 g/18 oz sugar with 500 ml/17 fl oz water for 1 minute. The thermometer reads 102 C/220 F and the saccharometer 28° Baumé (hot) and 30–32° Baumé (cold). This will make about 900 ml/1½ pints all-purpose syrup for ices, sorbets and sauces, and is the ideal consistency for a stock syrup.

Thread Boil 500 g/18 oz sugar with 250 ml/8 fl oz water to 106 C/223 F. To test: moisten the index finger and thumb with water and take a small pinch of syrup from the spoon. When the thumb and finger are opened and closed rapidly a 'short' thread is formed. If boiling is continued to 113 C/236 F a 'long' thread can be drawn. This highly concentrated syrup is used for fruit bottling and jam making.

Feather Boil 500 g/18 oz sugar with 250 ml/8 fl oz water to 112 C/234 F. Test by blowing cautiously through a small wire skewer which has been dipped in the syrup; small bubbles should form. If boiling is continued to 116 C/240 F a strong puff should cause large bubbles or a cluster of bubbles to appear. This density is called soft ball and is used for fondant or Italian meringue.

Firm Ball or Bullet Boil 500 g/18 oz sugar with 250 ml/8 fl oz water to a temperature of 118–121 C/224–250 F. Test by wetting the thumb and index finger in iced water, taking a little of the syrup from the spoon and plunging it straight into the iced water; it should be easy to roll it into a ball. Use for caramel or toffee.

Soft crack Boil 500 g/18 oz sugar with 250 ml/8 fl oz water to about 140 C/275 F. A little of the sugar poured into iced water should harden at once but still stay a little sticky. The more it is boiled after this the harder it will get and at about 153–155 C/305 310 F it has reached the 'hard crack' stage and is no longer sticky. Sugar boiled to crack is used for glazing fruits, for spun sugar and for making cake decorations.

Caramel Boil 500 g/18 oz sugar with 80 ml/3 fl oz water. At 160 C/320 F the sugar begins to brown and the colour can be deepened by further boiling up to about 180 C/350 F. Light brown caramel is used for making nut brittle or praline and for glazing pastries and puffs, and a slightly darker one for Crème Caramel. Caramel can also be made by melting the sugar without any water. Melt about one-third of the required quantity, stirring continuously, and dissolve the rest in it by degrees.

ALL THE WORLD'S FRUITS

From garden varieties to the rarest of tropical species

Since the beginning of time fruits have been available in variety and abundance, featuring in all accounts of the Garden of Eden and the Elysian fields, and in literature and legend from the tales of Pliny to Grimms' Fairy Stories. Some, like the golden apples of the Hesperides (probably, some scholars now tell us, the quince) promise eternal youth while others, like the fruit of the tree of knowledge of good and evil, entice us to sin. Somehow, fruits have always been around, as if created for our express benefit, waiting ripe and ready for the eating. They were the world's first convenience food and although even the early Greek and Roman writers do include them as components of meat and fish dishes (an idea which, interestingly, the Nouvelle Cuisine chefs have rediscovered for us) traditionally, fruits bring a meal to its end. Presented at their simplest or in the most sophisticated guise, it is upon fruit that the delicious flavour of most great desserts depends.

The ubiquitous apple, always available and ready to be turned to a thousand uses, from a warm crisp apple strudel to a simple fruit salad, has to be the founding fruit of our collection, if one of them must be singled out. The citrus family, also vast, and infinitely versatile, lends its subtle bite to sorbets, creams, soufflés and a variety of sauces. The berry fruits, from the exquisite wild strawberry to the more robust blackberry, give their unique flavour to our high summer and early autumn tarts. The stone fruits, from juicy plum to delicate cherry, lend their own luscious sweetness to compotes, preserves and pies. The truly exotic species, such as the passion fruit, the mango and their peers, owe their appearance in Europe, more often than not, to voyages of exploration or to royal patronage. For example, a charming portrait of Charles II shows him being proudly presented with the first pineapple raised in England by his gardener, John Rose. Georg Meister, Keeper of the Pleasure Grounds by gracious warrant to His Serene Highness the Elector of Saxony, in the course of his journeyings abroad became acquainted with the flowers, trees and fruits of India, Indonesia and Japan. He prepared drawings and detailed descriptions of everything he found, including the durian, mangosteen, pawpaw, coconut and many other species of fruit that are still relatively unfamiliar to us today.

It was the curiosity and perseverance of well-placed pioneers such as these that led the way for the cultivation in the temperate northern climates of Europe and the Americas of the exotic fruits, and in turn inspired that wider interest which the steamships of the Victorian age were to try to satisfy, at least as far as the wealthy were concerned. Today, air communication, advanced cold storage and deep-freeze technology, combined with our vastly increased knowledge of the exotic fruits of this earth, means that few of them remain undiscovered and the majority of them are available. With most varieties to choose from, you can make a passion fruit soufflé, a mango compote or a kiwi sorbet almost as easily as you would the more familiar delights such as a cherry clafoutis or a rum baba. The following pages will open your eyes to just a few of the many possibilities the world's fruits have to offer.

Exotic fruits can go wonderfully well with the more everyday varieties from your own garden – in a fruit salad, for example, piled inside a hollowed-out water-melon which, with a little ingenuity, can be turned into a fruit basket. Cut two segments out of the melon in such a way that an upright strip is left as a handle. Then the rim of the basket can be decoratively shaped with a semicircular scoop.

Why preserve your own fruit?

Opinions differ. Our grandparents' simple method of preserving fruit is no longer relevant, because commercial preserves are now so various, good and relatively inexpensive that home preserving is, for the most part, no longer worth the trouble.

What makes home preserving so attractive to the home cook, the gourmet and even the budget-conscious is that, whatever may be said for modern industrial methods of preserving, the fruit processed in the factory is seldom of top quality. Not even the most expensive jam or marmalade can match those made in small quantities with first-class fruits and following individual recipes. These are the two main reasons why, for the confectioner and for the housewife too, preserving can certainly save money as well, particularly if she does not include the cost of her own work. Individual fruits in season can be bought at their peak and preserved to special recipes by a variety of methods: for example, canning, bottling, freezing, in syrup or in alcohol.

Another very good preserving idea is to make fruit liqueurs, extending the principle of sloe gin with which most of us are already familiar. Fruits which are by their nature tender – raspberries for example – you can quite simply put into a preserving jar and top with a mixture of your chosen spirit and sugar in the proportion of two parts to one. Firmer fruits should be poached in syrup first.

Home-preserved fruit makes perfect sense. It guarantees a year-round choice of first-class fruit that can be used to create distinctive desserts economically, particularly when the fruit can be served out of season.

If it's tropical, preserve it yourself

Apart from the cost – for most of them are still quite expensive – tropical fruits can really only be processed at home. Not surprisingly, they are rarely used in commercial jams. But the same does not hold good for the commoner fruits, most of which are commercially canned or bottled to a very high standard: there would certainly be no sense in bottling expensive fresh figs, for example. It is occasionally useful to freeze tropical fruits, and by no means difficult in the case of those kinds which contain relatively little water.

In jam and marmalade making, on the other hand, there are immense opportunities for experimenting with tropical fruits either by themselves or mixed with other fruits. Mixing them with cheaper, less exotic kinds results not only in new, original and subtle flavours but also in a more reasonably priced jam. Moreover, using your own recipes gives you far more freedom to vary the end product, both in quantity and flavour. The possibilities for making use of such preserves are almost unlimited, whether they be plain bottled fruit, fine preserves or the most exclusive varieties steeped in alcohol. These can all be used in a wide range of desserts and sauces. No factory product can match what you make at home, or the combinations of flavours you yourself devise.

Deep-freezing, too, can be applied in quite new ways. In particular, individual berries of soft fruit in season, such as blackberries and red currants, may be frozen on the stalk, to be thawed and used as a decoration later. Wild berries, always in demand, also keep well in the freezer.

Rhubarb

The word 'rhubarb' is derived from the Greek *rha barbaron*, meaning 'stranger from the Rha' (a river known to us as the Volga), because the fruit came to Europe via its waters. According to ancient documents, rhubarb was known as a medicine in China about 5000 years ago. From there it found its way to Russia. The Greeks – or, more properly the Scythians – discovered it and brought it southwards. We treat rhubarb as a fruit although botanically speaking it is a vegetable because it is structured like the crown of a herbaceous plant. There are three groups, distinguished according to the colour of the stem and its flesh: 1. Stem and flesh both green; 2. Stem red, flesh green; 3. Stem and flesh both red.

Rhubarb is rich in vitamins, minerals and above all malic and citric acid, which makes it one of our purest natural medicines. Indeed, it was only at the beginning of the nineteenth century that rhubarb began to be enjoyed rather than merely administered to invalids and sickly children. The English can take the credit for this change of heart, for it was they who taught the rest of Europe how good rhubarb tarts and jams can taste. The addition of ginger, cinnamon, orange juice and rind will lessen its acidity, but there is little reason to do so, for it is that quality which makes a rhubarb dessert such an ideal end to a rich or heavy meal. Besides being used in cakes and tarts, rhubarb makes delicious creams, compotes, jams – and even wine.

Rhubarb's main season runs from April to September, but do choose wisely. Unlike many another fruit, (but quite compatible with its vegetable nature) it is only worth eating when young, at most adolescent. Mature rhubarb is coarse and too acid in flavour to be enjoyable. If you grow rhubarb, and cannot eat all your crop at the right stage, remember that it freezes well.

Name: rhubarb (*Rheum raponticum, Polygonaceaa* family). **Where from:** native of China. **Form:** long-stemmed herbaceous plant with large lobate leaves. **Colour:** shades of green and red. **Where cultivated:** in temperate climate, in deep, rich soil.

Wild Fruits

Sometimes brilliantly colourful, sometimes small and unpretentious, often perplexing in their variety, wild fruits were, for a long time, almost totally neglected. But their qualities and superb flavour are again winning for them the respect and attention of serious cooks.

The buckthorn (*Rhamnacae alaternus*) comes from Asia although it has been known in Europe for centuries. But it was only realised in 1940 that the fruit possessed an extremely high vitamin C content. The orange-yellow to red berries grow on a thorn bush with narrow, silvery leaves and form dense clusters around the stems. They ripen in the autumn and if eaten raw are rather sour but buckthorn juice and buckthorn purée are delicious in a dessert.

Rose hips are the fruit of the wild, or dog, rose (*Rosa canina*). The red, usually elongated, berries ripen in the autumn and are rich in vitamins. They should be picked after the first frost but care must be taken to remove completely all the many little hairy seeds which lurk inside because if touched they make the skin itch disagreeably. After de-seeding, the fruit can be made into rose hip purée, jam, wine or cordial.

The blackberry is perhaps *the* quintissential wild fruit, at its best equal in flavour to any of the cultivated soft fruits from the garden. For many of us their taste is no doubt intensified by their association with the best of country life – wild hedgerows, fresh northern air, long, late-summer walks with scones and blackberry jelly waiting for us at the end. They could be said to be the most amenable of all berries, available absolutely free of charge and adaptable to almost any treatment: on their own with cream, they are an unbeatable simple pudding; with muesli they will make any breakfast time; they add an edge to apple (or any other fruit for that matter) compotes and pies; and, as if all this were not enough, they make a fine sauce for duck and game.

Blackberries, raspberries, rose hips, buckthornberries, cranberries, elderberries and sloes are nature's own gift to us, treasures which we only have to accept gracefully and turn into our own particular culinary delights. Wild berries are not only prime sources of vitamins and minerals but they also possess the freshness and the flavour of the forests and hedgerows. Drinks, compotes, purées and delicious *eaux-de-vie* (like those made from the blackberry and the sloe), blackberry cordial, rose hip syrup, elderberry wine and the sparkling elder champagne – these are only a few of the ways in which we can enjoy those wild fruits which are ours literally for the taking.

Garden Strawberry

There are now more than 1000 varieties of the garden strawberry (*Fragaria ananasa*, a member of the *Rosaceae* family). It is descended from crossings between the scarlet strawberry and the large Chilean strawberry. In France it bears the name of Commander Frezier, who introduced it there in the mid-eighteenth century. In England it was first grown commercially in the 1820s, although it was already being raised privately a century before. Imported early strawberries are, surprisingly perhaps, full of flavour, but once the season has really begun there is no finer treat than English strawberries served with thick Jersey cream. Out of season, the frozen fruit makes a good sauce or a base for soufflés and ice cream.

White Currant

These white, sour-sweet tasting berries (*Ribes album*) have little commercial importance, but they do have their enthusiasts. Like their red and black relations, they are rich in vitamin C and fruit acids, but not at all easy to grow or process. Laxton's No 1 and White Versailles are two well-known varieties. At their best in July and August, white currants make good jellies, jams and unfermented juice.

Wild Strawberry

The true wild strawberry (*Fragaria vesca*, from the *Rosaceae* family) now deserves more than ever the title 'Queen of fruits' which the Roman poets Virgil and Ovid gave it so long ago. Its glorious flavour has endured through the centuries. But sadly, those we can buy are more likely to be alpine strawberries, which are cultivated and therefore haven't the same excellence of flavour and bouquet as the wild variety. Remember too, when choosing, that a large, good-looking fruit is no guarantee of fine flavour. And incidentally, what we regard as the fruit is really only the fleshy base of the flower, on which the actual fruit – consisting of numerous tiny seeds – is set.

Redcurrant

A native of Europe and Asia, this small, round red berry (*Ribes rubrum*) grows in bunches like grapes and has a sweet yet sharp taste. Two popular varieties are Laxton's No 1 and Red Lake. Like the white currant, the fruit is gathered in June and July and used chiefly to make syrup, jelly, jam, unfermented juice and redcurrant wine.

Black Currant

The black currant (*Ribes nigrum*) is the richest of all berries in vitamin C. The berries have a bitterish, tart flavour and not everyone likes to eat them raw. Two fine varieties are Laxton's Giant and the late-cropping Baldwin. In France the best blackcurrants flourish in the Dijon area, where they are used for making the well-known liqueur, Crème de Cassis – sometimes labelled Crème de Dijon. They are also much esteemed for their syrup, unfermented juice, purée, jam and jelly.

Gooseberry

The gooseberry originally comes from the western Himalayas and from southern Europe. Today it is widely distributed throughout the temperate zones. When ripe, the gooseberry has, after the grape, the highest sugar content of any domestic berry. The round, polyspermous berries are subdivided according to colour into yellow, red and green varieties and also into hairy or smooth-skinned types. The most popular garden gooseberry is Careless, which bears large green berries, and Whinham's Industry is a vigorous, dark red variety. Gooseberries make a fine summer fool, compotes and jams as well as an excellent wine.

Raspberry

This delicious fruit (*Rubus idaeus*) comes from Asia and Europe and will grow wild in any temperate climate. The cone-shaped berries are made up of numerous small fruits, and the garden varieties are protected by their thorns. Of course, the wild raspberry tastes – and is – better and is richer in vitamins, minerals and fruit acids than the cultivated variety and the higher up they grow the better they will be. Scottish raspberries are considered to be the finest in the world, for the northern summer suits them to perfection. Culinary uses for the raspberry are unlimited, although they are probably best appreciated when eaten just as they are, with cream and sugar.

Blackberry

Popularly known in the north of England and Scotland as the bramble, but botanically named *Rubus laciniatus*, the blackberry, like the raspberry, is made up of clusters of tiny berries. One of the finest native fruits, wild and cultivated blackberries can be found in most temperate climates; both kinds have an excellent flavour and are high in vitamin and mineral content. The dark, reddish-black fruits, which the Greeks call 'Titans blood', grow all over the world, but best and most plentifully in northern countries. They ripen in late summer and, for culinary purposes, are almost as versatile as the raspberry.

Cranberry

Oxycoccus macrocarpus is the botanical name for this large berry developed in America. It is rich in vitamins and minerals and is used in the same way as the cowberry. These two fruits are distinguished not only by their relatively large size but also by the shape of the blossom, the cowberry having a crenate crown and the cranberry a disc like the whortleberry. The European cranberry is a smaller fruit of a different species, *Oxycoccus palustris*, and is cultivated principally in Holland, Poland, the north of England and Scotland. They need to be cooked in order to bring out their full flavour, and they make a loud 'pop' when they burst.

Whortleberry

Also known as the bilberry or blaeberry, the ripened, blue-black berries of *Vaccinium myrtillus* are rich in vitamins and minerals. They are found mostly in Europe and northern parts of Asia. They tend to grow on high, deserted ground and this, added to the difficulty of picking them, has prevented them ever becoming popular in these islands. In France, however, it is quite a different story. There the berries are made into jams, liqueurs, sorbets, delicious tarts and other sweets. Cultivated wortleberries, though larger than the wild variety and perhaps more attractive to look at, cannot be compared with the latter for flavour.

Cowberry

This berry has entertaining nicknames: screwberry, hackberry, foxberry and cronesberry are but a few. Officially known as *Vaccinium Vitis-idaea*, these spherical, red berries grow on heaths, moorlands and sunny slopes and in upland forest clearings. They are rich in vitamin C, have a sourish, astringent taste, can withstand frost and ripen in August and September. It is only with cooking that their flavour develops, and are not good when eaten raw. Cowberries are found in the Upper Palatinate and the Bavarian Mountains and are also exported from Scandinavia. The aromatic little cowberry should not be confused with the big American cultivated cranberry.

Elderberry

The elder tree (*Sambucus nigra*) is in fact a bush that grows wild in Europe, western Asia and north Africa along the edges of woods, in hedgerows and by the roadside, but it is also cultivated, mainly in Denmark and Austria. Its round, black berries hang on umbellate stalks and are valuable sources of fruit acids and minerals and thus used also for medicinal purposes. The sprays of fruit are cut from September through to November. The flowers are used as an infusion to flavour other fruit preserves (particularly gooseberry, for which they have a special affinity). The berries are turned into syrup, juice, elderberry wine and brandy.

Cherry Time

In this country cherries are available from May right through to August. The cherry is a stone fruit and originally came from Assyria and Babylonia, where it was first cultivated. The Romans were already acquainted with wild cherries and in 74 BC, when returning from a Black Sea campaign, the Roman general Lucullus brought sweet cherry saplings back with him to Italy.

The cherry gets its name from the seaport town of Kerasos, whence the Romans brought it home with them. The cultivation of cherries soon spread to the rest of Europe and within some 200 years cherry trees were thriving on the banks of the Rhine, in Britain and in northern Europe generally.

Cherries are a valuable source of vitamins. They contain vitamins A, B, and C as well as potassium, phosphorus and iron. Sour cherries also contain vitamin A. The numerous varieties are divided into two main groups, the sweet cherry (*Prunus avium*) and the sour (*Prunus cerasum*), with a group of hybrid cherries, the Dukes, which fall somewhere between the two.

These indispensable and undeniable facts apart, the cherry is one of our choicest fruits. Its gloss, roundness and lusciousness, together with its arrival (in May) make it the perfect herald of summer's harvest of fruits.

The Sweet Cherry

This variety comes in a wide range of colours: dark, that is going from red through brown to black; bi-coloured, which is red on a pale background; and all yellow. Among the best-known varieties are Black Heart, Bigarreau Napoleon and Merton Favourite. Of the three groups of cherries – sweet, sour and hybrid – the sweet will obviously be the best for eating fresh from the bough, but they can also be used for cooking. Although of course not at all as valuable for this purpose as, say, the Morello, with a sharpening of lemon juice, and the reduction, or elimination, of sugar they do very well.

The Sour Cherry

This kind of cherry is either light or dark red and there are two main groups, consisting of tree and bush varieties. Examples of the tree sour cherry are Morello and Kentish Red, a bright red cerasus – as its name implies – with a most aromatic flavour. Bush sour cherries include Ludwig's Early and the Amarasca cherry from Dalmatia (once part of the Venetian Republic but now in Yugoslavia), which has a particularly subtle fragrance and is the best for making the well-known liqueur, Maraschino.

Hybrid cherries are crosses between sweet and sour varieties. The best known, and also the finest, are May Duke and Royal Duke.

The Uses of Cherries

For most purposes the sweet varieties are the more generally used. For home use they are bottled (that is, sterilised) and later turned into compotes, and tarts. In the factory they might also be stoned and preserved as candied fruit, jam, unfermented juice, dessert wine and kirsch. Commercially produced sour cherries are more usually turned into syrup, dessert wine and cherry brandy, if not frozen, canned or bottled.

Name: sweet cherry (*Prunus avium*); sour cherry (*Prunus cerasus*). **Origin:** Caucasia. **Shape:** round to heart shaped. **Colour:** black, red, yellow and shades of yellow and red. **Where cultivated:** in almost all temperate zones, especially in Europe (particularly Germany and Italy) and North America.

Sweet and sour cherries, a few members of a large family. **1.** A bright red sweet variety with creamy flesh, Merton Glory. **2.** One of the diversely coloured cherry varieties, Kent Bigarreau. **3.** Black Heart, a soft-fruiting sweet variety. **4.** Kentish Red, a sour variety suitable for cooking.

Two splendid examples of the dark red Morello cherry, which belongs to the sour cherry group.

Fruits of the Sun. Apricots, Peaches and Nectarines

These fragrant, juicy fruits with velvety or smooth skins are all stone fruits. They also share the same environmental needs in that they require a mild, warm climate and are extremely sensitive to frost. Accordingly, apart from a few areas in Germany, they are mainly cultivated in Spain, France (particularly Roussillon and the Rhône valley) and other Mediterranean countries, as well as Austria, south-east Europe, Israel, Australia, South Africa, North and South America. These very popular fruits have a great many uses, whether fresh or canned, in making desserts, pastries and cakes, or jams, preserves, cordials and wines. Even their stones are valuable: the kernels can be used to make liqueurs, or a paste – persipan – similar to marzipan, or an oil similar to almond oil.

Apricots first came to Europe from Asia in the time of Alexander the Great (about 330 BC), and until the end of the 17th century their golden-yellow fruits were thought to be early peaches. Their name can thus be traced back to the latin *praecox* meaning 'early ripe'. They are rich in vitamins A and C and calcium, phosphorus and iron. The most popular varieties are the Italian Ambrosia and the French Nancy, but by far the most popular – and also the best – English apricot is the Moor Park. It is interesting to note that over half of the total world exports come from Spain, France and Hungary, and that two-thirds go to West Germany and Switzerland. Fresh apricots are shipped from Spain, France and south-east Europe, canned ones from Australia and South Africa, and dried apricots from California, Turkey and Iran.

Peaches, Peregrine variety. This most reliable peach with an excellent flavour ripens in August. The yellow flesh comes away easily from the stone and is suitable for preserving in syrup. The depressed seam is well illustrated here.

An early-ripening, white-fleshed peach. These have a stronger taste than the yellow-fleshed varieties, although the latter are more popular on account of their more luscious appearance. In Italy the leaves are taken off the trees before these early peaches are harvested to expose them to full sunlight so that they will take on more colour.

The fragrant, velvety peach appeals to us no less than the apricot and nectarine. It was long supposed that this favourite summer fruit came from ancient Persia (hence its Latin name *malum persicum*, meaning Persian apple), but more recent research assigns it to China.

Whatever the truth may be, this delightful fruit can be troublesome to stone and so its various species are grouped accordingly: first, those with stones which are difficult to loosen are known as clingstone peaches. Early peaches are mostly cling varieties.

Name: apricot (*Prunus Armeniaca*). **Origin:** Armenia. **Shape:** round to oval; skin velvety with depressed seam. **Colour:** orange-yellow. **Size:** about the same as a plum. **Where cultivated:** in all mild, warm regions with a Mediterranean climate.

Name: peach (*Prunus Persica*). **Origin:** China. **Shape:** round; skin velvety with a more or less depressed seam. **Colour:** greenish to bright yellow, often flushed with red. **Size:** like an apple. **Where cultivated:** in all mild, warm regions with a Mediterranean climate.

Name: nectarine, belonging to the peach family. **Origin:** cross of peach with plum. **Shape:** spherical with seam; smooth-skinned with firm flesh that separates easily from stone. **Colour:** yellowish, flushed with red. **Size:** like a peach. **Where cultivated:** California, South Africa, Japan and, to a lesser extent, southern Europe.

Apricots and nectarines are hot-climate fruits. They blossom even earlier than the cherry and are in extreme danger from frost in colder latitudes. In Europe they thrive and ripen only in mild, warm areas such as those where wine is produced, and even there only in sheltered spots.

Then there are the smooth-skinned peaches: (a) nectarines with stones that come out easily, and (b) brugnoles with stones which are hard to separate from the flesh. Both of the last-named varieties are crosses of peach with plum and are distinguished not only by their smooth skins but also by somewhat firmer flesh. They are grown chiefly in South Africa, California and Japan.

Peaches and their cousins are rich in vitamins and minerals. The most important varieties are Early Rivers, a large fruit with excellent flavour, Lord Napier and Hale, an American variety. Unlike apples, however, we are unlikely to be able to buy our peaches by variety, but must rely on a good supplier to choose for us. Above all, avoid those which are soft or bruised, for this indicates an irredeamable woolly texture.

The Plum Family

With some 2000 different varieties to its name, many of which even experts can hardly tell apart, the plum˙ is a most perplexing fruit. It is, however, a fact that in character and pedigree the dark blue damson, the yellow-green greengage and the greenish-yellow mirabelle plum are subspecies of the plum family, and the European Economic Community has adopted standards accordingly.

The plum, regarded by us today as a completely European fruit, is in fact a native of the Caucasus, the region surrounding the Caspian Sea and Turkestan. Today's varieties derive mainly from cross-fertilisation carried out in the East. They can be distinguished by their colour, size and shape and whether the stone can be removed easily or not. Most plums have a plump, oval shape with rounded ends and a clearly marked seam. The colour ranges from reddish blue to deep purple. Its yellow or purplish flesh is very juicy and aromatic. In short, the plum is a first-class dessert fruit but it can also be stewed or made into jam,

deep-frozen or its juice can be bottled. Connoisseurs often preserve it in rum or make it into chutney. Its stone is rather hard to dislodge.

When choosing plums, avoid those that are bruised and/or whose skins have split or have been damaged in some way. For eating plain, it is advisable to remove the skin before consuming, if you feel acidity would upset your stomach. This is best done by pouring boiling water over them if the fruit is quite firm; the skin of ripe plums should come away quite ready without this brief blanching.

The varieties best known in England are Rivers Early Prolific, which ripens in July, the later Jefferson and Kirke's, whose richly flavoured fruit ripens in September – and, of course, the ever-popular Victoria.

The Damson

The damson's name is a shortened version of 'Damascene', that is, 'the plum from Damascus', as the crusaders called it when they brought it to Europe from Syria. In shape it is more elongated than the familiar plum, with comparatively pointed ends, and when ripe is blue rather than purple. There is no midline indentation. The damson has strongly flavoured, firm flesh that separates most readily from its stone. It is most often stewed or made into a purée but is also excellent when dried into prunes or made into plum brandy (the Yugoslavian slivovitz or the Bohemian slibowitz). The best-known English damson is the Merryweather Damson, which is very like a plum. A fine, late-harvesting variety is the Shropshire Damson, which ripens in September. Yugoslavia and Hungary are Europe's largest producers of damsons, with six fruit trees per head of population in the one and eight in the other. In winter all kinds of plums are exported from South Africa and Argentina.

The many varieties of damson and plum are often hard to tell apart. Here we have a damson which, like the Merryweather Damson, closely resembles a plum. Officially it would be adjudged a rather inperfect specimen because it has a suture and its ends are rounder than they should be. But they do taper somewhat towards the stalk end.

The Greengage is a very tender species, needing plenty of warmth and good, lightish soil. Greengage trees are very susceptible to changes in temperature and do best in a climate suitable for producing wine. Other varieties are yellow with a touch of red, or even golden yellow.

Name: plum (*Prunus domestica, Rosaceae* family). **Origin:** western Asia. **Shape:** oval with rounded ends. **Colour:** reddish-blue to purple, the skin frosted with a bloom. **Where cultivated:** Spain, Germany, North and South America, the Balkans (especially Yugoslavia and Hungary), Algeria and South Africa.

Name: damson (*Prunus oeconomica, Rosaceae* family). **Origin:** Syria. **Shape:** elongated oval, ends tapering, without perceptible suture. **Colour:** dark blue, with a silvery bloom. **Where cultivated:** as plum.

Name: greengage (*Prunus instititia* var. *italica*). **Shape:** spherical. **Colour:** green or greenish-yellow with a touch of red. **Where cultivated:** North America, throughout West Germany, particularly in wine-growing areas, France and England.

Name: mirabelle (*Prunus syriaca*). **Origin:** Syria. **Shape:** spherical, smaller than the plum. **Colour:** yellow with a red flush or small red speckles. **Where cultivated:** as greengage, especially in places where wine is made.

The Greengage

The greengage came from Italy to France where it was adopted by Claude (1599–1634), wife of François I. She gave her name to the fruit, which has been known ever since as the *reineclaude*. Its English name comes from that of the man who originally brought it into that country, Sir William Gage. It ranks as a fine-flavoured plum, being exceptionally sweet and aromatic, and is therefore a favourite compote fruit. The stone is unfortunately very difficult to remove. Great quantities of *eau-de-vie* ('*prunelle*' in French) are also made out of greengages and in Germany they are peeled, stoned, dried and preserved. Greengages ripen from about mid-July to September. Their distinctive flavour and tender flesh make them also an ideal filling for tarts, on their own or perhaps with a smooth almond cream base.

Fine flavour, bouquet and sweetness are essential in grapes, the fruits of the gods. The muscat grape provides two of France's most attractive dessert wines, Beaumes de Venise and Frontignan, and is also one of the best varieties for eating and cooking.

Greenish-yellow mirabelle plums, with their sweet juicy flesh already discernible from outside through the fine skin. They contain vitamin C and valuable minerals such as potassium, calcium, phosphorus and iron. Mirabelles are useful in the treatment of obesity as well as circulatory and gastric disorders (unless, of course, they have been preserved in rum).

The Mirabelle

The mirabelle is another fine-flavoured plum, though a good deal smaller than any of the others. Its shape is spherical and its colour yellow, flushed or speckled with red. The firm flesh is very sweet and hence the mirabelle is mainly used in compotes or for making the celebrated German Mirabellengeist *eau-de-vie*, but they are also excellent as a basis for an iced soufflé. Mirabelles ripen at the same time as greengages, from mid-July to mid-September.

Grapes

In the golden days of autumn when the grapes are full of heavy juice, how good it must be to live in a wine-making area. The first vines climbed up trunks of trees on the southern shores of the Caspian Sea – not quite in Europe. The Semites living in that region were very fond of fruit and brought the grape vine to the Phoenicians of Asia Minor. Thus it reached the Greek world, where in their turn the Romans appropriated the heavenly vine and furthermore, not wanting to be without it when campaigning in Gaul and Germany, grew it there as well.

Most of the grapes we eat are white (greenish-yellow, in fact). They are generally speaking larger than the black variety (really blue or reddish even in colour) which, though a little smaller, often taste better. There are also seedless varieties which so far have not been particularly successful. In all the infinite variety of our European grapes the muscat has captured the lion's share of the commercial market. For home growing under glass, Black Hamburg is a hardy, general-purpose variety and Buckland Sweetwater is a good, small sweet grape.

Muscat grapes have a faint odour of nutmeg and a very distinctive flavour. There are both white and black species. They are the foundation of a whole range of choice wines that often play their part in the making of desserts – notably Malaga, port and Marsala. The Merano Cure grape enjoys a widespread reputation in Europe. It has a very thin skin so is not very easy to transport and is mostly consumed where it is grown. Then there is the kind known as Hothouse Wine, which is grown in Belgium and Holland and is on the market from winter to early summer. The grapes are grown in glasshouses under controlled conditions of light and heat and look marvellous. But for taste and bouquet they cannot be compared with the naturally sun-ripened grapes grown outside and harvested from September to the end of November.

To eat grapes just as they are simply wash them first. In fruit salads, they should first of all be seeded, but otherwise left alone. For other cooking purposes they should be both seeded and skinned.

Name: grape (*Vitis vinifera*). **Origin:** central Asia. **Shape:** round berries borne in large bunches. **Colour:** greenish-yellow or blue-black. **Where cultivated:** in milder temperate and Mediterranean climate zones; also hothouse grapes from Belgium and Holland from winter to early summer.

Apples

The apple is one of the earth's oldest fruits. In Paradise it was (supposedly) the cause of man's great fall from grace, and the gift of an apple bestowed by Paris on lovely Helen gave rise to the terrible Trojan wars. It was always a symbol of beauty, of youth and of power: think, for example, of the 'Apple of Empire' gem among the German crown jewels.

The apple tree originally came from the area between the Black and the Caspian seas. From there it spread throughout the world, except for the tropics. Apple growing has always required considerable financial investment and therefore it largely fell to the pharaohs, kings and princes to promote and pursue this activity. Thus Rameses II (died 1225 BC) gained great renown for his apple plantations in the Nile delta. The Romans learned about apples from the Greeks and, as usual, spread them throughout their empire – although, as researchers into the lake dwellings on Lake Constance have shown, apples were already being cultivated there 5000 years ago. Later the planting of fruit, and especially apples, was encouraged by Charlemagne (768–814 AD).

Today, with 20 000 varieties worldwide, the apple is quite simply our daily fruit, in sickness and in health. Containing more than 20 valuable minerals, it is actually a 'medicinal' fruit and because of its fruit acids is referred to, more or less politely, as 'nature's toothbrush'. But these attributes, however worthy, are far too prosaic reasons for eating apples. Far better to enjoy them for the sake of the most delicious apple recipes: hot or cold, stuffed, baked, fried in butter, with or without calvados or other liqueurs.

Apples are officially divided into three groups: eating apples, cooking apples and all-purpose apples that may be eaten raw or cooked. Only the best varieties need concern us here, even though good plain dishes can be made with other kinds of apple; only the very best quality goes into our desserts. At the top of the English list comes the relatively new variety, Discovery and the old favourite, Cox's Orange Pippin. France produces the immensely reliable and widely exported Golden Delicious. Germany grows her apples chiefly in the north and on Lake Constance in the south – areas which give the best promise of an even climate with high humidity. There are major dessert apple orchards producing the Bell apple, Red and Yellow Boskop as well as the varieties mentioned above, in the Rhineland, the Palatinate and south Oldenberg. Apart from their uses in special desserts, apples may be stewed or baked, made into sauce, juice, jelly, cider, champagne cider and of course, calvados, the delectable

> **Name:** apple (*Malus domestica, Rosaceae* family). **Origin:** central Asia. **Shape:** round, flattening towards calyx and stalk. **Colour:** according to variety, from light green through yellow to brilliant red and dark red. **Where cultivated:** in temperate zones worldwide.

Epicure is a medium sized apple, greenish-yellow flushed with red. At its best it is delicious, sweet and juicy, and much appreciated either eaten as it is or cooked.

The Jonathan apple is noted for its beautiful red colour, rich flavour, and versatility as both an eating and cooking apple. Its skin is thin but tough and the flesh is wonderfully crisp.

Cox's Orange Pippin and Golden Delicious bring us the taste of summer sunshine. They are two of the most popular sweet and juicy varieties. But Cox's Orange Pippin is very particular as regards the kind of soil and attention it requires in order to give of its best and Golden Delicious is equally demanding; it needs a great deal of warmth in order to ripen fully so is not a variety for northern areas.

Buerré Hardy, a late ripening variety, is one of the choice dessert pears. It is a comparatively large fruit, cone-shaped at the stalk end and bellying out towards the calyx. It can vary from greenish-yellow to russet yellow, with a reddish blush on the sunny side. A very juicy, sweet pear.

Clapp's Favourite is the name of this medium-sized pear with a comfortably rotund shape, bred by Mr Clapp in Massachusetts in 1860. The smooth skin is coloured greenish yellow to golden yellow with fine red speckles. It is very juicy and has a delicately aromatic bouquet.

The Quince

The quince is truly a fruit for gourmets and connoisseurs. It comes from central Asia, where today it still grows wild. The Romans took quince shrubs away with them from Cydonia in ancient Crete (the modern Canea) and established it once more in more northerly regions. As a symbol of fertility it was in ancient Greek and Roman eyes sacred to the goddess of love. The Greeks were already preserving quinces with honey, the resulting confection being known as *melimelon.* The next we hear of the quince is in Portugal, where it is called *marmelo* and from whence it spread throughout the rest of Europe. *Marmelo* pulp is the origin of the German word *marmelade* (marmalade in English).

Quinces are rich in vitamins and minerals. Before being processed they must be cooked and thereafter can be made into such specialities as quince jelly, thick purée, quince cake, quince cheese or quince cordial, and the sliced fruit can be steeped in various kinds of liqueur. All in all the quince is something a sweet tooth may well fancy – whether simply preserved or in sophisticated desserts.

apple brandy. The Bramley apple is a variety grown specifically for cooking, and is the basis of the English favourite, apple and blackberry pie. France on the whole prefers to cook with dessert apples, and it is interesting to compare her Normandy apple tart – flavoured most likely with calvados – with the English pie.

Pears

The pear is a native of Asia: western Asia it may be, but Asia it is nonetheless. From wild pear and Persian pear there developed over the milennia many cultivated varieties, of which upwards of 1500 are known to us today. There are said to be over 700 in Germany alone.

The earliest cultivated pears of which we have knowledge grew in Greece in the Peleponnese, which for that reason was also called Apia – the land of the pear. Thence its cultivation spread through the Old World, primarily with the assistance of the Romans.

The pear has the lowest fruit acid content of all, but makes up for this deficiency with enough minerals to place it well ahead of the apple – it supplies calcium, potassium,

phosphorus and iron in abundance. Because of its rich potassium content it even reduces superfluous fat and has a very strong dehydrating effect. So it is anything but fattening. But the pear is not only good for you; it is also a juicy delight beloved by all discerning cooks and gourmets down the ages. It has inspired some of the world's loveliest desserts. These range from the simple deliciousness of a compote of pears in red wine to the grandeur of Escoffier's Poires Belle Hélène, a sophisticated confection of poached pears presented on vanilla ice cream, sprinkled with crystallised violets and served with chocolate sauce.

Pears do not ripen on the tree but only after they have been picked, when mature but still firm. It follows that they must therefore be carefully stored. They are gathered, according to variety, from July to the end of October. Not only do they need plenty of warmth to ripen them, but they are also very sensitive to frost at blossoming time, so are therefore best grown in mild, warm climates. Favourite English varieties are Conference and Doyenné du Comice. Pears can be preserved whole or made into jam, perry, juice, nectar and pear brandy, and notably into the superb eau-de-vie de poire.

Pear Quinces may be distinguished from apple quinces. Both have a very strong smell and should therefore be stored away from other fruit.

Name: pear (*Pyrus domestica, Rosaceae* family). **Origin:** western Asia. **Shape:** somewhat similar to an apple, but cone-shaped and pot-bellied. **Colour:** varies from green through greenish-yellow to golden yellow and roseate; some varieties are flushed with reddish brown. **Where cultivated:** in all mild, temperate climates from China, Australia, South Africa and North and South America and Spain to the rest of Europe.

Name: quince (*Cydonia oblonga, Rosaceae* family). **Origin:** central Asia. **Shape:** apple or pear shaped according to variety. **Colour:** deep yellow with a fine white down when ripe. **Where cultivated:** chiefly the Mediterranean countries, Spain, Portugal, the Balkans, North America and all central Europe in small quantities.

The Melon Family

The very thought of these big fruits, round or oval, with their multifarious shades of colour from green and yellow to orange and red conjures up pictures of sweltering cities and countryside enveloped in a shimmering haze of heat. Their name is derived from the Greek and simply means 'big apple'. Nevertheless, they are berries and, like the pumpkin, related to the families of climbing, creeping or clinging gourds; properly speaking, therefore, they are vegetables. They thrive in hot, sunny areas, but can be grown elsewhere quite successfully under glass.

The many varieties of melon which are on the market in western Europe fall into two groups, sweet melons and water-melons.

Sweet Melons

This group is of Asian origin, but now cultivated in all countries where the climate is suitable, principally Italy, Spain, Portugal, Cyprus, Israel, South Africa, Mexico and Chile. Smaller growing areas are found in south-east Europe also, particularly in Hungary, Yugoslavia, Bulgaria and Turkey. Generally speaking, the fruit reaches a weight of 1–4 kilos/2–8 lb. One of the most popular sweet melons is the Honeydew, which is oval, and yellow when ripe, with a faint ribbing on its smooth skin; it has whitish-green flesh and a delicate flavour.

The Cantaloup melon is round in shape with a rough skin and greeenish-yellow ribs; some specimens have a warted skin, whence it gets its other name 'wart melon'. The cantaloup is of Armenian origin and was brought from there by missionaries in the fifteenth century to Italy where it was first cultivated in a small village near Rome called Cantalupo, which means 'where wolves sing'. The Galia melon, related to the Ogen, has a greenish skin covered with a rough yellow net-like pattern.

The Ogen melon comes from Israel and was originally bred there for the home market. It is round and slightly flattened in shape, its colour green lightly streaked with

a paler green and its flesh aromatic. This melon gets its name from the Israeli kibbutz at Ha-Ogen in which it was first raised. Now it is grown throughout the world.

The Water-melon

The water-melon comes from the African desert, the Kalahari, where it still grows wild. Like the sweet melon, it serves the native inhabitants as a source of food and essential liquid, but it has also been cultivated for thousands of years around the north African countries of the Mediterranean and in the Middle East. Nowadays it is also grown in the Soviet Union, South Africa, the U.S. and China.

In contrast to the sweet melon, it will grow up to a weight of 15 kilos/32 lb. It is round and smooth-skinned and its colouring exhibits the most varied shades of green. The flesh ranges from pink to a brilliant red, is not too sweet in taste, contains a great deal of water and is therefore particularly refreshing.

Ogen melons. This variety is a hybrid from Israel now being grown throughout the world. These melons will not ripen in the open air in colder northern latitudes but do ripen under glass and in forcing houses, such as are extensively used in Holland. Ogen melons do not travel at all well and must be air-freighted over very long distances – a factor that has a considerable effect on the price. They are however a most delicious variety. Halved, scooped out into balls, mixed with strawberries and returned to the shell, they are an ideal summer fruit salad.

Melons from Europe. A few of the wide range of melons available include: **1.** Striped water-melon Crimson Sweet, sometimes known as the 'Russian melon'. **2.** Sugar Baby, a small early melon imported from Israel. **3.** The Honeydew. **4.** The Lavan, a small, round form of honeydew with a more pronounced flavour. **5.** Galia melon. **6.** Ogen melon. **7.** Two cantaloup melons, in the foreground the Charentais variety, the best of all.

Selecting and Serving Sweet Melons

To select a melon – of whatever kind – is a simple matter. A ripe fruit should yield slightly and spring back when pressed with the thumb at the blossom end and the same area should also have a strong, aromatic scent.

Melons are served fresh and well chilled, perhaps flavoured with sugar or a little liqueur, on their own or as part of a fresh fruit salad. The more distinctively flavoured varieties – the Ogen and cantaloup for example – make fine ice cream, particularly when perfumed with kirsch.

Melons from Sicily. Italy has, after Spain, the second largest acreage under melons. This Sicilian farmer proudly displays two magnificent specimens from his fields near Corleone, one a markedly ovate honeydew melon and the other a medium-sized, striped Miyako water-melon.

Water-melons in the Palermo market. They are often named after the district in which they are grown, and Palermitano is a popular variety of winter melon. But most Italian water-melons are grown in the Po delta. Florence is famous for her water-melons, unforgettable for their size and vivid colour – and the welcome chill of their flesh.

Melon harvest in Spain. Spain is the largest European exporter of sweet melons. Oval sweet melons, like those shown here, are exported as well as round honeydew melons. At the other end of the price scale from the precious Ogen, they can nonetheless be delicious themselves.

Name: melon (*Cucumis Melo, Cucurbitacae* family). **Origin:** western Asia. **Shape:** varies from a sphere to a pointed oval. **Colour:** yellow to greenish-yellow with rib or net markings. **Weight:** up to 4 kg/9 lb. **Where cultivated:** Spain, Portugal, all Mediterranean countries, Israel, South America, South Africa, Mexico, Chile, southern U.S., south-east Europe, and (under glass) in Holland.

Name: water-melon (*Citrullus vulgaris, Cucurbitacae* family). **Origin:** the African desert. **Shape:** spherical, but can be slightly flattened. **Colour:** great variety of shades from dark to pale green. **Weight:** up to 15 kg/35 lb. **Where cultivated:** Mediterranean countries, southern Russia, the Middle East, North and South America, China.

The Pomegranate

The praises of the pomegranate were sung in the Song of Solomon and long before Greek and Roman times its blossom and fruit were symbols of love and fecundity to the Phoenicians and Egyptians. Later the pomegranate spread widely in the Mediterranean world. It gets its latin name from the Romans themselves. In southern Spain the province of Granada, which was named after the fruit, is still its chief area of cultivation. The fruit also figures in the national arms of Spain. The pomegranate likes a warm, and not too humid, climate. The leathery, smooth skin is at first green or red and then becomes a brownish yellow. Its projecting calyx has six hard points and because of this feature it served as a model for onion pattern porcelain. The peel and rind are still used as a dye owing to their high tannic acid content.

The Persimmon

This Asian member of the ebony family was rarely seen in the Mediterranean region until the last century. Today it is cultivated in Italy as far north as Verona. Because of their high tannic acid content the juicy fruits must be eaten when absolutely ripe – it is only then that the rough taste disappears. The persimmon when ripe is however not only a sugar-sweet fruit but also one extremely rich in carotene and vitamin A. Dried persimmons are accordingly taken in Japan as a cure for hangovers on the morning after New Year's Eve. The main varieties available in Europe are *Diospyros kaki*, with a high tannic acid content, and *D. kaki Vanille*; the latter can also be eaten before it is quite ripe and has a slight taste of vanilla.

Japanese Medlar, Japanese Plum or Loquat

Somewhat curiously, this plant is, like the apple, the pear and the raspberry, a member of the rose family. It is a native of China and south Japan which came to Europe in the eighteenth century and is grown there principally in the Mediterranean region. We import the fruit both fresh and canned (then usually called loquats) from Italy and Spain. Japanese medlar bushes and trees produce a strongly scented white blossom in autumn and bear their brilliant fruits in spring. These are about as big as a plum but shaped like a pear. The flesh is firm but tender and juicy and has a sweet-sour taste which, depending on the variety, may resemble that of apricots, plums or apples.

Name: pomegranate (*Punica Granatum*, *Puinicaceae* family). **Origin:** Persia, Afghanistan. **Shape:** round, with projecting calyx, apple sized. **Colour:** reddish yellow to brownish; leathery skin. **Where cultivated:** Mediterranean countries, the Middle East, Israel, Canary Islands, Madeira, California, South America.

Name: persimmon (*Diospyros kaki, ebenaceae* family). **Origin:** Japan, China, Korea. **Shape:** similar to an orange. **Colour:** golden yellow to tomato red. **Where cultivated:** Mediterranean countries, southern France, Israel, California, Florida, South America, Japan, India, Australia.

Name: Japanese medlar, Japanese plum or loquat (*Eriobotrya japonica, Rosaceae* family). **Origin:** China. **Shape:** generally pear-shaped and plum-sized. **Colour:** ranging from yellow to golden yellow or apricot. **Where cultivated:** all Mediterranean countries, southern France, California, Florida, Central and South America.

The pomegranate is a false fruit. The real fruits are the red or pink seeds surrounded by yellow membranes. The little grains have a pleasantly acid taste and can be eaten with a spoon or used in desserts, sherbets or fruit salads, with or without a liqueur. Or they can be made into pomegranate juice and the excellent grenadine syrup.

'Plum of the gods' was another name for the persimmon. When the skin has a glassy look and the fruit feels soft it is ripe and then tastes wonderful. It has a slight flavour of apricots. You can spoon it out and eat it fresh or use it in fruit salads or other desserts, or make it into a purée, compote, syrup, juice or conserve.

The Japanese medlar is another false fruit. The shiny, dark-coloured, bean-like stones can be used like bitter almonds. The fruit must be peeled for the skin has a rough taste and contains tannic acid. It makes excellent fruit salads, jellies, creams, jams and syrup.

Prickly Pear or Indian Fig

The prickly pear is a native of the American deserts and was brought to the Mediterranean region from Mexico by Spanish seafarers in the sixteenth century. Today it also grows in tropical and subtropical climates. The immature, green prickly fruit is gathered from August onwards and must be left to ripen to a dark yellow, reddish or brown colour. It has a refreshingly sweet and somewhat pear-like taste.

Name: prickly pear or Indian fig (*Opuntia ficus-indica, Cactaceae* family). **Origin:** Mexico, Central America. **Shape:** roughly pear-like, with small thickenings on the outer skin in which the prickles are set. **Colour:** greenish, becoming orange to red. **Where cultivated:** south-western U.S., the Mediterranean area, tropics and sub-tropics, Australia.

Beware of the prickles when handling this delicate fruit; they are tiny, but very unpleasant. Using a fork to keep the prickly pear steady, slice the ends off. Then make an incision lengthways and run the knife underneath to prise back the rind. Do exactly the same to the other side and you will have neatly exposed the orange fruit.

Figs and Dates, Fresh or Dried

The fig (*Ficus carica*) belongs to the mulberry family and is a native of Asia Minor where in ancient times it was a very important article of diet. Not much later it was thriving all around the Mediterranean basin, and now we find it in North and South America, south-west Africa and Australia as well. In common with the date it has female and male trees and pollination is carried out by a gall-fly which only inhabits the male fruits. The fig tree fruits three times a year,

Dried figs form the main part of the trade in this fruit. Turkey, Greece and Portugal are important fig producing and exporting countries. The picture shows how in Greece the figs are air-dried on fibre mats laid on flat roofs. Afterwards they are pressed

beginning at 8–10 years old and then continuing for 40 years. Figs are false fruits and, depending on the variety, are light green or shades of yellow to purple.

'Feet in the water, head in the fire' is the best environment for the date palm (*Phoenix dactylifera*), according to an Arab proverb. It originates from Mesopotamia, where it was being cultivated over 5000 years ago, spreading to Iraq, Iran, North Africa and all the ancient civilisations of the Mediterranean basin. It has been grown for 200 years in California and is now found in almost all tropical regions throughout the world. The palms bear berry fruits when 8–10 years old and yield their largest crops from the 30th to the 100th year. We import most of our dried dates from Iraq, Iran and north Africa, and fresh ones mostly from Israel.

Smyrna figs from Turkey and Muscat dates from north Africa are the best known and best liked kinds of these exquisite fruits. Both have meltingly tender flesh and are rich in sugar, protein, minerals and vitamins A and B. In their countries of origin they are made into pulp, paste, schnapps and wine, and we can use them in fruit salads, compotes, confectionery (dates stuffed with marzipan, for example), creamy desserts, biscuits and a wide variety of cakes.

The Citrus Family

Starting with mandarins, which open the season in late autumn, and going on by way of oranges and lemons right through to grapefruit, the citrus family is so vast and so wide-ranging as to be almost impossible to comprehend: tangerine, tangelo, satsuma, lime, kumquat, ugli fruit – all these and many more delicious fruits have a common ancestor, the citron (*Citrus medica*). This can weigh between 1 and 2 kilos/2 to 4 lb and has a thickly padded rind. Whether it first came to man's notice in India, in ancient Persia or in Mesopotamia is uncertain. This fruit could have been that of the fabled tree of knowledge of good and evil, and a very sharp and tart affair it was too – as were all the forebears of our modern citrus fruits. However problematic this may be, it is fairly certain that the Jews became acquainted with it during the Babylonian captivity. They cultivated it in Palestine after the Persian conquest of Babylon in 539 BC. From 150 BC onwards, known as an etrog, it had its place in the ritual of the Jewish religion, figuring notably in the Feast of the Tabernacles. The etrog was also needed for ritual pruposes in the Jewish colonies all around the Mediterranean, which explains why it spread rapidly; it was also used by non-Jews for medicinal purposes and to make perfumes and flavourings. Today the citron is found in California, Brazil, southern Italy and Greece and on Corfu. The rinds are used to make candied peel.

The lemon, mentioned by the Chinese philosopher Confucius around 500 BC, is thought to have been brought by Arab traders, together with the bitter orange, from the southern Himalayas to the Mediterranean area where the etrog was already known. Its rich ascorbic acid content makes the lemon our biggest source of vitamin C. The bitter, or Seville, orange, sometimes called the 'unimproved' orange, and used of old as a decorative plant in royal households, is now used to make candied peel, orange liqueurs like curaçao and Grand Marnier, marmalade and preserves.

The common or sweet orange is another member of this family. Orange trees are said to have bloomed in the celebrated hanging gardens of Semiramis, Queen of Babylon, as early as 800 BC. In Europe they were first grown 400 years ago in the estates of Duke Antoine de Bourbon in the south of France. When orangeries were in vogue gardens were laid out in Spain and Portugal too, but not for commercial purposes until the end of the eighteenth century. The orange we know today is one of nature's marvels in the variety of fruit acids and sugars it contains, together with 13 different minerals and 14 vitamins. The rind carries 11 different aromatics.

The shaddock is not in fact a grapefruit, as was once thought. These large, somewhat pear-shaped fruits are still grown in the Far East. In China particularly they are an important part, especially for children, of the mooncake festival celebrations.

In Italy there are often three lemon crops in the year The first 'Primofiori' are picked when still a brilliant green, the second, 'Limoni' are left on the branch until turning yellow, and the trees come into blossom again for the last, the 'Verdelli'.

Oranges, lemons and grapefruit are easy to segment, but you need an extremely sharp knife for the job. Place the fruit upright on a board and pare off the peel and pith in even slices.

The segments are cut out individually, after the fruit has been peeled and all traces of white pith between the rind and the flesh have been carefully removed.

Blood oranges

belong to the second group of oranges, which are available for export in winter. The best known varieties are Sanguine and Mori. The juicy navel orange and the elliptical and very flavoursome shamoutis arrive earlier. Next after the blood oranges come the late oranges, among which the Valencia lates and navel lates are the best known.

The kumquat,

dwarf lemon or dwarf orange (*Citrus fortunella*) is a native of south-east China and Japan. First introduced as a decorative plant, it is used today – because of its sourish, spicy aroma – in fruit cocktails, fruit

The lemon (*Citrus limonia*) is grown in all the Mediterranean countries, North and South America, South Africa, Australia and Asia. Shiny green lemons are ripe but have been deprived of the cool nights which affect the colour of all citrus fruit.

The sweet orange (*Citrus sinensis*) once had a very bitter taste but is now one of the world's most delicious fruits. It is grown throughout the Mediterranean area and in all tropical and subtropical regions.

The mandarin or tangerine (*Citrus nobilis* var. *deliciosa*) is a strongly-scented fruit and easy to peel. A native of China, nowadays it is grown in all countries with a warm climate.

The pomelo used to be called the pamplemousse or shaddock and is of Javan and Malaysian origin. Although perhaps a little too coarse for our taste it continues to find favour in Far Eastern countries. However, a new and much improved strain is at present being put on the market by Israel.

The clementine is a cross between a tangerine and a bitter Seville orange, discovered in 1902 in the garden of Père Clément in Algeria. It is orange-red in colour, very sweet, and seedless. It grows in all areas where other citrus fruits thrive.

salads, jams and marmalade, and as candied fruit.

The rind of citrus fruits makes an ideal flavouring, but only if the fruit has not been chemically sprayed, as is usually the case with limes. It can then be finely grated or thinly peeled and shredded. The best way to do this is with a zester, which shreds rather than cuts off the rind in paper-thin strips.

The lime (*Citrus aurantifolia*) is not so sharp in flavour as the lemon. A native of the tropics, it will also grow wherever other citrus fruits do well.

The grapefruit (*Citrus paradisi*) is sometimes known by its Spanish name, *pomelo*. It is rich in vitamins, minerals and trace elements and has a somewhat sharp, bitter taste. Of the two main types one has greenish yellow flesh and the other pink, the latter having a rather milder flavour.

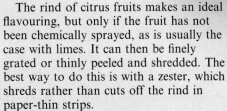

The Pineapple

The pineapple is held by many to be the queen of fruits and has been highly esteemed for the past 500 years. When Columbus arrived in the Caribbean island of Guadeloupe on his second voyage to the newly-discovered continent of America, friendly natives offered him this fruit with its compelling aroma and imposing crest of leaves as a fragrant gesture of welcome. Those pale-skinned savages called it *nana meant*: their forefathers had brought it with them from the South American continent, presumably from Paraguay, during their conquest of the Antilles. The name means 'the choice fruit'. The pineapple was truly the most prized of all the delicious fruits which Europeans were then tasting for the first time and, for many years after, every time a seafarer painted or sketched encounters with the West Indians, he included the pineapple with its characteristic spiky green top-knot in his picture. The Spaniards, no doubt

because of its resemblance to a fir cone, called it *pinon* and this was adopted into the English language as *pineapple*. The Portuguese, who later took the place of Spain in the struggle for colonies and sea power, gave the choice fruit its right name again, calling it *ananas*. But by this time the image of the pineapple had spread throughout Europe, whether as a botanical adornment in painting and architecture, on walls, pillars and small obelisks, or as a touch of grandeur on palace gates. It was also a familiar and sweet-smelling table decoration at banquets given by European princes and noblemen. At one of Madame de Maintenon's dinners in 1652, for example, six pineapples were displayed on her table, and that confirmed that the golden fruit from the new world had made the grade socially.

As living standards began to rise after the end of the Thirty Years' War, the pineapple, and a lot more fruit besides, spread from France to influence the culinary and cultural history of Europe generally. By the end of the nineteenth century pineapples grown under glass featured in an ever-increasing number of recipes for creams, jellies, parfaits and moulds. Yet in 1911 a chef was still heard to complain that 'they are not available in sufficient quantity . . . they deserve to be as popular as oranges and lemons'. This has now largely come about, thanks in no small measure to the arrival of tinned pineapple from Hawaii. An English nurseryman had introduced a thousand or so pineapples to the island in 1886, and thus laid the foundation of a first-class industry.

The pineapple is the multiple fruit of a shrub with spear-shaped, sharp pointed leaves. At blossoming time an 'ear' about 30 cm/12 in long sprouts from the clump of leaves and on this appear numerous pink flowerets. Each of these later forms a berry which coalesces with the fleshy axis of the flowerets into a single fruity mass. From the outside nothing can now be seen of the individual berry except the hard scaly part together with the small, hard leaf. The plants like damp heat and abundant water, and no wind or cold or shade. Hence in the Azores they are mostly grown in greenhouses. There, ideal

Annanas.

p.119.

The pineapple (*Ananas comosus*, from the *bromeliaceae* family) is a good plantation crop. Suckers or the leaf-knot crowns of the fruit inserted into prepared soil will quickly root. Nowadays it is cultivated in tropical regions the world over, especially in Hawaii, the Caribbean, Mexico, Brazil, the Azores, Africa (Kenya, Ivory Coast), Australia and Asia.

To peel a pineapple, grasp it by the leaves and make an incision lengthways with a sharp knife. Then, holding the knife at an angle, thinly pare off the rind by revolving the pineapple. Slice both ends off and prick off any remains of the rind with a sharp pointed knife. To remove the woody core, quarter the pineapple and cut it out lengthways. Cut the quarters into chunks as and when required, but do not store in the refrigerator.

climatic conditions are created by the systematic opening and shutting of windows, which enables the plants to bear fruit faster and more often. These pineapples are said to have the best flavour, but they are more easily bruised in transit than those grown out of doors. Should you need to ripen them after picking it is best to hang them up by the leaf-tuft. They are ripe when the rind no longer has any green areas, yields a little when pressed and when small leaves can be easily plucked out. Besides vitamins A and C, iron and calcium, the pineapple contains bromelin, a ferment which splits up protein and is used today in the treatment of alimentary disorders. It is also used as a medicine by the natives of Paraguay.

The Annonas

Anyone who has ever eaten a ripe cherimoya is enthralled by its magical flavour. The white flesh, sometimes with a bluish shimmer, tastes like a mixture of strawberries, raspberries and pears, perhaps flavoured with a hint of cinnamon. It is one of the best fruits in the world. No wonder then for us, it has something of the aura of a treasure from a vanished world, for its hard, glistening black seeds have been found by archaeologists in ancient graves; the Incas are known to have cultivated this delicious fruit. It was rediscovered in the northern Andes and in the high valleys of Ecuador and Peru and today, together with the other species of annona, is found everywhere that citrus fruits can grow successfully; but the cherimoya does need a mountain climate and in the lowlands lose some of its aroma.

The other important annona, which is grown in California and Florida, is the custard apple. It grows to a larger size than the cherimoya and its flesh is even creamier, with a suggestion of oiliness so that it has even more potential for making desserts than any of the other varieties. The sweet flesh, reminiscent of strawberries and cream, is excellent for making creams of all sorts – which are delicious laced with champagne, sparkling white wine, liqueur or lemon juice – and for fruit sauces and iced desserts. But it is very important not to keep any of the annonas in the refrigerator for they deteriorate rapidly in the chill.

The cherimoya (*Annona cherimola*) has a particularly high grape sugar content and is rich in vitamin C. The skin is patterned in thin scales and is green, soft and leathery, becoming brown to blackish as the fruit ripens. If the fruit is small you can slice off the top and eat the flesh with a spoon – and a little cream perhaps.

The sweet sop (*Annona squamosa*) is mostly marketed under the name 'annona' – incorrectly, since that is the generic name. The skin has strongly marked scales with warty thickenings. It has a very sweet taste reminiscent of juicy pears lightly flavoured with cinnamon, but sadly, few of us will be able to sample it since hardly any appear in our markets.

The sour sop (*Annona muricata*) is an elongated fruit with spiky bumps. The juicy, rather sharp-tasting white flesh is mostly made into ices and cooling drinks. Some variants, however, are not so acid.

The custard apple (*Annona reticulata*) has pale flesh, or rather pulp, with a few seeds. Strained of these, it can be added as it is to all kinds of desserts. The custard apple is very popular in India and Indonesia. Should it be readily available to us, we would prize it as a perfect, natural fruit fool.

Avocado

This tropical fruit (*Persea americana* or *P. gratissima*, from the *lauraceae* family) is one of the oldest of the new world. Excavations of burial grounds in Aztec and Maya territories have revealed that the avocado tree was being cultivated in these ancient empires 8000 years ago. The name is derived from an Aztec word *ahuakati*, and its other name, *palta*, comes from the Paltas, an Indian tribe of the Andes, who also grew the fruit.

Among 400 varieties of avocado only three kinds are suitable for systematic cultivation: the Mexican, the Guatemalan and the Caribbean. In the Mexican avocado the leaves smell strongly of aniseed and the fruits are small and thin-skinned with the same kind of scent. The Guatemalan avocado does not smell of aniseed and has middling to large fruits with a thick, leathery skin. The Caribbean or West Indian avocado – the kind suited to lowland cultivation – has no aniseed smell and the fruits are relatively large with a thin, leathery skin.

Most varieties bear fruit in two or three years. The fruit is hard when ready for harvesting and will soften with keeping. Avocados are cultivated nowadays in all tropical and subtropical areas from the Americas to Africa and the Far East. Being extremely sensitive they must be sent by cold-storage ship or by air freight. Europe imports them chiefly from Israel. There too several quite different varieties are grown, such as the pale green Ettinger, the very rough-skinned Fuerte, the round Nabal, and the small, oval Hass with a wrinkled skin that is almost black.

The name 'butter-fruit' sometimes given to the avocado distinguishes it as one of the most nourishing of the tropical fruits. In addition to minerals, plenty of protein and vitamins A, B, C and E, it contains up to 30 per cent oil, consisting of unsaturated fatty acids. The yellowish-white flesh has a creamy consistency and a mild flavour of nuts. It is usually served raw with either a savoury or a sweet dressing. For desserts avocados are creamed with lemon juice, red wine or sherry, or flavoured with liqueur or brandy. Matched with coffee or cocoa they make a very distinctive ice and they can also be added to white rum to make a liqueur.

The flesh of the avocado turns an unappetising shade of brown when exposed to the air, so it is wise to purée it only a short time before serving. If you are going to present it cut or halved, and need to keep it a little while, rub the cut surface with lemon.

The Tree Tomato

Also called the tamarillo, this is the fruit of the tomato tree (*Cyphomandra betacea*) belonging to the nightshade family. This fruit was cultivated for many centuries by the Indians in the northern part of South America. The 'tree' is really a shrub, but can grow to a height of 3 to 5 metres/9 to 15 ft. The leaves are heart-shaped and up to 40 cm/15 in long. With its beautiful, large, pink or white flowers it is one of the wonders of the Andes mountains. The egg-shaped berries, brilliant orange to scarlet in colour, hang mostly in threes, rather like grapes, on their long stems. The skin has a bitter taste and should not be eaten; the flesh is juicy and rich in vitamins, its flavour sweet-sharp with an aroma like that of apricots. Use tree tomatoes fresh in fruit salads and iced desserts, or make them into a purée or jam.

The tree tomato is now found in almost all tropical or subtropical countries as far as the foothills of the Himalayas. It is grown commercially all over South America, in Africa (especially Kenya), and in Sri Lanka, Indonesia, New Zealand and Australia.

The Banana

Its enemies are flying foxes and elephants, it has up to thirty fingers on its eight-to-fourteen hands and it crooks these fingers so that the sun can reach them on all sides. From childhood onwards we carry around a completely erroneous picture of the banana, for at the greengrocer's bunches of them are invariably displayed upside down, curving *downwards*: bananas do not in fact hang downwards but grow upwards like a series of crowns fitted one into another.

The banana, a member of the *Musaceae* family, is found today in such a bewildering number of varieties as to defy formal botanical classification. It is however one of the oldest cultivated fruits known to us. From the Himalayas more than 200 varieties of it came to the Near East, Africa, the Canary Islands and Madeira, whence it presumably travelled to the West Indies in the sixteenth century. Although in former times it could not. when ripe, survive much more than a day's journey unless it had first been dried, it was celebrated in Hindu epic poetry several centuries before our time and its image adorned Assyrian and Javanese temples and pyramids. Chinese mandarins and Roman naturalists alike described this nutritious, satisfying and health-giving

A typical banana plantation on the western side of the island of Martinique. The rather fragile plants are much at risk from the storms and hurricanes of these latitudes, which can destroy whole plantations in a few seconds.

fruit. Alexander the Great met with it on his march from Persia into India. Then, at the beginning of the fifteenth century, the Portuguese planted bananas on the Canary Islands.

But not until the 1880s did it become possible to ship fresh bananas to Europe. Then, with faster ships and improved methods of cold-storing the perishable fruit to delay ripening, its steady advance into the markets of Europe gained momentum. This was helped by the fact that bananas are always available because they blossom, set fruit and can be harvested throughout the year, irrespective of the seasons. But they do need the damp heat of the tropics in order to do so. All the varieties of banana, be it our well-known dessert banana or the dwarf banana, grow in the same way. From buds on the root-stock (rhizome) or suckers, that is to say, the false stems reach a height of up to 10 metres/ 31 ft in 12 to 14 months. They have no woody stem: the leaf-stalks merely sheath and enfold each other to make it appear so. Out of their centre grows a single inflorescence which may be 1½ metres/4½ ft long, on which blossoms open and fruits grow like hands with their fingers. That is why Arab traders gave

the fruit its name, *banan* being the Arabic for finger. A cluster of bananas consists of 8 to 14 hands, each with 10 to 20 bananas. Once harvested, the plant is cut down and a new one grown from the young suckers.

Bananas are soft and have their best flavour when the skin is a deep yellow with small brown spots or streaks. They keep best in a cool place but may well lose some of their flavour in the refrigerator. They complement well any fruit that has a slightly sour taste. In general they are excellent for making creams and ice creams and, when fried and flambéed, as accompaniments to all sorts of desserts.

A last word about eating bananas. In spite of the foregoing sensible directions, there is tremendous debate and disagreement as to what stage they are at their most delectable. Wildly personal preference apart, it is undeniable that green bananas must be treated as vegetables, that pied yellow ones are perfect for eating straight, and the quite brown ones are best in ice creams, milk shakes and mousses.

Dwarf bananas from South East Asia are only 10 to 12 cm/4 to 5 in long. This Asian variety is now cultivated in tropical America also. Unfortunately it does not travel well, so we have little opportunity to taste the sweet and fragrant flesh.

A banana cluster with small, unripe fruits which have not yet bent upwards. The flower, which in South East Asia is stewed and eaten as a vegetable, can be clearly seen. It makes a very fine dish, similar in inspiration to our elderflower fritters.

How bananas grow – in clusters of hands with the fingers bent upwards, always pointing towards the sun. They do not like the shade. Those shown here are unripe and it will be some time before they are ready to eat or to export.

Red sugar-bananas in Sri Lanka. We have little idea of the banana *colour* range, which even includes purple, because only the yellow varieties are really transportable, but the quality of their flesh is fair compensation for us northerners.

The Guava

Citrus fruits used to be the great providers of vitamin C. But this has changed with the appearance on the market of an increasing supply of exotic produce. Many of these have a higher vitamin C content, but the guava (*Psidium guajava*, *L.*, from the *myrtaceae* family) is a vitamin C bomb and may contain up to five times as much as citrus fruits do. It is also rich in vitamins A and B, calcium, iron and phosphorus. Its fine flavour was described in a monograph of 1535 about the new world, which at once prompted the Spaniards and the Portuguese to extend its culture to the Philippines and the Indian littoral.

Guavas have spread from there to all the tropical and subtropical regions of the world. They originally came from the tropics of Central and South America and mainly from what are now Mexico, Peru

and Ecuador. The fruits of the small guava tree, which grows to a height of 8 metres/25 ft, can be round, egg or pear-shaped, and the size of a medium-to-large apple. Yellowish, waxy skin encloses the delicate flesh, which may be white, yellow, pink or red. The once numerous hard seeds have been much reduced through selective breeding and some varieties are even seedless. The fruit has a very soft, delicately acid smell. The flavour, which is hard to define, combines those of the quince, the apple and the pear and, depending on the kind of guava and the place from which it comes, one or other of these will seem to dominate. The biggest guava orchards outside Mexico and Brazil are in California, Florida and South Africa, and there are also some in the Middle East and Israel.

Guavas can be eaten raw, peeled but with their seeds, when their texture is unusual and pleasant.

The guava can be put to all sorts of uses, but it must first be thinly peeled and the seeds removed. It is excellent in fruit salads, compotes, jellies and jams and the juice, syrup and purée do wonders for creams, flummeries and ices. Guava liqueur is made by macerating the fruit in brandy and spices.

Kiwi fruit

Also, but now less familiarly, known as the Chinese gooseberry (*Actinidia chinensis*), the kiwi is a member of the *Actinidiaceae* family. There are several important varieties: *Actinidia chinensis Planchom* (small and round like the European gooseberry), *A. Arguta* ('Kokuwa', a large-fruiting Japanese variety that tastes of honey and is very popular) and *A. Chinensis Hayward* (another cross-bred variety grown chiefly in New Zealand and California; this one also grows, together with the newer varieties, in France, Italy, Corsica and Spain): a hardy variety has even been bred in Russia.

The kiwi is a tropical climber, native to China since ancient times, whence it spread from the Yangtse valley as far as the Himalayas, and was first planted in New Zealand in 1906. It gets its modern name from the kiwi, a wingless New Zealand bird related to the ostrich whose body shape and colour the fruit resembles. It has an exceptionally high vitamin C content and also contains vitamins A and D, iron, calcium, tannic acid and a protein-dissolving enzyme so that in addition to its other uses it will tenderise meat. The fruit is ripe if it gives slightly when pressed with the finger. It may be picked before it is ripe and shipped in cold storage, but it will ripen instantly if even the smallest amount of ethylene gas is emitted in its vicinity (this gas is present in the kiwi fruit's own stalks and in car exhaust fumes and in the scent of apples and pears). Eaten raw, just as they are, kiwis are a feast fit for the

gods. They may be halved, spooned out and flavoured with liqueurs, or thinly peeled and sliced. The flavour is a subtle combination of strawberry, raspberry and gooseberry with, of course, variations. They are excellent in fruit salads, preserved in rum, in creams and ices, and either fresh or as a compote in flummeries, hot baked puddings and fruit sauces.

Lychee, Rambutan and Longan

The lychee (*Litchi chinensis*, from the *Sapindaceae* family), favourite fruit of Chinese emperors of the earliest dynasties, ranks as southern China's finest fruit; it has been cultivated in the Far East for 3000 years and nowadays of course is also grown in other subtropical regions such as India, Indonesia, Australia, Madagascar, South Africa, Kenya, Brazil and Florida. It grows, like its cousins the rambutan (*Nephelium lappaceum*) and the longan (*Euphoria longana*) on tall, shrub-like trees from which the fruits, round to oval in shape and about the size of a mirabelle plum, hang in panicles of up to 30 on twigs. The skin of the lychee is divided into small segments with a small tubercle on each and is thin and brittle, wine-red in colour but eventually goes brown, especially in cold storage. Inside the fruit is a black, inedible stone enveloped in a thick, pearly-white aril. The flesh has a delicate sweet fragrance and a flavour reminiscent of nutmeg. Lychees should not be picked unripe, since they will not ripen afterwards, but they are harvested somewhat ahead of time in order to facilitate storage and unfortunately the flavour suffers. The lychee's relation, the rambutan, comes from Malaysia, and looks more like a hairy creature than a fruit, but its flavour is equally fine.

Lychees are a very versatile fruit, adapting their flavour to the dishes in which they are served. Thus they are often eaten with meat. In China whole clusters of lychees are dried in the sun and sold as 'lychee nuts'. Fortunately for us, they are also one of the few fruits which are successful in canned form. For dessert purposes they are much esteemed, as are also the rambutan and the longan, as a compote, in fruit salads and fruit cups. They can also be used in creams, blended with cream cheese, with rum, or flambéed to accompany soufflés and dessert ices.

The Cape Gooseberry

Physalis peruviana is no relation of the common gooseberry, nor of the Chinese gooseberry or kiwi, but belongs, like the tomato and the potato and also the Chinese lantern, to the nightshade family. In its wild state it is found chiefly in Mexico and Guatemala and South America below the equator, where its fruits were esteemed as long ago as the time of the Inca and Aztec empires. But it was in quite another continent that it first underwent cultivation, for it was brought by seafarers to South Africa some 200 years ago and reared there as an antiscorbutic. Resourceful planters soon recognised its full value, however, and today it is cultivated, both as a dessert fruit and for jam making, in Kenya, Madagascar, southern India, Java and Australia. Inside its husk, which is the colour of raw silk, the Cape gooseberry is similar in shape and size to a cherry and grows on a bush which reaches a height of 70 to 90 cm/2 to 3 ft. When the fruit is ripe the husk has a yellowish-grey tint and the berry is deep yellow. The flavour is very refreshing and the fragrance calls to mind a mixture of pineapple and pawpaw, both of which qualities make it a fine fruit salad ingredient.

The rambutan thrives only in damp, tropical heat. It has long, soft red hairs on its skin and is oval in shape, but is otherwise much the same as the lychee and longan, with a refreshing, sweet-sourish flavour. Unfortunately it perishes quickly once picked and is seldom to be had fresh in this country.

The longan, the 'Chinese dragon's eye', was also much esteemed long ago in the Far East. It is a little smaller, orange-yellow in colour, later flecked with brown and slightly sharper in flavour than the lychee. Like the rambutan, its fruits will not keep long and generally speaking are only found in tins in this country.

The Cape gooseberry, ground cherry or jamberry, also known as the tomatillo, is rich in vitamins A, B, and C and in calcium and iron. It is used for jams, fruit cups and fruit ices and as a pie filling, as well as compotes and custards. The raw berries should be pricked before adding sugar, to allow it to penetrate the smooth skin.

37

The fruit of the mango tree, a gift to us from the tropics, is, after the banana, the most important article of diet for the inhabitants of the tropics. For us it has proved to be a very versatile fruit but it has such a consummate aroma that in desserts it is best not to put other fruit with it. Mango with cream or ice cream, mango cream flavoured with vanilla or cream cheese and mango flummery are all delicious, and it also makes an excellent pie or tart filling. It can, too, be eaten as a compote, puréed and made into ice cream, and all sorts of drinks.

The Mango

The evergreen mango tree (*Magnifera indica*, from the *Anacardiaceae* family) is a native of the area extending from the Indo-Burmese monsoon belt up to the foothills of the Himalayas. Buddha himself rested in its shade; in India it has been cultivated for at least 4000 years and it is a familiar domestic plant in Sanskrit writings. It figures largely in Indian mythology and in Buddhist ritual. Indian rulers always greatly esteemed the tree and its fruits and had large plantations of it laid out. The best varieties which we know today seem to have existed in the sixteenth century. In the fourteenth and fifteenth centuries, with the help of Portuguese seafarers, the mango tree finally arrived in West Africa and Brazil. Now it has spread all over the tropics and in some subtropical regions as far as California, Florida, Egypt and Israel.

The fruit of the mango is extremely rich in vitamins A, B and C. In shape it looks something like a gigantic plum, about 10 cm/4 in long, with sides somewhat flattened, but can be kidney or pear shaped too, and sometimes roundish. The colour ranges, according to the variety, the climate and the nature of the soil, from green to yellow with darker patches, others having red cheeks or being red all over. Because of this diversity the ripeness of a mango cannot be judged by its colour. If it yields when pressed gently, gives off a pleasant sweet fragrance and in some cases also shows small brown speckles, it is ready. The leathery skin is not edible. The golden yellow flesh encloses a large, flat stone, to which it closely clings, creating various difficulties in the preparation of the fruit for the table. This is a rather messy business in the case of very ripe mangoes as they contain a lot of juice, and mango stains are not easy to remove from clothing. In some fruits a faint taste of turpentine can be noticed. This will not be apparent if the fruit is served chilled, but not ice-cold. After eating mango, neither milk, water nor alcohol should be taken for two hours since for some unknown reason they may cause stomach pains which, though not dangerous, are uncomfortable.

Ripe mangoes bruise very easily, and those we import are therefore gathered before they have ripened but will ripen at room temperature. The best-known varieties are Langra, Alphonso, Kent (usually red in colour), Mango Blanco, Harden and the exquisitely fragrant Sangra.

Unless you feel inspired, the best way to eat mango is the simplest, just as they are or in a fruit salad.

How to peel a mango. Slit the skin with a sharp knife four or five times from top to bottom: it can then be drawn downwards, held between thumb and the knife, if the fruit is ripe and still firm. If the fruit has fully ripened the only thing to do is to cut it open and spoon out the flesh.

Opening a mango is no easy task. Since the stone is very flat a slice should be taken off each of the two broader sides above and below it and as close to it as possible and then the flesh remaining around the stone cut off separately. The fruit can then be diced or puréed as the recipe requires.

The Coconut

The fruit of the coconut is in reality a stone-fruit, for what we buy as a nut with its brown, fibrous hair is the unripe kernel or seed; the leathery skin and thick fibre coat have already been removed. So-called 'fresh' coconuts should have sweet and snow-white flesh and the milk inside must make a gurgling sound if you shake one. If you hammer a nail into at least two of the small dimples (plumules or eyes) under the hair, the milk can be poured out first. The hard shell should then be tapped all over to loosen the flesh, the woody sheath smashed or sawn open and the flesh scraped out.

As the coconut palm produces everything that inhabitants of the tropics originally needed in order to sustain life it was called 'the tree of life' or 'tree of heaven' in the South Seas and in India: the milk of unripe coconuts made it possible to survive on islands devoid of springs and rainwater. The flesh of the ripe nut has a considerable oil content and therefore satisfied hunger. The outer skin is made into bowls, water pipes and carvings. The fibre coating supplies material for ropes and fishing nets. Palm wine or 'toddy' is obtained from the flowers. Young shoots are cooked as vegetables and the mature leaves woven into mats and roofing materials. The stem serves as timber for building and carpentry and as firewood.

The coconut palm (*Cocos nucifera*) grows faster than the other species of palm and may reach a height of 30 metres/90 ft. The stem is flexible enough to withstand even the tropical hurricanes. It bears 15 to 20 nuts which take a little more than a year to ripen from the flower and can be harvested continuously up to a total yield of 120 nuts a year. Fully ripened nuts are principally used to make coconut oil and copra from the oil-rich flesh. Coconut milk appears in many recipes from the tropics, but this does not mean the natural liquid inside the nut. Coconut milk or cream, like almond milk, is made by soaking grated coconut in boiling water and squeezing it out again. In American recipes the nut is halved and placed first in a moderately hot oven (200 C, 400 F, gas 6) for 15 minutes. Its juice is then topped up with a little water to make the amount of liquid equal to the amount of nut flesh and both are puréed together in a blender or food processor and then passed through a sieve.

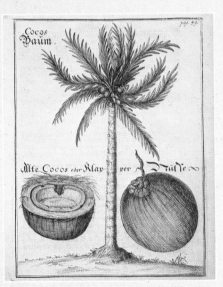

The 'coconut tree' was thus described by the German writer Georg Meister in 1692: 'The fruit of this tree and its precious juice is food and drink alike to hungry and thirsty Indians, and to Europeans, and it shields and protects them from the sun's great heat.'

Ripe coconuts complete with outer covering. Only the inner nut, or seed, gets into the shops, together with a few of the fibres. Coconut milk is found only in the unripe fruit, and dries up when it ripens.

The king coconut (*Cocos nucifera aurantiaca*). Inside it is more than 600 ml/1 pint of exquisitely aromatic and refreshing juice. Cut off one end of the bright yellow outer covering, which is fairly soft, and drink until you have emptied the fruit.

The mangosteen is a sumptuous fruit in more senses than one. Even in South East Asia it is not cheap. This picture was taken at Ambalangoda in Ceylon, the modern Sri Lanka, where, in the high season of the mangosteen (July-September) the precious fruits are sold in the main streets on mats of plaited wood. It is of interest that the local people only eat them raw because for them the flavour is too delicate to spoil by adding other ingredients.

Mangosteen

The mangosteen tree (*Garcinia mangostana*) belongs to the *guttiferae* family. It hails, as do many related species, from Malaysia, and presumably it was cultivated in South East Asia long ago. Still hardly known in Europe, the mangosteen is esteemed in Asia as one of their most delicious fruits. But today planting is no longer limited to the Asian monsoon belt and the mangosteen has settled down in tropical South America as well. Large-scale cultivation however still presents problems, since the rate of success in propagating the plant has not been very high. The tree, over 10 metres/30 ft high, also needs 10 to 15 years in order to produce its first crop.

The fruits are about the size of a tomato or an orange, being round but slightly flattened at the top and bottom. The sepals curve in around the stalk rather like a ruff. The reddish-brown to brownish-purple skin is fairly thick and hard. The flesh is gleaming white or cream and looks somewhat like that of a lychee, from which it differs in that it is divided into four or more plump, juicy segments each with a number of green seeds inside.

There is no way of describing the flavour of a mangosteen. It is really only possible to apply enthusiastic phrases to it like 'indescribably good', 'out of this world' and 'exquisite'. For us Europeans the mangosteen must be the most aromatic and in point of flavour the most precious of all the tropical fruits and, accordingly, once it has made the long journey here it should be treated with great care. Because of its hard skin it keeps well and after travelling may be kept in the refrigerator for a few days, but despite the toughness of its skin it is in fact extremely sensitive and must be kept in an absolutely airtight container, or its aroma will be completely destroyed.

It is sad that this fruit, by reputation as fine as the mango, should be so little known outside its native land. But there does seem to be a very good reason for this: its slow rate of growth makes it almost impossible to develop on such a scale as to make it an economical success. All the more reason to treasure the few which come our way.

Should you be lucky enough to come across a mangosteen, you must eat it quickly. With a sharp knife, slice it across horizontally and remove the upper half of the shell to expose the fruit. Prise this away gently and enjoy it straight away, for it discolours rapidly on contact with the air.

As a dessert fruit, if not served raw, the mangosteen is particularly good in light, airy creams or made into a fool with cream, or in ice creams. A mangosteen sorbet cannot be bettered.

Pawpaw

Pawpaws are round, tropical fruits about the size of a melon and are set close to the trunk of a tree which grows taller than a man and has no branches but only a thick, leafy crown at the top. Also called tree melons, they put forth flowers which smell like lily of the valley and the fruits, green at first, gradually assume the shape of a pear. They can reach a weight of 9 kilos/about 20 lb but are gathered when they weigh about 500 g/1 lb. The skin should then no longer be green but streaked with yellow. If a fruit is cut through, hundreds of sticky black seeds can be seen in the middle; these are the size of a peppercorn and have a sharp taste like watercress, although they are not eaten with the fruit. The flesh is as firm as that of a pumpkin and tastes of apricots or raspberries with a hint of woodruff.

It should also be said that the pawpaw is rich in vitamin C and contains a hydrolysing enzyme called papain and that its flavour, somewhat insipid when not quite ripe, can well be sharpened with lemons, limes and other citrus fruit and supplemented with fresh coconut, bananas and pineapple. Unripe pawpaws are cooked as vegetables in the countries where they are produced; they can also be used in soups or grilled.

Pawpaws thrive in all tropical regions. They are of Mexican origin and their delicate fruit have only reached the green-grocers of the northern hemisphere thanks to air transport from Hawaii and Israel.

In the British empire of old the pawpaw was christened 'the breakfast fruit'; you cut one freshly gathered in half, took out the seeds, sprinkled the flesh with sugar and ate it with a spoon. In Caribbean cooking a considerable number of recipes for jams and marmalades have evolved, whereas the wives of German farmers settled in Africa made fruit tarts with pawpaw filling, and slices of fresh pawpaw are served with the classical Indonesian rice table to cool the tongue in between, or at the same time as eating, the hot dishes. In all tropical countries, where the meal nearly always ends with fresh fruit, halved pawpaws have their place, often with other fruit.

This fruit is gradually beginning to be familiar in Europe, although *Larousse Gastronomique* has only a few laconic words to say about it: 'Its fruit is sweet and easily digestible owing to its enzyme content.'

In America, where the name is sometimes spelled 'papaw', it is esteemed for its low calorie content, 77 calories to every 11 grams/½ oz of fruit. If the fruit is too green American cooks recommend that it should be left to ripen for a day or two – not in the refrigerator but in a warm, damp place away from direct sunlight. Ripe pawpaws have a predominantly yellow skin, give a little when pressed and after buying should be kept in the refrigerator for a few hours at the most but preferably eaten without delay.

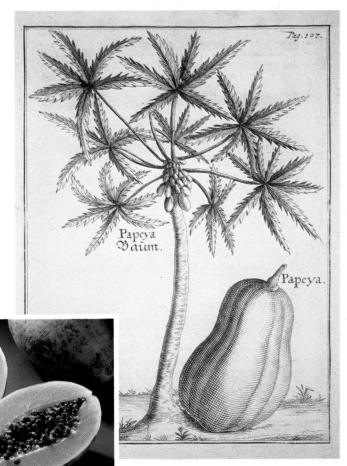

Of pawpaws, the *East Indian Gardener* says that, 'The fruits look like German melons, greenish-yellow with many black seeds inside, and have a hot taste almost like mustard.'

The pawpaw (*Carica papaya*), a member of the *caricaceae* family, was called the 'tree of health' by the Caribbean islanders because of the ability of its milky sap to heal wounds and the beneficial effect of its fruit on the stomach.

The flesh of a ripe pawpaw is very juicy but the seeds must be removed. For breakfast, sharpen it with a little lime juice, and for dessert flavour it with brandy or port. It is excellent also in creams or ice creams and in fresh fruit salads.

Passion Fruit

This fruit belongs to a very large family of tropical climbing plants, the *passifloraceae*, over 300 species of which are known, most of them in the wild state and in the main producing inedible fruit. But the flowers of every species are extraordinarily beautiful. Shown here is the enchanting flower of the purple granadilla (*Passiflora edulis*). The 'passion flower' has been known to us since the seventeenth century, having been given its name by Spanish missionaries who recognised in its open flower the instruments of Christ's passion. Some varieties of passion fruit, including the purple granadilla with its three-lobed leaves, are plants long cultivated by the South American Indians, as evidenced by archaeological discoveries in Peru. The fruits of the purple granadilla (the Spanish name means 'little purple pomegranate') are about the size of a hen's egg but round and deep red to purplish-brown in colour. The skin is somewhat leathery and shrivels quickly, so that the fruit should not be kept long. When they are cut in half a large number of small seeds are seen within, each enveloped in a jelly-like and very juicy mass of fruit cells. This pulp has a sweet-sharpish taste with a full, strong fragrance that is reminiscent of several different tropical-fruits. On its own it will transform an ordinary fruit salad into a rich and rare dessert.

The yellow form of the purple granadilla is considerably more productive. The fruit is larger, has a smooth, yellow and somewhat thicker skin and tastes almost as good. It does not thrive in cold climates but is now grown commercially all over the tropics. Another variety, also very productive, is the Jamaica-honeysuckle or water-lemon (*Passiflora laurifolia*). In contrast with the purple and yellow granadillas it has long, ovate leaves. Passion flowers usually open in the afternoon and close at about 10 o'clock in the evening, during which time they may be pollinated. This is normally done by insects and mainly by a particular species of bee, but if the creature is not present – and most of the planting is done far from the country of origin of the plant – the flowers must (as can be seen in the second picture) be pollinated by hand individually, particularly in Africa and Asia. The colour of the apple-sized fruits is officially yellow but can vary from lemon through ochre to reddish-orange, depending on the area and climate in which the fruit is grown. The fruits illustrated come from Sri Lanka but orange-coloured specimens of the same variety are produced in Brazil. Lastly, there is the curious 'giant granadilla' (*Passiflora quadrangularis*) which can grow to 26 cm/10 in long and looks like a big, oval pumpkin. But it lacks the tropical aroma of the passion fruit and the flavour is insipid. Passion fruit are grown nowadays in California, Florida, Brazil, Africa, India, New Zealand and Hawaii.

The three first-named varieties can be used in much the same ways, even though the modest-looking purple granadilla substantially excels the other two in aroma and flavour. The fruit should be spooned out raw and added to flummeries and puddings or used in fruit salads. It will also make a particularly luxurious and perfumed soufflé. Particularly important to us is the concentrated maracudja juice (*maracudja* being the Guadaloupe name for the passion fruit), a luxurious flavouring for creams, ices, jellies, shakes and other drinks. And there is also the well-liked maracudja liqueur with its irresistible 'nose' which makes the simplest dessert into a delight and should not be overlooked.

Exotic Rarities

Travellers in South East Asia, in the African tropics and sub-tropics, in the Caribbean and in Central and South America discover many kinds of paradise. What astonishes particularly is the abundance – or rather, the prodigality – of fruits which nature provides there. Exotic rarities beyond compare, full of luscious sweetness, are everyday fare for those who live there. One or another of these rare fruits may turn up once in a while in this country in a highly specialised delicatessen, but too often disappear again as quickly. Others really do 'get off the ground' – witness the success of the kiwi and the mango. The fifteen rare and exotic fruits listed over the page represent a fine selection of fruits which may never come our way (we must export ourselves to them!). The durian's personality, for one, is obviously so infectious that few carriers would convey it. On the other hand, the sweeter-tempered (and much prettier) carambola is a versatile fruit which might one day be much better known.

Apart, however, from cultivated tropical fruits, which are grown mainly for export, there exist innumerable species either growing wild or in private gardens, which are still completely unknown to us Europeans. Among these are a good many which should certainly be grown commercially too. There are as well a number of fruits of purely local importance which are marketed in preserved form, for example the bael fruit from Sri Lanka. But some of these, despite their quality, have difficulty establishing themselves on the

A market stall on the outskirts of Singapore. A rich display of the finest fruits, some of them familiar, some not so familiar: the durian for example, the prickly fruit in the foreground, has a smell which causes even the bravest gourmets to wrinkle their noses when faced with it. Nonetheless, even in its own country it is a highly priced delicacy.

markets of the industrialised countries. As for the question of whether we shall have in the near future new desserts made with now unknown exotic fruits, the answer has to be a qualified 'yes' as far as we, the potential importing countries are concerned, for not all tropical rarities reach the consumer in the right condition. But the majority of these fruits are excellent dessert material, even though extremely few recipes are available from their native lands. The reason for this is simple: in these tropical regions the fruits were – and are – scarcely processed at all or given additional flavour, but just eaten fresh off the tree. It is a very strange fact that in the best restaurants in the midst of a paradise of tropical fruits,

whether in South East Asia, Africa or Central and South America, imitation European or American desserts should be made with cream and butter under extremely unfavourable conditions and with predictably mediocre results, when in Paris a simple mangosteen sorbet has become a favourite ending to a meal. In those far-away places the fruit is, so to speak, at the door, but it is left often to the European or American cooks to put these divine gifts to imaginative use. In fact, ice creams, sorbets and granitas and the fluffy egg-based creams are just what tropical fruit should be used for – and of course fruit salads too. But interested cooks and pastry chefs, using traditional basic recipes as their starting point, have innumerable opportunities for using them creatively. There is no way of guessing future availability; even among the tropical fruits listed below some are included which will not make the grade commercially, at any rate in this country. Conversely, we will certainly see some kinds that are not mentioned here, for, as we have already stressed, it is not only the difficulty of transporting fresh fruit that inhibits their export. The outstanding canned fruits from Sri Lanka are a good example: they travel well, yet they are not to be had in quantity. However, whatever the situation is now or may be in the future, we shall suggest ways of breaking with culinary tradition and experimenting with the unknown and the exotic. It is well worth the trouble. But it should be borne in mind that there is often great confusion with regard to the names of the individual fruits: it is not unusual for the same one to have several, derived from the native language of the country of origin and from that of various colonial rulers. Naturally this does not help clarify things, but need not deter us from making use of these wondrous fruits. But always remember that exotic fruits, like any other, should be bought with discrimination and not just for the sake of novelty. Very often overripe fruits are offered for sale, or, even worse, downright 'green' ones – something that often happens with the pawpaw which then, despite leaving them on a sunny window sill, never ripen properly and are therefore quite useless.

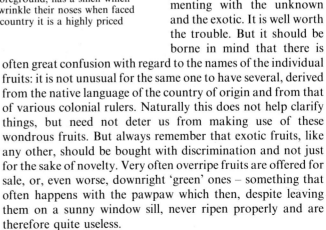

Barbados Cherry

Also known as the acerolas, the Barbados cherry (*Malphighia glabra*) is quite unrelated to our European varieties of cherry and flourishes in the tropics and subtropics of Central and South America. It is of West Indian origin. The shrub-like tree produces pink or purple flowers and red cherries 2 to 3 cm/1 in in diameter with three seeds. The fruits have the highest vitamin C content of any known fruit or vegetable in the world – they have at least 30 times that of the lemon. They have a sweet-sour aromatic flavour and are made into syrup as well as eaten raw in the countries in which they are grown.

Bael Fruit or Bengal Quince

Botanically known as *Aegle marmelos*, the bael fruit flourishes in the tropics and subtropics of South and South East Asia principally. It is of Indian origin and grows most extensively in that country. The fruit is the size of an orange and has a hard shell like the coconut. Its orange-yellow flesh is soft and has a refreshingly sharp and very aromatic flavour. When puréed it is an excellent ingredient for ice creams, sorbets and fruit creams. Rich in vitamins A and C, in India the bael fruit is eaten raw, made into drinks or cut in slices and sold as dried fruit. A puréed version, sweetened with sugar and sterilised, is produced and canned in Sri Lanka under the name 'Beli cream'.

Bael fruit or Bengal quince

The Cashew Apple

Anacardium occidentale is a fruit cultivated in ancient times by the Indians in the region of Mexico. Spanish and portuguese seafarers brought it to East Africa and India. The 'apple' is in fact oval, 8 to 15 cm/3 to 6 in long, the skin shiny and yellow to reddish in colour. At one end hangs the cashew nut, which is the real fruit, the apple being nothing but the thickened stalk of the nut. This 'fruit-stalk fruit' has a sharpish,

astringent taste but when sugar is added to it develops a very delicate aroma. Syrup, jelly, wine, liqueur and jams are made with it.

The Date Plum

This fruit belongs to the *ebenaceae* family and is related to the persimmon. *Diospyros lotus* comes from the Himalayas and is now grown all around the world from California through the Mediterranean to Japan. The cherry-sized berries range in colour from yellow to blue-black and are sweet to the taste. As syrup and purée they are useful in cream cheese or creamy puddings and also in ice cream.

The Durian

This is a member of the *bombacaceae* family. Its home was originally on the islands of South East Asia but now it is also grown in tropical Africa and South America. Owing to the smell given off by the skin, which resembles that of sewage, it is not allowed on public transport in Asia. The prickly fruit, as big as the head of a child, is an expensive delicacy even in its own country. The flesh is pale yellow with numerous seeds, and tastes creamy and aromatic. In Asia it is made into sweetmeats and marmalade.

Durian

The Feijoa

Known also as the pineapple-guava, *Feijoa Sellowianus* belongs to the *Myrtaceae*, or myrtle, family. The small and very drought-resistant tree thrives in the subtropics of South America but is today also cultivated in the corresponding regions of Africa and Asia. With its green skin it bears a superficial resemblance to the avocado, but carries several seeds instead of a single large one. The yellowish flesh is rich in vitamins, has a sweet, aromatic flavour and the purée is good in creamy desserts. In

the countries where it is grown the feijoa is usually eaten raw.

Feijoa

The Coco Plum

This rare fruit has its home in tropical South America. *Chrysobalanus icaco* is about the size of a plum, the colour varying from yellow through to red to reddish-brown. Inside are lodged several stones. The flesh has an austere but sweet flavour. The coco plum is usually made into a compote and can also be bought in candied form. It is also suitable for making into ice cream and creams.

The Jaboticara Tree

Related to the myrtle family, the jaboticara (*Myrciaria cauliflora*) flourishes in the climate of the tropics and is a notable fruit tree in Brazil. The cherry-sized fruits are attached by tiny stalks directly to the trunk, measure about 2 to 3 cm/1 in across and have a dark blue, purple or black skin which is very tough and not eaten. The pulp is full of vitamins and has a sweet-sour and very aromatic taste. The fruit may be eaten raw together with its small seeds, or made into syrup and jam. As a compote or added to iced puddings and creams it enriches our range of exotic desserts.

The Carambola

This most elegant fruit, *Averrhoa carambola*, is of Malaysian origin, and now widespread throughout the tropics. The few we get here come mainly from Brazil. The fruits grow to 10 or 12 cm/4 to 5 in in length and when fully ripened are dark yellow in colour and the flesh translucent. They are divided lengthways into five angular segments. Much esteemed in the tropics, they contain plenty of vitamins but have a somewhat dull, though sweet, flavour. They are easy to peel but the skin can also be eaten, as can the little seeds.

Carambolas are eaten raw or made into syrup, jam and candied fruit. With lemon or lime juice added they are also very suitable for fruit salads and iced puddings. Sliced crossways they make a star-shaped fruity decoration which looks pretty floating in wine or punch.

Carambola

The Lawalu

The lawalu, (*Chrysophyllum roxburghii*) comes from South East Asia, it is about the size of a lemon. When ripe it has mealy but very sweet flesh, the colour of pale ochre, under a thin skin. Since it contains very little fruit-acid, lemon or lime juice should be added before it is eaten raw or used for making desserts. The purée makes a very pleasant addition to sorbets, creams and iced puddings. Sadly, it has yet to be imported into this country.

Lawalu

The Melonfruit

Occasionally exported from its home, Chile, the melonfruit is ripe when the skin is coloured orange-yellow, sometimes with brownish-purple patches. It peels easily, the flesh is refreshingly juicy and tastes like honeydew melon and therefore fits in admirably with fruit salads and desserts served with a sharpish sauce.

Melonfruit

The Marmalade-Plum or Sapodilla

This species, *Achras zapota*, is the subject of much confused debate. Innumerable varieties are in cultivation, making it very hard to classify. Cultivated originally in ancient times by the Indians of tropical Central America it is now grown in all tropical regions across the Caribbean and Africa and on to South East Asia. The oval fruits, 6 to 8 cm/2½ to 3 in long, have a yellowish cinnamon-coloured and rather tough skin which encloses juicy, salmon-pink flesh and several dark seeds. The sweet-sharp taste is reminiscent of honeydew melon and therefore goes well in sorbets, creams and iced puddings – and of course also in fruit salads. Because of its tough skin it will travel well if gathered before it is fully ripe.

Sapodilla

The Star Apple

Called 'Kaimito' by the Indians, *Chrysophyllum cainito* is an old Indian-cultivated fruit. The tree comes from tropical Central America and is grown today in the other central areas of America and in the West Indies. The fruits are reddish purple and have a hard skin, inside which is the soft, white, gelatinous flesh with a few seeds.

When the fruit is cut crossways the star pattern which gave it its name appears. The flavour is very pleasant and sweet. Unfortunately the fruits ripen fully only on the tree and then spoil rapidly. But they are very good indeed for sorbets, creams and iced puddings as well as for jam.

The Tamarind

Also called the sour date, *Tamarindus Indica* hails from the tropical African summer rain forest, but today is cultivated in the tropics and subtropics all over the world. The pods may grow up to 20 cm/8 in long and they have a hard, brown shell. The flesh is white and juicy but extremely sour and is therefore usually made into syrup or stewed before anything else is done with it. The purée is used in cold drinks and to flavour sweet fruit sauces, sorbets and ices.

Woodapple

The Woodapple

This is a gigantic tree, *Ferolia elephantum*, from Sri Lanka which bears orange-sized fruits. Their shell is brown with darker streaks and is as hard as a coconut's. The fruit is ripe if it feels loose in its shell. The reddish-brown to purple flesh has a somewhat unpleasant sourish smell but with the addition of sugar develops a unique and delicate aroma. The fruit makes first-class creams, sorbets and ices and also blends very well with yoghurt. In Ceylon, now Sri Lanka, the flesh is sterilised with sugar and marketed as 'woodapple cream', which is an excellent product exported mostly to Australia.

45

SPICES AND FLAVOURINGS

Dessert flavourings from aniseed to vanilla

It is precisely because all creams, milk puddings and steamed puddings promote a mood of such contented well-being, that they are the ideal foils for the numerous flavourings which over the centuries have found their way into our kitchens. Some of these are classic: pears poached in wine flavoured with cinnamon; chocolate pudding or a red fruit jelly cooked with split vanilla pods; a peppermint flummery sauced with melted chocolate; or a wine punch spiced with lemon rind and cloves. Some other combinations have more to do with magic and medicine than with the art of cooking: we have almost forgotten that the pungent scent of cloves was supposed in the Middle Ages to ward off the plague. More practically, a pungent, spicy smell would mask the indifferent quality or stale condition not only of the rudely made red wine of those times but also of cream, butter, fruits or flour.

Anyone who could afford to buy pepper – the name given to all the spices on which the 'pepper men' grew rich (and also the landed gentry who reserved for themselves the privilege of dealing in spices), and by implication anyone therefore who could dip deep into his own store of cardamom, nutmeg or whatever – gave proof of no mean fortune.

We live today in an age in which the aroma of the fruits that we buy in shops and even from the market grows weaker and fainter, largely because the fruit has been gathered too early and insufficiently ripe. Transportability takes precedence over flavour and fragrance. But we can – and must – compensate for this deficiency with spices, with alcohol and with herbs. Dairy products on the other hand have fared better in that butter need no longer be rancid nor cream go sour in the refrigerator. The very standardisation of these products thus requires flavourings to vary it, and perhaps even a dash of strong liqueur or dessert wine. The classic English trifle is a prime example. Here macaroons or sponge cakes are first soaked in brandy and wine, covered with an egg custard gently perfumed with vanilla, then spread with fresh raspberries or raspberry jam and finally with wine-flavoured syllabub. A sweet sponge mixture and a bland blending of milk and eggs are thus enlivened by the sweet and sour taste of the fresh fruit or jam, by the alcohol and the various flavourings. This is a classic recipe, which ought to be quite strictly adhered to. However, what goes with which should not always be so firmly laid down by tradition as to rule out experiment – nothing can be more exciting than to stand convention on its head and flavour apples with ginger or ice cream with cinnamon. But with dessert flavourings as with all others the golden rule should be that discretion is the better part of valour – or in this case, extravagant meddling. A flavouring is like the accompanist at the piano: you cannot do without him, but he must not drown the soloist.

Vanilla and cinnamon are the undisputed leaders when it comes to flavouring sweet desserts. And vanilla is the basic flavouring, simply because it has such a subtle aroma and is fully compatible with almost all other flavours, including the alcoholic ones. On its own it is the indispensable flavour that determines the character of a delicate cream, and practically all basic recipes for egg or milk creams call for vanilla, whether it be English custard, confectioner's custard, whipped cream or cream caramel. It is the vanilla that gives them all their incomparable flavour, and it can at any time be mixed with chocolate, coffee, nuts or other ingredients without any risk of the vanilla not harmonising with them.

Exotic Spices and Home-Grown Herbs

The very thought of spices and herbs evokes in us certain concepts and imaginary perfumes. We sniff around after the scent of vanilla, a breath of cinnamon and cloves, the powerful aroma of bitter almonds, or the freshness of mint. Yet, within the broad category of sweet things, desserts are somewhat hard to accommodate: the choice of spices and herbs is in fact relatively narrow if we leave aside the many possibilities for using spirits and other ingredients such as nuts, chocolate, coffee and the wide variety of fruit derivatives. By way of compensation we do have the major flavourings, such as vanilla and cinnamon, which are very versatile.

Aniseed

This is the dried seed of the anise plant (*Pimpinella anisum*). It is one of the world's oldest spices and is believed to have originated in Egypt. On account of its strong flavour it is used sparingly in desserts, but goes well in baked sweets, puddings and compotes. It is exported nowadays from Spain, Italy, Greece, Bulgaria and the Soviet Union.

Bitter Almonds

Bitter almonds are the fruit of the almond tree with reddish blossoms (*Prunus amygdalus amarum*). Predictably, it is called for whenever you want to give a dessert a stronger flavour of almonds. It also suits all sorts of stone fruits like apricots, peaches and plums – the stones of which can also be cracked open and the kernel used similarly.

Ginger

Of tropical Far Eastern origin, ginger (*Zingiber officinale*) can be bought in this country in the following forms: the dried root (either whole or ground), preserved ginger in heavy syrup, crystallised ginger and the fresh root. The last-mentioned is to be preferred, since its flavour is more delicate yet at the same time more concentrated; when buying, care should be taken that the roots are tight and firm. Preserved ginger is at once both a flavouring and an ingredient, and the syrup can also be used, notably in fruit salads. Ginger is quite compatible with other flavourings.

Cardamom

Cardamom (*Elettaria cardamomum*) hails from the humid regions of India and produces in its seed capsules a spice known in Europe since the Middle Ages. It goes with every dessert that contains coffee and, together with cinnamon and cloves, may be added to apple, pear or plum compotes.

Mint

Peppermint (*Mentha x piperita*) is a European herb, the culinary uses of which were discovered by the English. Only fresh mint should be used for desserts. Small bunches wrapped in kitchen foil are easy to freeze. Its faint menthol flavour suits fruit salads, fruit ices and fruit sauces.

Nutmeg and Mace

The nutmeg tree (*Myristica fragrans Houtt*) originates from the tropical rain forests of the Banda Islands and Moluccas. Until the Middle Ages mace and nutmeg were brought to Europe by Arab traders. Both are used, particularly in English-speaking countries, in creams, sorbets and compotes.

Poppy

Papaver somniferum comes from Asia Minor and has been known ever since ancient times. The flower develops a pod which carries hundreds of bluish-grey seeds. The poppy seed is both a flavouring and a flavouring ingredient: it is used sparingly as a decoration on breads and small cakes and in quantity as a filling in Austrian strudels, dumplings and pastry horns.

Cloves

This ancient Far Eastern spice is the dried flower-buds of the aromatic clove tree (*Syzygium aromaticum*) and originates – like the nutmeg – from the Moluccas. Once a year the red buds growing on the flower umbels are plucked and then dried over a low fire or in the heat of the sun. The oil glands with the characteristic clove aroma are located in the sepals. For dessert purposes cloves are used, in powdered form, in creams and also in compotes, as well as with fresh fruit recipes and fruit sauces.

Saffron

This old-fashioned flavouring and colouring plant from Asia Minor (*Crocus sativus*) is today cultivated all around the Mediterranean. For desserts, because of its strong and not universally popular flavour, saffron is largely relied on as a colouring for creams and sauces. But remember: saffron spoils the flavour of vanilla creams.

Woodruff

This herb of May (*Galium odoratum* or *Asperula odorata*) grows widely in Europe. Its delicate, yet concentrated, aroma gives an attractive taste to creams and fruit jellies. It is compatible with dry white wine, but not with other flavourings.

Two spices in one fruit. The peach-sized fruit of the nutmeg tree opens at the seam as soon as it is ripe. Under the soft covering of fruit lies the first spice, brilliant red and, incorrectly, sometimes called the flower of the nutmeg. It encloses the hard shell within which rests the second spice, the nutmeg itself.

Fresh, young ginger, as harvested by this Indian farmer, can be found in oriental markets in spring. It has a more concentrated aroma and is not so hot. When peeled and sliced or, better still, finely minced it makes an ideal dessert flavouring.

Woodruff all the year around. This freezes well and retains all its aroma. Experience has shown that it is better not to tie it up in bundles, in the way it is usually sold, but to freeze it loose in foil containers. It can then be used in the same way as fresh woodruff.

Vanilla

The queen of spices, vanilla (*Vanilla plani-folia*) is a liana of the orchid family which hails from the primeval tropical rain forests of Mexico. Its yellow flowers are pollinated in plantations by means of bamboo wands, a task which must be performed very rapidly, since each flower opens for a few hours only. To obtain the spice the fruit capsules must be gathered before they are ripe and while still greenish-yellow. They are then drenched with hot water, packed in containers and left to sweat in the tropical sun. After some weeks the vanilla sticks take on a deep brown colour but remain soft and pliable. The Aztecs of old used vanilla to flavour their cocoa drink and it was there that Spanish conquistadores became acquainted with both. For 300 years the coveted vanilla was a Mexican (Spanish) monopoly, but at the beginning of the nineteenth century the Dutch and the French succeeded in laying out plantations on their island colonies in the Indian Ocean with cuttings taken from botanical gardens. Today vanilla is exported mainly from Madagascar, Réunion, the Comores Archipelago and Indonesia. For the pastry cook it takes precedence over all other flavourings, even though its incomparable aroma develops to the full only in combination with sugar. It imparts its unmistakable taste to all delicate creams and sauces made with egg and milk or cream and, of course, the 'nicest of all ice creams'. It is also ideal for blending with other flavours, being very compatible with cinnamon, cloves, chocolate and most of the spirits used to flavour desserts.

Vanilla pods are imported in bundles for commercial use. Otherwise the valuable pods, which are very liable to become desiccated, are sold individually or in powder form, with or without sugar. When mixed with sugar the proportion of vanilla powder must be not less than 5 per cent.

Cinnamon and Cinnamon are Two Different Things

The evergreen cinnamon tree belongs to the laurel family. The bark of only two can be used as a spice: the Ceylon cinnamon (*cinnamomum zeylanicum*) and the Chinese or cassia cinnamon (*Cinnamomum aromaticum* or *Cinnamomum cassia*).

Ceylon cinnamon (the picture at the top left shows the sticks being dried) is light brown and has a delicately sweetish fragrance and flavour. The thinner the bark, the fuller the aroma. Both sides curl up when it is dried and when ground it remains light in colour and lightly scented. Ceylon cinnamon comes also from southern India, the Seychelles or Madagascar but is not of such good quality as the originating sticks in Ceylon (now Sri Lanka).

Cassia cinnamon is a native of southern China, Indochina and Indonesia, the best kind being the *cassia vera* from plantations in western Su-

matra. The picture below left shows cassia being harvested. The bark within reach is first peeled off the standing tree, which is then felled. Dried cassia is darker in colour, the bark hard, the scent less cloying and the taste stronger. When ground it still has the characteristic darker colour and the strong, rather pungent smell. The quality of cassia is in no way inferior. It is just a different kind and has different uses.

So can you choose one or the other? Certainly: both kinds are very compatible with sugar and therefore make ideal dessert flavourings. Light creams or custards call for the sweet and soft tone of Ceylon cinnamon. But stronger preparations like a red wine sauce or compotes of home-grown fruits are better spiced with the more pungent cassia.

Pure cinnamon oil is distilled from the dried, unripe fruits, bark fragments and leaves of the cassia tree. Cinnamon is, incidentally, the oldest spice in the world.

Rum

If there is an ideal spirit for dessert flavouring it is, without doubt, rum. It is compatible with almost all other flavourings, and often increases their effectiveness.

Unfortunately perhaps, no other spirit has such uncritical consumers as rum, whether light or dark. But the best rum is extraordinarily hard to come by. It is pure sugar cane distillate of incomparable aroma. And, since quality alone makes a dessert excellent, finding a good rum is really important.

Brandy

Practically every kind, be it French Cognac or armagnac or German, Italian or Spanish brandy, makes a good flavouring for desserts. The aroma of grape brandy complements particularly well the taste of fruits low in acidity and also rounds off pleasantly the flavour of a custard. Also brandies made from grape skins, the residue of the wine press, like Marc de Champagne, or the Italian *grappa*, are an excellent flavouring for fruit salads and compotes. In a refreshing sorbet they are first-rate.

Clear Fruit Eaux de Vie

Their fragrance would be enough but we will happily settle for their alcoholic content. In addition they are very simple to use. Every distillate suits its own fruit – kirsch with cherries, bananas with rum, and so on. Especially with whipped cream, the aroma of *eaux de vie* in combination with the appropriate fruit is peculiarly effective. Nevertheless, they should be used more sparingly than other forms of alcohol. This also goes for fruit salads, which must be given no more than a breath of them.

Liqueurs

Liqueurs are so many and various that no rules on flavouring with them can usefully be made. And strict standards of quality are essential. Those which have a basic flavour, such as apricot brandy, the orange and almond liqueurs and so on, present no problem: they go anyway with their own fruit and mostly they blend well also with chocolate and vanilla. Liqueurs made with a large number of aromatic ingredients are more difficult: they usually have so characteristic a flavour that they will not tolerate the company of any other flavouring in a dessert. In such cases you have to rely on

the given recipe, or occasionally try out something new yourself, which often works out well if you have a good idea of the liqueur's aroma.

Wine

Wine may in a given recipe be either a major flavouring in itself or a substantial ingredient that determines the final flavour of the dessert: it just depends on the quantity used. For example, in a wine jelly which naturally consists mostly of wine it will dominate. But used in a lesser quantity, as in a zabaione, it will be more of a flavouring ingredient. In choosing wine for cooking the greatest attention must be paid to quality. For the very reason that the amount called for in a recipe is often more than merely a flavouring, the best is only good enough.

Champagne and Sparkling Wine

Either of these communicates its fizziness to the dessert, and still wine can in no way be substituted for it. For example, one test with a granita will clearly show the difference. Again, as with all ingredients, it is quality that finally determines the finished result. All the same, champagne should only be used in those desserts in which its strength would be fully appreciated. Moreover, the dessert should be enjoyed right away –

just like a freshly filled glass of champagne – whether it be an airy zabaione or a sorbet. Champagne will not go with any other flavouring, except fruit, for which it makes an admirable partner.

CREAMS

The foundation of a good dessert

Cream – the very word has a soft and pleasing sound, perfectly descriptive of this most agreeable of desserts which literally melts in the mouth. *Bavarian cream* could stand as the symbol of royal puddings, for one thing because in a figurative sense the cream means the choicest or best part of anything. In the purely culinary sense the word embraces a wide range of somewhat heterogeneous groups of dishes with only one thing in common – namely that cooked or uncooked cream or milk constitutes their principal ingredient. Nevertheless, some kind of systematic classification can be made, according to the methods used in making them, so that there can be agreement on what is what. For a start, 'English custard' is the internationally accepted name for the basic egg cream which is the foundation of a whole series of creams and sauces. Next come the baked custards, known everywhere as cream caramel or, in an even finer form, as *petits pots de crème*. A third kind is the Bavarian cream, a cream custard with whipped cream set with gelatine, which fell into oblivion during the lean war years but is now deservedly fashionable again. The fourth group comprises the *crèmes françaises* – foamy eggs beaten over the heat till just below simmering point then set with gelatine. And finally there are the *crèmes pâtissières*, which used to be cooked with flour and used instead of whipped cream. All these creations made from eggs, cream and other fine ingredients have always had their place in the perfect menu, whether it consisted of three courses or a dozen. Looking at old menu cards one sees that the accompanying wine was changed once again for this dessert. The red wine which had been drunk with the roast and vegetables was followed by champagne, a muscatel or a Marcobrunner or by *punch à la romaine* – a cooling dish made with champagne and ice cream which could also be a popular entrèe when served before the meat. It is largely because of the nature of the ingredients that such old recipes have stayed in fashion: this means they can be reproduced quite unaltered, except of course that the quantities given for a banquet with 48 guests do need to be halved or quartered. It is also quite permissible to do as our grandmothers used to do, that is stir and beat and mix the flavours with great patience and care. Anyone who has ever prepared two or three different creams for a big family occasion or a celebration and served them with a plate of flaky petits fours knows what delight and admiration is their reward.

Considerations of fashion apart, the Bavarian cream does happen to be one of the most delectable and versatile desserts around, a blessing and a boon to anyone's repertoire. As well, the basic technique of English custard making which underlies it is one of the most invaluable to the learner cook. One of its greatest assets is that the Bavarian cream can be as light or as sumptuous as you require for the particular occasion. Made with fresh orange as a flavouring, for example, sharpened or not with a dash or two of Cointreau, it will refresh the palate after a rich and heavy main course. Whereas, made with chocolate it will be a dessert of quite another colour and character. At the other end of this particular scale lies the zephyr-like cream caramel – the airiest of all creams, fit to please the jaded, the invalidish and the sensitive palate alike. As for confectioner's custard, it is aptly named indeed, for it is perhaps the most useful recipe the pastry cook can master. As it is, it fills and greatly flatters that other great and favourite standby, the profiterole. On its own it is a fine sauce. And as well, spread on the base of fruit-filled pastry shells, it will both protect the pastry from being soaked by juice and add an extra, richer dimension to the finished dessert.

A basic cream

English Custard

Crème à l'Anglaise

This pleasant, thickly flowing cream is the foundation for a whole range of desserts, the Bavarian cream for example, but it is better known simply as the traditional 'vanilla sauce'. It is indispensable for serving with compotes, mousses, flummeries and for various hot desserts. At the same time it is the foundation of all kinds of fine ice creams. But, whichever way it is used, its composition varies little: the main ingredients are always milk (sometimes with added cream), egg yolks, sugar and flavouring. The coagulation of the egg yolks thickens the liquid, thus making a light coating sauce. But the whole of the egg must not coagulate completely, or the thickening will be undone and the sauce will curdle. This factor must be kept in mind throughout. It is also very important that no trace of egg white should be left with the yolks when they are beaten up with the sugar, or it will form small clots when the sauce is heated. Next, the hot milk is added, little by little, to the egg yolks – this makes it less liable to curdle – and the mixture can be set directly on the hob. But it must on no account be allowed to boil.

Ingredients for the basic recipe are:

6 egg yolks
100 g/4 oz sugar
600 ml/1 pint milk
¼ vanilla pod

1 **Separate the eggs.** Crack open the shell on the rim of a cup. Tip the yolk over the cup from one half of the shell to the other, letting the white drain off into the cup. Carefully remove the gelatinous thread clinging to the yolks and place the yolks in the mixing bowl.

2 **Add the sugar.** Weigh out the quantity required and add it to the bowl with the egg yolks. Carefully whisk it in, slowly at first and then a little faster. It is best to stand the bowl on a damp cloth to stop it slipping around on the work surface.

3 **Cream the egg yolks and sugar.** Do not use an electric beater for this process, only a balloon whisk. The sugar must dissolve slowly and blend with the egg yolks into a creamy (*not* frothy) mixture otherwise there will be too much air in the custard. Neither should the whisking be too rapid.

4 **Add the vanilla-flavoured milk.** Put the pan of milk on the heat, cut the vanilla pod open lengthways and scrape the seeds and pith into the milk. Bring to the boil and while still hot ladle it slowly onto the egg and sugar mixture, stirring continuously.

5 **Pour the custard into a pan.** The custard may just as well be poured into the milk saucepan, provided that the milk has not stuck to the bottom. Stand the pan on the heat and cook the custard, stirring all the time. Be careful not to let it boil, otherwise it will curdle and spoil the finished result.

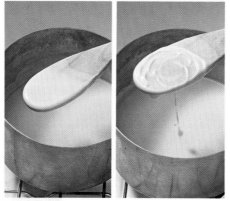

6 **Giving the custard the rose test,** as the experts call it. It is sufficiently cooked when it has thickened just enough to coat the wooden spoon or produce a rose-like pattern on it when blown upon. On grounds of hygiene the former method is to be preferred, and is at least as efficient.

7 **Strain the custard through a fine sieve.** This may well strike some people as superfluous, but it is not. Any small clots that may have formed will in this way be removed. Straining enhances the quality of the custard; a first-class cook will insist on it, so this procedure should be followed unless you are very short of time.

Illustrating another cooking method
for egg custards

Cream Caramel

Crème caramel

The ingredients – milk, eggs and sugar – are the same as for English custard, though in different proportions. This custard, however, is baked in the oven, protected by a water bath. Basically it is no more than the familiar *royale* as the French call it, a savoury mixture of eggs, milk and seasoning that is cooked to setting point in a water bath. The firmness of the setting depends – as also in the sweet versions – on the proportion of egg white used. This determines whether the custard will be creamy or half-set or, as in our example of cream caramel, can be turned out of its mould.

Beyond doubt, the most exquisitely delicate members of this family are *petits pots de crème*, which are quite unjustifiably overshadowed by cream caramel. Not only have they an especially smooth consistency through containing a minimum of egg white; they are also immensely versatile. The custard mixture is put into little ramekins or ovenproof pots which are then stood in a large, deep pan. Hot water is carefully poured around them to come halfway up the sides of the pots, the pan covered and the custard allowed to set for about 20 minutes in a moderate oven (180 C, 350 F, gas 4). It should be well cooled before serving. The custard itself can be flavoured in a great many ways, for example with coffee, melted chocolate, grated nuts and all sorts of liqueurs. There are likewise many possible combinations with fresh or stewed fruit and fruit sauces.

Compared with this half-set custard those that are to be turned out have a greater proportion of egg white, and often also a greater proportion of milk to egg. They are therefore somewhat firmer, but should melt in the mouth too and are no less delicious.

For the caramel glaze:
100 g/4 oz sugar
1 tablespoon water
a little oil to grease the moulds

For the custard:
500 ml/17 fl oz milk
¼ vanilla pod
100 g/4 oz sugar
3 eggs plus 2 egg yolks
This quantity is sufficient to fill 6 moulds
holding 100 ml/scant 4 fl oz each.

Preparing and pouring caramel into the moulds. Heat the sugar in a saucepan. Begin to stir when it starts to melt around the edges, then stir slowly but continuously. When it is fully dissolved add the water all at once and pour sufficient caramel into the lightly greased custard moulds to cover the bottom by about 3 mm ⅛ in. Any left over can be boiled up with water and served as a caramel sauce.

Only the milk is boiled up with the vanilla pod. The eggs and egg yolks are thoroughly beaten with the sugar but not allowed to become frothy. Then the hot milk is stirred in gradually and the custard passed through a fine sieve and poured into the moulds. These are then placed in a water bath (the water should be at a temperature of 80 C, 150 F) and left to cook for about 20 minutes in a moderately hot oven (200 C, 400 F, gas 6). Let the custards get thoroughly cool, and run around the inside of the mould with the point of a knife before turning them out.

Cream caramel should be turned out and served right away, for it tastes best when cool and fresh on the plate. The dissolved caramel will still be adhering to the top and caramel sauce may be served as well. Incidentally, cream caramel does not have to be made in the traditional cone-shaped timbale moulds: brioche or other moulds are equally suitable as long as they have a level bottom so that the layer of caramel sits well on top when the custard is turned out.

Whipped Cream

Crème Chantilly

Whipped cream is not just a binding agent. Whipped up with sugar, and perhaps with vanilla too, it is in itself a cream of extraordinary versatility, useful as a filling for desserts, a decoration, or simply an accompaniment – to a compote or ice cream for example. Whipped cream is also a lightening ingredient for a whole range of creams and chilled desserts. It may only be lightly whipped and thus used at a pouring consistency, or else stiffly beaten and folded into creams; in this form it can also be used to lend body to fillings.

Always chill cream well. It is usually no problem to work with if just a few basic rules are observed. Fresh cream is concentrated milk that has had fluid removed from it by centrifugal force. True fresh cream, sadly, has vanished from the market, its beautiful flavour now just a memory. Nowadays cream is usually heated to improve its keeping quality and this, unfortunately, has had no good effect on its flavour.

The butterfat content must be at least 30 per cent, and the higher it is the lighter the cream will whip. When speaking of 'fresh cream' a ripening time of 2–3 days is implied, but it usually takes this long anyway to get from producer to consumer. It is then in perfect condition for whipping, incorporates a large amount of air and doubles or triples in volume. But it must be worked when it is as cool as possible: the cream itself, the utensils, and – if possible – the room itself should all be cool. It will then take in more air and be more flexible so that the danger of its turning into butter will be substantially reduced. Should it be too warm – that is, about room temperature – the unhappy result may be that the fat will separate from the liquid.

Newly whipped cream tastes best. Although it will keep in the refrigerator for up to 12 hours it will then need to be whipped again for a few moments before using. Artificial agents for keeping whipped cream stiff which are on the market only make the fluid in it settle more slowly. It will still in time become limp and of course the flavour will not be improved. Using cream as soon as possible after it is whipped is the only way to ensure its quality. It is also important to store it in a refrigerator.

Unwhipped cream – and whipped cream still more so – must be in an absolutely airtight container when stored in the refrigerator with other, strongly smelling foods. It is extremely sensitive and absorbs other aromas very easily – an attribute which, in the case of onions for example, has nothing to recommend it but becomes a considerable asset when crushed, freshly picked wild strawberries are stirred into it. No other cream could do as much to enhance their flavour.

1 **Can cream be whipped with an electric beater?** Yes, but only at a slow speed, because if the result is to be as light and airy as that achieved with a balloon whisk it must be given time to take in enough cold air. Add the sugar to the liquid cream so that it can dissolve as the cream is whipped.

2 **Working in circles will very largely prevent uneven whipping.** Otherwise the cream increases its volume only around the paddle and remains fluid in the rest of the bowl. And remember: chill all utensils before use and work in a cool room if possible, because these are the optimum conditions for this particular exercise.

3 **Finishing by hand is the surest way to avoid over-beating,** because with the balloon whisk you are much more sensitive to the exact condition of the cream. You can feel as the cream gets stiffer and reaches its correct texture. Also, any cream that splashes up around the inside of the bowl can be incorporated much more easily with a wire whisk.

Bavarian Cream

Crème Bavaroise

This is basically an English custard, lightened with whipped cream and bound with gelatine. It ranks as one of the classic international desserts and in its simplest form derives its character solely from its fresh ingredients (eggs, milk, and cream) and the vanilla flavouring. Another, centuries old, moulded cream, prepared in the same way, is the classic blancmange which has the added aroma of sweet almonds warmed in milk and then squeezed out. The basic cream, and thus the eggs, are dispensed with in this recipe; instead, whipped cream lightens and gelatine binds the dessert. A Bavarian cream can however also be flavoured in all sorts of ways – with coffee, chocolate, hazelnuts, almonds and most kinds of fruit. Filling the mould with layers of differing flavours adds interest both for the palate and for the eye.

Vanilla Bavarian Cream with Raspberry Sauce
500 ml/17 fl oz milk
1 vanilla pod
4 egg yolks
100 g/4 oz sugar
7 leaves gelatine or 15 g/½ oz powdered gelatine
600 ml/1 pint double cream

Make the basic Bavarian Cream mixture in exactly the same way as the English custard on page 63. The quantity of gelatine is sufficient for a moulded Bavarian cream that will turn out, but it can be made lighter for serving in glasses. In that case 5 leaves of gelatine will suffice.

1 **Soak the gelatine leaves in cold water and squeeze them out well.** Warm the basic cream mixture a little and put in the gelatine leaves or powder. Stir until it has completely dissolved; if it does not do so as readily or as quickly as you wish the whole mixture can be stirred over heat to dissolve the last remnants.

2 **Pass the basic custard through a sieve to filter out any possible lumps.** For this have ready a large bowl half filled with ice cubes and cold water and stand a smaller bowl in it. This should be large enough to hold both the custard and the cream that will be folded into it at a later stage.

3 **Set this bowl into the one containing iced water** and stir until the cream mixture is cold. Do not beat with the balloon whisk but just stir slowly. The basic cream must not froth. Meanwhile, whip the cream. When the basic cream is cool and beginning to thicken lift its bowl out immediately.

4 **The critical point.** The basic cream must not be too warm and runny, or the whipped cream will liquefy in it too. Should it already be too cold, the whipped cream which is also cold will cause it to set straight away and the resulting mixture will not be homogeneous.

5 **An ideal consistency** is achieved when the cream flows heavily off the spoon. While filling the mould, tap it a few times on the work surface to allow any air bubbles to escape. Chill well, and dip the mould quickly in hot water to turn it out. Serve with raspberry sauce.

Confectioner's Custard

Crème pâtissière

This is a virtually all-purpose basic custard, but the specifications can vary widely and easily lead to confusion. The chief ingredients, however, are milk and sugar, bound with cornflour, and vanilla is the usual flavouring. Add egg yolks and you have a flummery or, in everyday language, a moulded cream, one of Europe's favourite desserts, perhaps partly because of the simplicity of its preparation.

Confectioner's custard can be stirred till cold after it has been cooked and will still retain its creamy consistency. Or it can be left in a bowl to cool, when it will set firm and will need to be stirred to make it creamy again for further use or, better still, passed through a sieve. This makes it once more an ideal, spreadable, basic custard for use in every recipe which calls for a creamy coating or filling, such as fruit tartlets. It is also used to lighten butter cream, and with whipped cream beaten in becomes a richer whipped cream filling. But it should, on principle, be eaten fresh, as it will not keep for more than 2 days even if well chilled.

100 g/4 oz sugar
40 g/1½ oz cornflour
4 egg yolks
500 ml/17 fl oz milk
½ vanilla pod

1 **Prepare the thickening.** Put half of the sugar and the cornflour into a small bowl. Separate the egg yolks very carefully from the whites because any traces of white will inevitably form small lumps when the custard is cooked. Add about a quarter of the milk.

2 **Beat with a small balloon whisk.** Do this carefully: all the ingredients should be well blended, so that they will form an even-textured, effective liaison. Meanwhile, bring the rest of the milk and sugar to the boil, together with the split and scooped out vanilla pod, in a small saucepan.

3 **Thicken the boiling milk.** First give the cornflour mixture a good whisk through, as it has a strong tendency to settle in the bottom of the bowl. Then pour it slowly and evenly into the boiling milk, at the same time whisking it in over a constant heat.

4 **Boil up the confectioner's custard,** stirring it through evenly with a whisk as you do so. This procedure is critical to the success of a good custard. When the custard has bubbled up a few times, and become quite homogeneous, take if off the heat immediately. If it is to be used as a basic custard pour it into a bowl and sift icing sugar over the surface to prevent a skin forming as it cools. A sugar coating should also be used to prevent this unappetising skin if the custard is poured into a mould to be turned out later as a pudding.

Custard filling with egg white. This is an extra-light variation of the basic recipe on the previous page. The basic custard is lightened with beaten egg whites. While the milk is coming to the boil 3 egg whites are beaten into stiff peaks with 50 g/2 oz sugar. When the confectioner's custard has thickened correctly leave the pan on the heat and stir in the beaten egg whites with the whisk until the whole has bubbled up once or twice. It is this action which gives the filling its body: the egg whites coagulate and at the same time blend with the custard. It must be used quickly because its creamy consistency lasts only as long as it is hot and the mixture will congeal as soon as it cools. It is an ideal filling for fancy cream slices particularly, and for desserts that can be served fresh and eaten immediately.

Confectioner's Custard with Whipped Cream

Crème pâtissière à la crème chantilly

Here it is shown as a filling for profiteroles. A. Stir the basic custard to a smooth consistency and beat it together with an equal volume of stiffly whipped cream and any additional flavouring. This makes a light and airy custard which can be made in very small quantities, but it will keep fresh for a few hours only. B. The addition of gelatine makes the custard keep better but it must be made in larger quantities. This would be a classic custard filling, made according to the basic recipe for confectioner's custard but with only 35 g/1¼ oz cornflour and with the addition of 6 dissolved leaves of gelatine.

1 **Extra stiffening with gelatine.** Prepare the custard as in the basic recipe, bringing it smoothly to the boil with the cornflour thickening. Then reduce the heat and stir in the water-softened and squeezed-out leaf gelatine until dissolved. Pour the custard into a bowl and sift icing sugar over it.

2 **Push the custard through a fine sieve.** After it has cooled, weigh out the required amount and pass it through the sieve. Or it may be beaten with a hand-held mixer till smooth. Next warm the custard, stirring continuously, until the gelatine has dissolved.

3 **Fold in the whipped cream.** For a good custard filling it is crucially important that the basic mixture should be at the right temperature: it should almost be cool to the touch but still semi-fluid. Stiffly whip the chilled cream and blend it into the custard with a wire whisk.

4 **Fill the profiteroles.** First open them on the underside with the point of a knife then pipe in the custard, using a piping bag fitted with a plain nozzle. Keep any unused custard at room temperature till needed, so that the gelatine does not take effect.

5 **First cool the filled profiteroles,** to let the custard set a little. Chocolate sauce is a classic accompaniment, but almost all fruit sauces will go with the neutral taste of vanilla. And the custard itself can also be made with additional flavourings, such as chocolate or coffee.

SWEET PASTRIES AND MERINGUES

Basic preparations illustrated step-by-step

If this chapter title were to be taken literally all the sweet and some of the unsweetened pastries would have to be included. The realm of desserts is so wide that in it we find almost every sort of pastry, whether it be 'only' a leaf-shaped *pâte aux tuiles* decoration for a sundae, a sorbet or other ice, or the sponge fingers which surround a superb charlotte. The entire pastry repertory could be brought into play, from the simplest sponge cake to the very special batter from which we make Normandy crêpes, but the chapter that follows is confined to the basic pastes which can be used for a whole series of recipes in this book. For example, the sponge for a Swiss roll can be spread with jam in the usual way, rolled up, sliced and used to line a *charlotte royale*; but the slices can also form the base of an ice cream dessert or, if the sponge is not rolled up, it can be cut into strips for sandwich slices or stamped into other shapes.

Other pastes which are just as versatile are *pâte aux tuiles*, choux paste, shortcrust pastry and meringue. There is the advantage, particularly in the case of shortcrust pastry dough or *pâte aux tuiles*, that if wrapped in foil they can be kept in the refrigerator for quite long periods. Thus a tartlet can be rolled out and baked in no time, a decoration for an ice cream bombe quickly made with the prepared *pâte aux tuiles*. Choux paste too, when baked into an éclair or puff, can be frozen and crisped up again at any time very successfully. Meringue halves, once they have been properly dried out in the oven, will keep a long time – but for this a dry, well-ventilated place away from smells is absolutely essential since they pick up extraneous smells very easily.

You will find in practice that this and the preceding chapter are virtually interdependant. Chantilly cream, for example, is a perfect – and for some the one irresistable – companion for meringues, plain or decorative; and choux puffs are at their best when filled with an appropriately flavoured custard.

One of the prettiest uses for almond biscuit paste (page 66) is for making flower-shaped cups. These store well in airtight containers and are an exquisite – and exquisitely useful – container for ice cream. The trick of making them once mastered, they are simple to produce, out of very ordinary ingredients, and very impressive. There is too a charming logic about biscuits that manage to be ice cream wafer and bowl all in one. The meringue mushrooms, while rather more frivolous in inspiration, again once mastered can be made in quantity, keep very well for a long period in airtight containers and will transform in a trice a sensible looking dessert into a sensational looking one.

It goes without saying that best quality ingredients are important in pastry as in other things, for they alone guarantee a perfect result. Today, we are deluged with an enormous number of preparations, especially for sponge mixtures, which guarantee a good-looking result but are hopelessly lacking in flavour. Puff pastry as well, widely available frozen (and now marketed in ready-rolled form) rises impeccably and is easy to work with. But, needless to say, you will not taste any fresh butter. In practice, it is only too easy to turn to ready-made preparations such as these, but it is an unavoidable fact that a first-class result in terms of integrity and excellence of flavour will only be achieved if ingredients of the highest possible quality are used.

Quality and tradition still count when making baked desserts, even though the pace of our lifestyle today does not easily leave time for either. Pastry recipes, whether for shortcrust, sponge or choux have not changed materially over the years, and fine desserts continue to depend on the use of fresh, high-quality ingredients.

Sponge Fingers

Biscuits à la cuiller

These are airy sponge biscuits ideal for serving with many different desserts, or form part of one, for example a *charlotte russe*. This recipe for sponge fingers is also suitable for chocolate-covered sponge cakes, petits fours and in fact all biscuits. The familiar finger shape can be varied according to the purpose for which they are to be used: they can be quite straight, without any broadening of the ends, or broad at only one end – or adapted in many other ways. To make sponge fingers successfully, all utensils should be clean and free from grease, the ingredients must be absolutely fresh and scrupulous care taken over each stage of the operation.

The quantities in the following recipe are enough for about 70 sponge fingers. They can of course be halved if desired.

12 egg yolks
250 g/9 oz sugar
½ vanilla pod
8 egg whites
100 g/4 oz cornflour
150 g/5 oz flour
icing sugar for dusting

1 **Add only a quarter of the sugar to the egg yolks,** after the eggs have been cracked open one by one over a cup and the yolks separated from the whites. The egg white must be free from all trace of yolk. When the sugar has been stirred into the yolks add the seeds from the vanilla pod.

3 **Beat the egg whites to a snow.** In an immaculately clean and grease-free bowl beat them to an airy froth. Then little by little let the rest of the sugar trickle into the bowl (it is best to use a piece of greaseproof paper folded into a funnel shape for this). Again, if using an electric mixer start at the lowest speed and increase it gradually.

4 **Fold the cornflour into the meringue base.** Sift it first onto a sheet of paper and then work in carefully with a wooden spoon. The cornflour must be added little by little and must blend completely with the stiffly beaten egg whites without making them fall in.

5 **Incorporate the foamy egg yolk and sugar mixture into the meringue.** Stir around the bowl with a wooden spoon while letting the mixture run in slowly. A tip: after each circular movement with the spoon turn the bowl a little in the opposite direction.

8 **Dust with icing sugar.** This is not strictly necessary but it will make the tops crisper and they will taste better. Now bake then in a moderate oven (180 C, 350 F, gas 4). Check after 8 to 10 minutes how they are coming along. When they are light gold in colour, remove from the oven.

9 **Take the finished fingers off the paper.** There is a simple way of doing this: draw the strips of paper over the edge of a square baking tin or large biscuit box, or even the edge of the kitchen table. This automatically dislodges the sponge fingers without breaking them.

Sponge for a Swiss Roll

Biscuit pour une roulade

8 egg yolks
100 g/4 oz caster sugar
a generous pinch of salt
grated rind of 1 lemon
4 egg whites
75 g/3 oz flour
25 g/1 oz cornflour

Making the sponge is not a problem in itself. But if it is to be filled with whipped cream you have to ensure that the sponge does not break after it has cooled, and here opinion differs as to the best way of doing this. Some cooks roll it up as soon as it is baked, others let it cool first.

2 **Whisk the egg yolks and sugar until foamy** with circular movements of the whisk and without actually beating. If using an electric mixer start at the lowest speed and increase it only when some of the sugar has been mixed in. The sugar must dissolve completely, and the mixture should turn a pale yellow.

6 **Lastly, stir in the flour.** The flour is weighed and sifted over the sponge mixture. Then, again with a circular motion, draw it carefully into the mixture. The paste must stay firm, or the sponge fingers will lose their shape in the baking.

7 **Pipe the sponge fingers.** Cut cooking parchment or greaseproof paper into strips 10 cm/4 in wide and lay them on the baking sheet. Fit a piping bag with a large nozzle and pipe the fingers onto the paper. Here the ends broaden out into a tongue shape but you can vary it as you wish. Should no suitable paper happen to be available the fingers can be piped directly onto the baking sheet provided it has first been lightly and evenly greased then sprinkled with flour. Once cooked, however, they must then be lifted off the baking sheet with a spatula while still warm, or they will stick and get broken

1 **Adding the egg yolk mixture to the stiffly beaten egg whites.** First beat the yolks with a spoonful of sugar and the salt and lemon rind but they must not become foamy. Fold them into the meringue. Sift together the flour and cornflour and stir them in.

2 **Spread out the sponge mixture evenly,** having covered the swiss roll tin with cooking parchment or baking paper. It spreads best with an angled palette knife or spatula.

3 **Roll it up while still hot,** if it has a jam filling. Turn the sponge out onto a damp cloth or one sprinkled with sugar and at once spread it with jam and roll it up. For other fillings cover it with a damp cloth and let it get cold.

Meringue

Baiser/Meringue

Egg whites and sugar make the sweetest and airiest paste imaginable. But the basic meringue formula can be varied both as to sugar content and by flavouring with coffee, chocolate, hazelnuts, almonds, etc. It can be baked to make firm meringue shells and meringue bases, or just quickly browned as the coating to an ice bombe. It can also be shaped into balls and poached in liquid (*oeufs à la neige*), or piped and baked as a decoration, as shown on the opposite page.

A basic meringue recipe:
250 ml/8 fl oz egg whites
(about 8 eggs)
250 g/9 oz caster sugar
200 g/7 oz icing sugar
25 g/1 oz cornflour (only if the
meringues are to be baked)

Beat the egg whites lightly and continue to beat while slowly adding 200 g/7 oz of the caster sugar. When this has dissolved the icing sugar, mixed with the remaining 50 g/2 oz caster sugar, must be carefully folded in with a wooden spoon. If you are making meringue shells or cases the cornflour should be added as well (it will ensure that they stay dry). The meringue should then be baked in a very cool oven (120 C. 250 F, gas ½) for about 3 hours. At this point the oven door must be opened a fraction. After baking the meringues should be left to dry overnight in the switched off oven. If you prefer them lightly browned with a slight taste of caramel bake them at 150 C, 300 F, gas 2. But check them after not more than 1 hour. These quantities are sufficient for about 30 small meringues.

Italian meringue is added to fruit ices and sorbets. As in the basic recipe, beat 200 g/7 oz sugar slowly into the egg whites. Then boil 250 g/9 oz sugar with 150 ml/5 fl oz water to the soft ball stage (112 C, 234 F), pour it in a thin trickle into the meringue mixture and stir it in.

1 **Be sure to separate the eggs one by one,** for the smallest amount of yolk escaping into the egg white will make it useless for beating. If this happens when the egg is separated individually over a cup only one egg white has to be discarded. In addition all utensils must be absolutely clean and free from grease.

4 **Until the sugar is all used up** the egg whites are beaten at a steady rate, preferably with a balloon whisk. The colour should be satin-white and the sugar crystals completely dissolved. Stiff peaks have formed when a point on the end of the lifted whisk will hold its shape without falling.

Meringue for decoration

This meringue mixture is beaten in a warm water bath. It develops less volume but is particularly delicate and smooth. It is especially well adapted for piping small decorations because the line will not break with even the finest of nozzles.

5 egg whites
200 g/7 oz icing sugar

Dissolved instant coffee or cocoa powder may be added where a change of colour or flavour is required. It will not make the meringue more liquid – it will still retain its firmness. But do not heat the oven above 110 C, 225 F, gas ¼.

2 **Begin to beat the egg whites,** preferably using a balloon whisk. With a hand-held electric mixer the quality of the beaten egg whites will not be so good. Start at a slow speed first and increase it gradually. When the whites have formed soft peaks, gradually add the sugar.

5 **Continue carefully, using a wooden spoon.** Do not beat any more, or the mixture will collapse. Sift the icing sugar together with the cornflour, if your meringue requires it, onto a sheet of paper, add the rest of the sugar and draw it all carefully into the beaten egg whites with the wooden spoon until the mixture is smooth.

1 **Beat the egg whites over warm water.** The egg whites and icing sugar are stirred well together and then beaten over a warm water bath. The 'snow' will slowly change in texture to a creamy foam, losing some of its airiness. The mixture is ready when stiff, at about 45 to 50 C, 113 to 122 F.

3 **Let the sugar trickle in slowly.** The best way is to put it onto a clean sheet of waxed paper, fold it and while beating add the sugar in a thin stream. If this is done quickly the egg whites will not take in enough air and will become 'gluey'.

6 **Fill the piping bag** with any meringue mixture that is to be piped. Fold the top of the bag well back, use a spatula to fill up with the mixture, pull up the top, shake the mixture down and close the bag. Hold the bag in one hand and guide the nozzle with the other.

7 **Pipe the meringues onto the paper.** Line a baking sheet with cooking parchment or greaseproof paper, sticking the corners to the sheet with a little meringue mixture to prevent it slipping. The mixture made with this recipe is very airy and light and particularly suitable for meringue shells and meringue bases.

2 **Now beat the meringue to cool it.** The stiffness will continue to increase without loss of volume. Both the warm and the cold beating can be done with a hand-held electric mixer without impairing the quality. But for best results finish off the operation with a balloon whisk.

3 **A stock of meringue mushrooms** will keep well in airtight containers. For the stems, pipe a blob of meringue and then, without squeezing the piping bag, draw it upwards to a point. The caps are piped in hemispherical shapes and dusted with cocoa powder before baking.

Almond Biscuit Paste

Pâte aux tuiles

This is an ideal paste for desserts and decorations of all kinds, as it can be shaped easily after being baked, so long as it is still warm. The German name for it, *hippenmasse*, is taken from the word *hohlhippen* which means hollow wafers (*cannelons* in French), those crisp and brittle biscuit rolls most often eaten with ice cream or filled with whipped cream and coated with chocolate. This versatile paste may be made with or without almonds. In the recipe below they are added as almond paste.

75 g/3 oz sugar
25 g/1 oz almond paste
pinch of cinnamon
pinch of salt
1 large egg
65 g/2½ oz flour
1½ tablespoons cream

The method, as the sequence of pictures shows, is quite simple, the essential requirement being that the mixture is smooth and spreadable. After the sifted flour has been stirred in, it must be left to rest for at least an hour. It can of course be kept in the refrigerator for much longer, if well wrapped in foil. But the cream must be added only just before baking. Once baked, the pastry can be handled easily as long as it stays warm, but it becomes hard and crisp very quickly, so you have to work with the utmost speed. When the edges begin to brown, draw the baking sheet half out of the oven and work quickly on the individual biscuits. This applies equally whether you wish to make cups out of the discs of paste or cigarette biscuits, with the help of a wooden spoon handle or other convenient tool. Fancy shapes for decorating can be made by spreading the paste through stencils. After these have been baked interesting three dimensional variations can be achieved if, for example, a pattern of leaves is laid on a curved surface to cool.

Set the oven at 180 C, 350 F, gas 4. After the first 3 to 4 minutes, take the baking sheet out of the oven and let it cool a little. Then continue baking till the pastry is done, keeping a constant eye on its progress.

These quantities are sufficient for about 20 pastry discs with a diameter of 10 cm/4 in.

1 **Cream together the sugar, almond paste, flavourings, and the egg** with a hand-held mixer. Low speed is essential, for the mixture must not froth.

2 **Stir in the sifted flour,** working once more with the hand-held mixer, till the mixture is quite smooth. In order to ensure that there are no lumps it can then be pushed through a fine sieve. Cover the mixture and leave it to rest for an hour in the refrigerator. Only then stir in the cream.

3 **Spread out the mixture.** Grease a baking sheet lightly all over and dust it with flour. Mark out the chosen shapes, then spread the mixture thinly and evenly so that each one bakes to a similar colour. Let the baking sheet cool off after 3 to 4 minutes in the oven and then put it back to finish baking – about 1 minute.

4 **Now you have to work quickly.** Slide the baking sheet half out of the oven, lift the discs off with a palette knife, drop them quickly into brioche moulds or cups and press them home with a small glass. The pastry cups will set in about a minute. Take them out and continue in the same way with the rest.

5 **All sorts of shapes can be made with stencils.** Patterns can be cut out of 1 to 2 mm 1/10 in card. Draw the motif and cut it out with a scalpel or very sharp knife, taking care to include a 'handle' for holding the stencil. There is no limit to the variety of shapes you can devise.

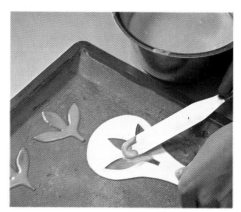

6 **Lay the stencil on the baking sheet,** ready-greased and dusted with flour. Spread the mixture onto it with a round-tipped knife or small palette knife, removing ragged pieces of paste with the knife blade held vertically. For bigger designs use a dough scraper.

Choux Paste

Pâte a choux

125 ml/4 fl oz milk
50 g/2 oz butter
pinch of salt
pinch of sugar
90 g/3½ oz flour
2–3 eggs

This makes a really airy paste, ideal for tiny profiteroles, for example, or éclairs filled with mocha cream. Choux paste is also suitable for special desserts but must be a little firmer, that is to say fewer eggs should be added. It must also be passed through a fine sieve so that it can be piped paper-thin. Once the baking sheet is in position, pour a glass of water on to the floor of the oven and shut the door. The resulting steam makes the pastry rise nicely. Bake for 15 to 20 minutes at 220 C, 425 F, gas 7. These quantities make 60 miniature éclairs or profiteroles.

First sift the flour onto folded paper. Put the milk, butter, salt and sugar into a saucepan and bring to the boil. Now shoot the flour all at once into the pan, stirring all the time with a wooden spoon or spatula. Cook this until the paste comes away from the side of the pan and forms a lump, then take the pan off the heat and let it cool a little. Put the paste into a bowl and stir in one egg, which must be completely blended in before the next egg is added, and so on until all the eggs have been incorporated. The paste is ready when it has a silky sheen and is supple and easy to pipe. When preparing prifiteroles, éclairs or other shapes which need volume, bake them in a preheated oven with steam to ensure an excellent rise.

Shortcrust Pastry – with or without sugar?

We will avoid altogether the age-old controversy about whether or not to include sugar by giving two recipes. The (almost) unsweetened pastry goes well with a filling of fresh, sweet fruit or with sweet creams, while the sweet one makes a very good lining for most fruit tartlets. This pastry moreover can be baked unfilled without the help of dried beans and without shrinking away from the tin, provided that it is a reasonably shallow one. In both cases it is very important to give the paste enough time to rest in the refrigerator – for at least an hour and preferably overnight.

Both recipes are prepared in the same way. Sift the flour onto the work surface, make a well in the middle and put in the softened butter, the flavourings and the egg and start blending them all together with the fingers. Then quickly work in the flour and finally add the milk. A little more or less milk may be used to obtain the desired consistency. Do not work the paste too much for it is apt to become crumbly. Should this happen, knead an egg white into it. Bake at 200 C, 400 F, gas 6, adjusting the cooking time according to the size and thickness of the pastry case.

Recipe with almost no sugar:

250 g/9 oz flour
125 g/4½ oz butter
1 teaspoon salt
1 tablespoon sugar
1 egg
2–3 tablespoons milk

This will make 450 g/1 lb pastry, enough for about 12 tartlets of 10 cm/4 in diameter.

Recipe with sugar:

400 g/14 oz flour
200 g/7 oz butter
125 g/4½ oz icing sugar
good pinch of salt
1 egg yolk
2 tablespoons milk

This will make 800 g/1¾ lb pastry, enough for about 20 to 25 tartlets.

SAUCES AND GLAZES

– and ideas for decorations

A cook is judged by his – or her – sauces. The phrase was originally coined with the gravy for the roast in mind but is just as true of those which accompany a dessert or glaze the surface of some other mouth-watering morsel. And, just as with the savoury sauces, it is also true that every spoonful of sauce and every glaze is as good as its most minor ingredient: that is why the chocolate we melt in a water bath should be the best chocolate and why we should select the strawberries for our sauce with as much care as if we hoped to win a prize with every one. And, above all, every combination of flavours adds new interest. Why, for instance, should raspberry sauce inevitably be served with semolina pudding or vanilla ice cream? Why not hot orange sauce for once? Or why shouldn't home-made nut brittle be flavoured with cinnamon or cardamom? Or a chocolate custard with raisins and rum? Better still, why not serve several different sauces with the same dessert, so that everyone can help themselves as they please? Not only does it broaden the cook's repertoire, it is also a challenge to the imagination, on which sauces have never ceased to have an especially stimulating effect.

It was a great milestone in culinary history when people first began to give up the practice of eating with their fingers at banquets and dipping them into the communal bowl of soup or mush, and instead switched to using flatware and to having individual plates of different sizes for different purposes, complete with knife, fork and spoon. They were now equipped for adding sauces to their food and, thanks to the blossoming of trade with new colonies, had something more exciting than baked apples and mashed elderberries on their new-fangled china plates. And, though it be true that hunger and scarcity make every sauce more appreciated, culinary perfection does not necessarily depend on a glut. And if scarcity, as in the Second World War, taught us again to boil up wild fruits to make a purée, we learn today from a good many packet sauces that ease and speed are sometimes achieved at the expense of the delicious fruitiness which only time and the freshest ingredients can provide. Thus, sauces and glazes have always added a refinement to our meals which in this case need not mean making simple food into something complicated. In the farmhouse kitchens of northern Europe summer fruits have always been – and still are – simmered together in subtle and interesting combinations, sieved and sweetened and then eaten with porridge and milk or cream. And that is as simple and tasty a recipe as any of us could wish for. But if this is a pairing of familiar ingredients, less likely marriages can give just as good a result. Herein lies the secret of these ingredients, the source of perfect harmony: what is added to anything must go with that thing, for a sweet sauce should be the ideal companion, adapting its flavour to that of the dessert so that the whole character of the dish is enhanced.

In the following pages an attempt has been made to group the sweet sauces under basic recipes. The extent to which this can be done is limited, however, because the basic combinations can be varied in many different ways. Nonetheless, it was felt to be important to retain some precision of method and description.

Fresh ingredients of the highest quality are essential to all sweet sauces, and particularly fruit-based ones. The fruits themselves make it relatively easy for us to choose the best, for we have to be guided by their availability. The choicest and juiciest strawberries, for example, come in June and the sweetest plums in September.

Fruit Sauces

This is a theme on which there are countless variations. Almost all fruits can be made into a sauce, and their association with other flavourings, for example liqueurs, produces an immense number of possible combinations. These are multiplied again by the different methods of preparation to which certain fruits lend themselves. With fruits from all over the world as readily available as they are nowadays it is really up to every creative cook to decide on the formula for his or her 'special' fruit sauce. But it is precisely this abundance all the year round that should argue in favour of sauces that are made with fresh fruits. They are the simplest and most economical to make and retain the greatest purity of flavour. Choosing well-ripened fruit will reduce the amount of sugar needed. Some kinds of fruit are more suitable than others for making a fresh fruit purée, but most berries are ideal, as are also apricots, peaches and plums. Among exotics there are several especially delicious kinds, such as the mango and the kiwi – not forgetting the mangosteen, guava or passion fruit.

Fresh Fruit Sauces

These are often made of what the market has to offer and usually on the spur of the moment or, as the French say, *à la minute*. Such creations cannot be regulated by exact recipes in that they must be adapted to the sugar content of the particular fruit. Thus a really ripe mango when puréed makes an excellent sauce, without any added sugar. Hence the recipes that follow are simply basic formulae, which may be varied both in respect of the sugar content and in the flavourings used. A further advantage is that fresh sauces can be quickly prepared even in very small quantities: 60 to 100 ml/2 to 3 fl oz per serving should be allowed for desserts. Sugar syrup is the most practical sweetener, since it blends immediately with the fruit purée and can also be flavoured in advance. You can simply bring it to the boil with a vanilla pod, the juice or grated rind of a citrus fruit, a cinnamon stick or some cloves and allow it to cool again. If no sugar syrup is available, icing sugar may be stirred into the fruit.

Boiling down with sugar

This causes some fruits to develop a stronger flavour and of course the sauce is then much sweeter and more substantial. Above all, lemon juice boiled to a syrup with sugar produces wonderful sharp sauces, which will keep well.

Quick variations on these sauces can be concocted from any kind of jam or jelly.

This can be blended with wine, fresh fruit juice or a liqueur and when no fresh fruit is available they make a perfectly good substitute.

Grape Sauce

Sauce aux raisins

Bring to the boil 200 ml/7 fl oz white wine, 75 g/3 oz sugar and 4 small slivers of fresh ginger root. Peel and quarter 225 g/8 oz white grapes, remove the seeds (this should yield about 150 g/5 oz), add to the liquid and simmer for 3 minutes. Cool and stir in 2 tablespoons marc de Champagne. Makes 4 to 6 servings.

Elderberry Sauce

Sauce aux baies de sureau

Cook gently 350 g/11 oz elderberries with 60 ml/3 fl oz water, 100 g/4 oz sugar and 2 tablespoons lemon juice until they are tender. Purée them in the blender and pass through a sieve. Serve hot or cold. Makes 4 to 6 servings.

A cornflour liaison

This will turn any fruit juice or thin fruit purée into a creamy sauce. But these sauces with few exceptions get the lowest marks for flavour. The amount of liaison should in any case be as small as possible and the cornflour boiled as thoroughly as possible. But they do have the great advantage that they need very little sugar.

Kiwi Sauce

Sauce aux kiwis

Peel 3 kiwi fruit, purée them in the blender and pass them through a sieve. Stir in 3 tablespoons maple syrup and 1 teaspoon lime juice. Makes 4 to 6 servings.

Plum Sauce

Sauce aux prunes

Boil together 200 ml/7 fl oz plum juice with 50 g/2 oz sugar. Blend in 1 teaspoon cornflour with a small quantity of the juice, stir this into the rest and let it cook well through. Chop very finely 1 plum in ginger pickle and stir in. Makes 4 servings.

Lemon Sauce

Sauce au citron

Bring to the boil 200 ml/7 fl oz Sauternes with 4 tablespoons lemon juice. Blend 1 teaspoon cornflour with a little of the liquid, stir into the rest and let it cook thoroughly. Makes 6 to 8 servings.

Blackberry Sauce

Sauce aux baies de ronce

Purée 250 g/9 oz fresh blackberries with 75 g/3 oz icing sugar and then pass them through a fine sieve. Stir in 2 tablespoons *crème de cassis* and finally fold in 75 ml/2½ fl oz lightly whipped cream. Makes 4 to 6 servings.

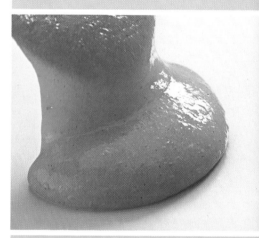

Pineapple Sauce

Sauce à l'ananas

Chop up 400 g/14 oz pineapple flesh (this will mean a medium-sized fruit) and purée two-thirds of it. Bring to the boil 125 ml/5 fl oz sugar syrup (20°) with ½ vanilla pod and cook in it the remaining small pineapple chunks for 1–2 minutes. Add 2 tablespoons brandy and the fruit purée and allow to cool. Makes 6 to 8 servings.

Orange Sauce

Sauce à l'orange

Strain 200 ml/7 fl oz freshly-squeezed orange juice into a saucepan and reduce for 3 to 4 minutes with the shredded rind of a well-scrubbed orange. Then stir in Grand Marnier to taste and allow the sauce to cool. The sauce may be served with or without the shredded rind. Makes 4 to 6 servings.

Hot Raspberry Sauce

Sauce aux framboises

Purée and sieve 200 g/7 oz well-ripened fresh raspberries. Bring to the boil 75 g/3 oz sugar and 75 ml/2½ fl oz full-bodied red Burgundy with a small piece of lemon rind. Add the raspberry purée and reduce for about 3 to 4 minutes. This sauce can also be served cold. Makes 4 to 6 servings.

Apricot Sauce

Sauce à l'abricot

Blanch, skin and stone 250 g/9 oz well-ripened apricots. Purée in a blender with 3 tablespoons sugar syrup (20°). Stir in 2 teaspoons fresh lime juice, 2 tablespoons apricot brandy and 2 teaspoons brandy. Makes 4 to 6 servings.

Persimmon Sauce

Sauce aux kakis

Halve 3 well-ripened persimmons and spoon out the flesh (this should yield about 300 g/11 oz). Process in a blender with the juice of 2 limes and 40 g/1½ oz icing sugar. Stir in 2 tablespoons Cointreau. Makes about 6 servings.

Wild Strawberry Sauce

Sauce aux fraises de bois

Take 250 g/9 oz fresh wild strawberries and purée half the quantity with 1½ tablespoons lemon juice. Pass the purée through a sieve and bring to the boil with 50 g/2 oz sugar. Add the rest of the strawberries and cook for 1–2 minutes more. Add 1½ tablespoons brandy and leave to cool. Makes 4 to 6 servings.

Fresh Fig Sauce

Sauce aux figues

Peel 300 g/11 oz ripe figs, purée them in the blender and pour in 2–3 tablespoons Sauternes. Heat up 4 tablespoons sugar syrup (20°) with 1 tablespoon lemon juice and 1 teaspoon coarsely chopped pink peppercorns. Leave to cool and mix with the reserved fig purée. Makes 4 to 6 servings.

Cranberry Sauce

Sauce aux airelles rouges

Cook 300 g/11 oz cranberries in 100 ml/3 fl oz sugar syrup for about 5 minutes until soft. Push through a sieve, stir in 2 tablespoons dark rum and a generous pinch of cinnamon. Finally, combine with 75 ml/2½ fl oz crème fraiche or yoghurt. Makes 4 to 6 servings.

Strawberry Sauce

Sauce aux fraises

Purée 250 g/9 oz ripe strawberries and push them through a sieve. Bring 50 g/2 oz sugar to the boil with 4 tablespoons water, add the shredded rind of half a well washed orange, reduce for about 2 minutes and add 1½ tablespoons dark rum. Blend the mixture with the strawberry purée when cold. Makes 4 to 6 servings.

Vanilla Sauce

Sauce à la vanille

This is the classic sweet sauce and at the same time the foundation of a whole series of other cream sauces. It is a mixture of milk, egg yolk, sugar and vanilla in which, when heated, the egg yolk becomes the binding agent; it is made in exactly the same way as an English custard (page 54).

6 egg yolks · 100 g/4 oz sugar
600 ml/1 pint milk · ½ vanilla pod

Combine the egg yolks and sugar with a balloon whisk, slowly add the vanilla flavoured milk and proceed to heat the mixture until it coats the spoon lightly. (This, if you are new to the technique of egg-custard making, and are therefore perhaps lacking a little in confidence, can be done in a water bath, otherwise over very carefully controlled direct heat.) The custard will thicken shortly before boiling point is reached, the sauce becoming noticeably denser through a very slight curdling of the egg yolk. If this moment is missed the egg yolk will break up into curds, in effect making sweet scrambled eggs. This process can be remedied, if it has not gone too far, by standing the pan in cold water and giving a good stir with a hand mixer set at maximum speed.

When vanilla sauce, as a foundation sauce, is combined with other flavourings it can of course be made without vanilla. But often only a part of the sauce will be so modified and likewise the delicate aroma of the vanilla will enhance the effect of the added flavourings (for example, coffee, pounded nut brittle, nougat or liqueurs).

This classic vanilla sauce should not be confused with another sauce of the same name which is thickened with cornflour and so can do with less egg yolk or none at all and is also very easy to make. Although it can never rival English custard in quality of flavour it is duly esteemed where restraint in the use of sugar and egg yolks is indicated.

Vanilla sauce with cornflour thickening:
600 ml/1 pint milk
40 g/1½ oz sugar · ½ vanilla pod
15 g/½ oz cornflour · 2 egg yolks

Set aside 2–3 tablespoons milk to mix with the cornflour and bring the rest to the boil with the sugar and vanilla pod. Meanwhile beat the cornflour well into the reserved milk and egg yolks. Take the vanilla pod out of the boiling milk, scrape out the seeds and thicken the sauce by stirring the creamed cornflour and egg yolks into it with a balloon whisk. Let it boil up a few times, and stir it as it cools. Makes 6 to 8 servings.

Tea Sauce

Sauce au thé

25 g/1 oz Ceylon or Assam tea
3 tablespoons water
300 ml/½ pint vanilla sauce
300 ml/½ pint double cream
50 g/2 oz sugar

Brew the tea with the boiling water, let it infuse for 5 minutes, squeeze the liquid through a linen cloth and blend it with the vanilla sauce. Lightly whip the cream with the sugar and stir it into the sauce. Makes 12 to 15 servings.

Almond Sauce

Sauce aux amandes

1 tablespoon Amaretto (almond liqueur) or sweet sherry
150 g/5 oz almond paste
600 ml/1 pint vanilla sauce

Stir the Amaretto and the almond paste in little flakes into the hot vanilla sauce until smooth, then pass it through a fine sieve. Makes 12 to 15 servings.

Hot Chocolate Sauce

Sauce au chocolat

250 ml/8 fl oz cream
2 teaspoons honey, or to taste
½ vanilla pod
200 g/7 oz plain chocolate

Bring the cream to the boil with the honey and vanilla pod. Remove the pod and scrape out the seeds. Melt the chocolate in a water bath and stir in the hot cream a little at a time. Makes 6 to 8 servings.

Pour the vanilla-flavoured cream into the melted chocolate, stirring all the time and with the heat switched off completely. Serve this sauce hot. To make cold chocolate sauce add 100 g/4 oz chocolate that has been melted in a water bath to vanilla sauce made according to the basic recipe, and stir it in well.

Wine and Egg Sauces

Sabayons

Wine-and-egg punches form a large family of sauces. From a single basic recipe with only minor variations a whole series of international sauces can be made: hot or cold, with dry white wine or strong red Burgundy, Marsala or patrician champagne, some on the light and airy side, others heavier and more creamy. There are all sorts of names for them: in French, *sabayon*, in Italian *zabaione*, in German (accurately) *Weinschaumsaucen* and in the Austrian usage (rather less accurately) *Weinchaudeau* from the French *chaud*, meaning hot. This expression is seldom used in France since it only denotes a hot sauce, but in Austria there is apt to be confusion on this very point, because a *Weinchaudeau* may well be served cold. Sometimes these sauces are called creams – and not inappropriately so when they are served as a dessert on their own (as they usually are in Italy where zabaione – not necessarily made with Marsala – is the most popular of desserts).

A wine-and-egg sauce is so simple to make that it will admit variations which are well worth trying. Thus the juice, and sometimes the grated rind, too, of citrus fruit are used to round off the flavour admirably. And concentrated fruit syrups like raspberry, strawberry or apricot result in excellent fruit and wine sauces. But the taste of the wine must remain perceptible.

Out of a multitude of different recipes three examples are given here, all of them the same as regards method of preparation but all very different in composition.

Classic French Sabayon

This is made only with egg yolks, sugar and very dry white wine, preferably from the Champagne region.

6 egg yolks
200 g/7 oz sugar
250 ml/8 fl oz very dry white wine

The basic rule is that the egg yolks and sugar must always be creamed together first. The bowl is then placed in a water bath and the wine added to the mixture of egg and sugar. This basic recipe is extremely versatile, as the dry white wine blends happily with any added fruit flavour. Substituting champagne for the white wine gives a noticeably racy finish to the whole sauce. Serves 6.

Italian Zabaione

Made with rich Marsala this is a recipe familiar to everyone. But a 'Spanish' variant can very well be made with a cream sherry. Add some puréed fresh raspberries to this Spanish version and you have an exceptional delicacy.

3 egg yolks
1 whole egg
125 g/4½ oz sugar
6 tablespoons Marsala

This is made in the same way as the French sabayon and as shown in the step-by-step pictures. Serves 6.

An Austrian Weinchaudeau

This sauce is always somewhat lighter than the two previous examples and must therefore be served at once or its whole charm will be lost.

2 egg yolks · 1 whole egg
125 g/4½ oz sugar
250 ml/8 fl oz dry white wine

In this recipe the high proportion of wine necessitates that all the ingredients be beaten up together. And although this ought to be done in a water bath experienced Austrian cooks do it over direct heat, that is over a low gas flame. But great care has to be taken that the egg yolks do not curdle. Briefly taking the pan off the heat from time to time, while continuing to beat, helps considerably to increase the volume. Serves 6.

1 **Cream the egg yolks and sugar well** but do not beat them. The mixture must not become foamy. Place the bowl in a water bath, taking great care that the bottom of the bowl containing the egg and sugar mixture does not touch the hot bottom of the pan beneath.

2 **Pour in the wine** as soon as the bowl is in the water bath, stirring continuously. The water should not come to the boil again but be kept just below simmering point. Now beat the mixture energetically with the balloon whisk until it froths and has doubled in volume

3 **Cold zabaione** is beaten over iced water after its original heating. The quick cooling process ensures that the sauce does not lose too much of its volume; it stays more foamy than if beaten until cool at room temperature.

4 **Foam falling from the spoon** is the sign of a successful zabaione. The hot sauce has a naturally lighter and airier consistency than the cooled version. The proportion of wine to egg-and-sugar mixture also has its effect on the firmness of the sauce.

Apricot jam and sugar syrup are brought to the boil together. The jam should previously have been passed through a sieve. Let them continue boiling for 8 to 10 minutes until they have reduced by about one-third. The liquid must be clear and transparent when tested with a wooden spoon.

Royal icing for piping through a paper bag. If you are making a small quantity of this it should be blended with a spoon. The hand-mixer makes it too frothy and the thread too inelastic and liable to break. Increase the proportion of sugar until the icing ceases to be runny.

Warming fondant in a water bath. The temperature of the water should not rise above 40 C/104 F. Add a little sugar syrup and egg white according to the consistency required and stir until uniformly fluid. It should not exceed 35 C/95 F or when set it will have lost its shine.

Apricot Glaze

Glace à l'abricot

This is principally used as an insulating layer between cakes and other glazes. But it is also a convenient and quick glaze in its own right, although it will never set quite firmly. It must be worked while hot and is thus unsuitable for desserts that are extremely sensitive to heat.

100 g/4 oz sugar
75 ml/2½ fl oz water
1 tablespoon lemon juice
200 g/7 oz apricot jam

Bring the sugar, water and lemon juice to the boil and strain. Pour it onto the sieved apricot jam and boil fast to thicken. If a transparent glaze is required it may be passed through a hair-sieve as well. The sharpish apricot flavour harmonises with almost everything, but this glaze can also be made with other kinds of jam. The glaze can suitably be flavoured with a fruit *eau-de-vie* or a liqueur.

Royal Icing

Glace au blanc d'oeuf

This is made to a simple formula and is easy to prepare.

150 to 175 g 5 to 6 oz icing sugar
1 egg white
2 teaspoons lime or lemon juice

Stir the sifted icing sugar with the egg white and lime juice until a smooth, satin-sheened icing is obtained. The simplest method is to use the hand-mixer set at its highest speed. The consistency of the icing can be adjusted by thinning it with egg white or thickening it with icing sugar. Always cover the bowl with a damp cloth, since the surface of the icing dries out quickly.

Fondant Icing

Fondant

This is a pure sugar icing, for which sugar is boiled to the 'soft ball' stage, i.e. 113 C/235 F. The syrup must then be poured onto a marble slab and worked continuously with a palette knife until it becomes milky-white. You can however spare yourself the trouble, because good quality fondant icing can be bought commercially.

This firm fondant needs only to be warmed in a water bath and suitably thinned. For this purpose sugar syrup or egg white, or alternatively milk, can be used. As flavouring any strong alcoholic liquor will do well. It is important that the icing should be stirred all the time and not allowed to heat above 35 C/95 F, or it will crystallise and lose its satiny texture when set. To guard against this the top of the dessert or cake should first be sealed with a layer of apricot glaze which will prevent the moisture from soaking into the cake and keep the fondant glistening.

1 **Finely chop the couverture** and melt half of it in a water bath at about 50 C/122 F. Add the rest and remove the bowl from the water bath. Stir while it melts and the temperature of the whole is reduced. If necessary cool it in the refrigerator until it thickens.

2 **Slowly warm the cooled, thickened couverture** in a water bath at about 40 C/104 F, stirring continuously till it reaches 32 C/90 F. It is best to do this in stages, so that it does not get too warm. Test it by lifting some out on a palette knife: after 2 to 3 minutes it should have become smooth and acquired a silky sheen.

Draw a leaf through tempered couverture and let it set on waxed paper. If the leaves are to be curved, lay them on a rolling pin wrapped in waxed paper. When the chocolate has set strip away the leaf, and the chocolate leaf will show even the finest details.

Chocolate

Chocolate is indispensable to sweet-making and highly important to desserts, whether used as an ingredient or as a glaze (hence the French word *couverture*, meaning covering). However, couverture is not entirely without its problems, as it has to be 'tempered' first in order that it may taste and look as it should.

Why does couverture have to be tempered? Couverture chocolate consists of cocoa solids, cocoa butter and sugar. The ratio 60/40 denotes a medium quality and means 60 per cent sugar. Couverture melts at over 35 C/95 F and is suitably fluid for working at 32 C/90 F. But it must first be brought to a much lower temperature because the cocoa butter only binds properly if the couverture is brought up slowly from a cool temperature to the necessary 32 C/90 F and never the other way around. That, for the handling of couverture, is the cardinal rule.

Should the couverture be warmed up beyond 32 C/90 F the whole process must begin all over again. Cool it again and

temper it slowly. While you are working with it you can keep it fluid in a water bath at 30–32 C/86–92 F. It should however be stirred every now and then to ensure that none of the cocoa butter separates. The ideal temperature for desserts which are to be dipped in couverture or have it poured over them is around 20–24 C/68–75 F. Keeping to the rules for tempering, which incidentally are also valid for milk or cream couverture, will guarantee both an even glaze and the true flavour of fine chocolate. As with all high-class ingredients there exists a substitute for chocolate, namely chocolate cake covering. It is simple to use as it does not have to be tempered but its composition – since it is based on vegetable fat with a low percentage of cocoa – means that its flavour is not to be compared with that of couverture.

Chocolate Leaves

This is a very simple trick which can be done with fresh leaves, providing a decoration for almost any dessert which can moreover be produced and stored in quantity for future use. All it requires is tempered couverture and some leaves with a smooth surface, free from small hairs which would cause them to stick to the solidified chocolate. Good results are obtained with bay leaves, rose leaves – which are particularly effective on account of their saw edge – and the leaves of small orange trees. Hold them by the stalk and draw them over the surface of the couverture. Take off a little to avoid too thick a coating, then lay the leaf on waxed paper and leave it to set. Once the couverture is firm the real leaf is simply stripped away leaving a chocolate leaf showing all the minutest veins of the natural model. These leaves can of course also be made with milk chocolate couverture and also with white chocolate, although this does not set quite so firm and stable as the others.

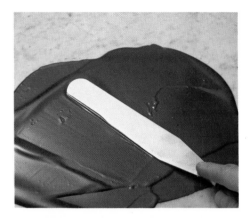

Spread the couverture on a marble slab, working very quickly so that it does not firm up before it is all evenly thin and does not harden before being formed into curls with a spatula. Hold the spatula at an angle and push it forward 2 to 3 cm/1 to 1½ in at a time.

Fill the moulds with tempered couverture and pour it back at once into the bowl, then lay them upside-down on a wire rack to set. When the couverture has firmed a little cut away the projecting edge with a pastry knife. When completely cold loosen the chocolate cups from the moulds.

The liquid couverture must fall heavily from the spoon, thick enough for the thread not to run out of shape when it is piped. Filigree patterns should be piped onto waxed paper or cooking parchment. The outlined shapes, as in these flowers, can be filled with liquid couverture.

Chocolate curls

These are a universal decoration, their flavour going with almost every kind of dessert. What is more, they are easy to make because it is not absolutely necessary to temper the couverture. That occurs quite automatically through its being spread out thinly on a marble slab or a completely smooth work surface. The spreading should continue until it sets. Then while still supple it must be 'rolled up' very quickly with a knife, or preferably a metal spatula. Apply this obliquely and the chocolate will roll up by itself. These chocolate curls will remain soft for a while and should be allowed to harden completely before being used for decorations or put away in an airtight container.

Chocolate Cups

Tempered couverture can be easily cast into thin hollow shapes which make ideal edible containers for creams, ice creams or sorbets. Many differently-shaped moulds are suitable – those for brioches, tartlets and timbales among others. Fill them to the brim with the couverture and pour it out at once. A thin coating of chocolate will remain inside the mould. Thus a chocolate container from a mould holding 50 g/2 oz should not weigh more than about 15 g/½ oz. The rim formed by the couverture as it drains away should be trimmed off. Allow the chocolate cups to harden completely in the refrigerator and then carefully detach them from the moulds. If necessary tap the mould first on a hard surface to loosen it.

Chocolate for Piping

This requires tempered couverture and it must be worked at a constant temperature 32 C/90 F. To make it thick enough to pipe stir in 40 g/1½ oz sifted icing sugar and a few drops of water to 200 g/7 oz couverture. This calls for some caution, since too much water would make it too thick and therefore useless. The required designs can be drawn beforehand and the paper for piping the decorations laid on top. Supplies of these chocolate filigree decorations can be stored, but they are very brittle. If outlined shapes, like the flower petals, are filled with liquid couverture they are considerably strengthened. Milk couverture and 'white' chocolate look particularly attractive. This couverture for filling in should be kept as thin as possible so that it flows readily. If necessary stir in a little melted cocoa butter to make it more fluid.

Make a piping bag from folded cooking parchment. 1. Fold a square piece diagonally. Hold the triangle in the middle of the longest side with the thumb and forefinger of the left hand and roll the paper towards the left with the right hand. **2.** Go on rolling it while holding the point of the bag with the left hand. **3.** Fold the projecting corner inwards to hold the bag together. **4.** Fill it with the icing, taking care to keep it away from the top of the bag. **5.** Fold the bag together with the seam – that is, the straight edge of the paper – facing away from you. First press the air out of the bag and then fold the ends together inwards. **6.** Cut off the point with a sharp pair of scissors. The size of the opening will determine the thickness of the piping thread.

Working with a simple paper piping bag looks more complicated than it is. Whether royal or chocolate icing is being piped it is important that it should be strong and elastic, ensuring a thread that will not break. Hold the bag touching the paper or dessert, press a little icing through to expel the air then lift the bag upwards, squeezing it steadily so that you can 'draw' with the thread thus formed. But only curves can be drawn in this way; to draw angles you will have to go back to the surface of the paper or dessert and start the next part of the pattern afresh.

A stock of decorative shapes can be made and stored. This is very simply made with piped chocolate icing, since it can be removed from the paper after a few minutes when it has set firm. In the case of piped royal icing the shapes must be left to dry overnight so that they can be loosened from the paper without breaking. This is done by drawing the paper over a hard edge and the decorations will loosen themselves. The piping thread must not be too thin however, or the filigree shapes would be too fragile. They are much more stable if outlined spaces are filled in with a little thinned icing which may be coloured according to taste. Piped royal icing and chocolate icing can also be combined. Other suitable ornaments are gold or silver sugar-plums, crystallised rose or violet petals, pistachio nuts, glacé fruits and generally anything that is sweet and decorative. For solid flowers the point of the piping bag should be cut off a little higher up and the petals piped inwards from the outside with a narrowing thread. One more tip: flavour the icing with a few drops of a liqueur with a good strong bouquet.

FLUMMERIES, GRITS AND JELLIES

The pudding that isn't quite a pudding, plus other moulded desserts

In its original form, the English flummery was a somewhat stolid affair, a cereal (normally wheat or oatmeal) based jelly, whose set was supplied by the addition of isinglass, a precursor of gelatine made from fish bladders. The Germans adopted it (spelling it *flammeri*) and turned it into Guelph pudding and tutti frutti. Basically they used the same process, which was to exploit the capacity of cereals and other thickeners with a high carbohydrate content to expand in hot liquid. The more finely milled the starch, the faster it can soak up the liquid and the shorter accordingly will be the cooking time. Thus a rice dessert takes quite a long time, but a flummery made with cornflour can be made in a matter of seconds.

Until well into the 1930s a flummery was duly called a *Flammeri* in all German textbooks for technical and vocational colleges and in cookery books. But ever since 1910, when Dr Oetker's first *Manual of Cookery* was published, it had been possible by following his Recipe No. 7, to boil, using 'pudding powder' – which was then quite a novelty – a 'Semolina and Cornflour Pudding', although this was properly speaking a flummery. And after the First World War, when this earliest convenience dessert was divided into cornflour, semolina, jelly and sago pudding powders, this way of making a 'boiled pudding' met the current general economic and social needs: it was quick, it was cheap and it did not use other much-needed ingredients such as eggs, butter and sugar. This was all the more helpful during and immediately after the Second World War when all able-bodied women were at work and had no time to make elaborate or time-consuming desserts.

Another member of the flummery family is a sweet which, in northern Germany and Scandinavia only, is not called a *flammeri* but *Rote Grutze* (red grits), while in central European cookbooks it appears under names which mean either 'fruit juice flummery' or 'red fruit pudding'. It is simply fruit juice thickened with cornflour, semolina or sago. *Rote Grutze* really was originally made from grits, and oatmeal porridge and mashed rye are still eaten in the southern parts of Germany and Europe as a whole, sometimes with milk, sometimes with cream. By regional or family tradition people still enjoy fruit flummeries that are almost as clear as rubies, some with fresh or stewed fruit inside.

In this chapter we have also included some fine jellies made in the classic tradition, with clear fresh fruit juice or wine, and set in castellated moulds. These stand on their serving dishes as proudly as they must have done when they were one of the most important cold sweets on grand banqueting tables. They lost their prestige when ready-flavoured jellies came on the market, and are now rather more of a children's party treat. But it is well worth making them in the old manner, for they combine a handsome appearance with a delicacy and freshness of flavour that is most welcome to the palate after a rich meal.

Beautiful decorative moulds made of earthenware, china, copper and nowadays, of course, plastic, have turned the simple flummery into a sophisticated dessert. Rice or semolina flummeries too can be moulded in this way, although when made to a lighter consistency they may also be served in bowls or glasses.

Chocolate Flummery

Flamri au chocolat

The flavouring of our chocolate of course may be exchanged for vanilla, coffee or other flavouring ingredient. But these variations will need a little more binding. The amount of cornflour should be increased to 50 g/2 oz.

Caramel flummery is an especially good variation: melt the sugar to a medium brown colour and boil it with the milk.

2 egg yolks
100 g/4 oz sugar
40 g/1½ oz cornflour
600 ml/1 pint milk
½ vanilla pod
65 g/2½ oz couverture
2 leaves gelatine or
1 tablespoon powdered gelatine
1 600 ml/1 pint mould

for decoration:
a little cream
chopped pistachio nuts
vanilla sauce

Beat the egg yolks, sugar and cornflour with a little of the milk. Bring the rest of the milk to the boil with the vanilla pod, and then add the couverture which has been melted in a water bath. Stir the blended egg yolk and cornflour mixture into the chocolate milk and let them boil through quickly while stirring continuously. Remove from the heat and stir in the softened and squeezed out leaf gelatine or the powdered gelatine until it is completely dissolved. Rinse out the mould with cold water, pour in the flummery and leave to set in the refrigerator for 2 hours.

After turning out decorate with whipped cream and chopped pistachio nuts. Serve a vanilla sauce with it.

Serves 4.

Semolina Flummery with Blackberries

Flamri de semoule aux baies de ronce

600 ml/1 pint milk
1 vanilla pod
the grated rind of 1 lemon
50 g/2 oz semolina
8 leaves gelatine or
25 g/1 oz powdered gelatine
5 egg yolks
100 g/4 oz sugar
300 ml/½ pint double
or whipping cream
2 tablespoons icing sugar
1.25 litre/2½-pint ring mould
a little vegetable oil
450 g/16 oz fresh blackberries

for the sauce:
500 g/18 oz apricots, puréed
250 ml/8 fl oz cream
1 tablespoon sugar

Bring the milk to the boil with the vanilla pod and the grated lemon rind, strain through a fine sieve, pour it back into the pan and bring to simmering point. While continually stirring add the semolina all at once and continue cooking over a low heat until it starts to thicken, then stir in the softened and well squeezed-out leaf gelatine or the powdered gelatine. Beat the egg yolks with the sugar until creamy and stir them into the semolina a little at a time. Stand the pan in iced water and stir till cold, and finally fold in carefully the cream, stiffly whipped with the icing sugar. Put this finished mixture into the lightly oiled mould, level the top with a palette knife and leave in the refrigerator for 6 hours to set.

Turn out the semolina flummery onto a dish and serve with the blackberries, apricot sauce and cream whipped with the sugar.

Serves 8 to 10.

Trautmannsdorff Rice

Riz Trautmannsdorff

1 vanilla pod
100 g/4 oz long grain rice
500 ml/17 fl oz milk
100 g/4 oz sugar
pinch of salt
450 g/16 oz jar sour cherries
3 tablespoons kirsch
1 piece cinnamon stick
½ teaspoon cornflour
250 ml/8 fl oz double or
whipping cream

Cut the vanilla pod open lengthways and scrape out the seeds. Put the pod, the seeds and the rice into the milk. Bring to the boil, cover and leave over gentle heat for about 1 hour for the flavours to infuse. Then stir in 50 g/2 oz of the sugar and salt and allow to get cold.

Drain the cherries and reserve the juice. Sprinkle the cherries with the kirsch, cover and leave to macerate. Bring half the cherry juice to the boil with the piece of cinnamon stick and the remaining sugar, stir in the cornflour, blended with a little water, and let it all cook through. Add the macerated cherries.

Stiffly whip the cream with the tablespoon of sugar and fold it into the cold rice mixture. Put layers of rice and cherries into individual glass dishes and decorate each with a few cherries. Trautmannsdorff Rice should be served well chilled.

You can ring the changes on this traditional German rice dessert, for example with stewed fruit such as plums, apricots or gooseberries. Nicest of all are sweetened fresh fruits, especially mango, wild strawberries or blackberries.

Serves 6

Zigzag-cut melons. This is quite easy to do with a small pointed knife, but must cut well into the middle of the fruit each time. The ring can be marked out with the point of the knife beforehand. For melon balls or oval shapes a round or oval cutter is used.

Fresh Fruit as Dessert

A fresh, ripe apple selected from a basket of fine fruit can be truly delicious and a complete dessert in itself. But it does have to be good and perfectly ripe. That is the only secret wherever desserts of fresh fruit are concerned. Only the best is just good enough and the best arrives at harvest time when that fruit is most abundant. This not only makes the price more reasonable but first and foremost guarantees a better flavour. For example, apricots, peaches or cherries are no longer a rarity in the shops in December but their flavour cannot be rated highly and they at best serve to give the fruit basket extra colour and variety. The seasons therefore should be respected (except in the case of some exotics like kiwi fruit) and only fruit which is really ripe and fresh should be used. That is self-evident as regards raw fruit salads but is also true of fresh fruit compotes, which should on no account be confused with conserves since

there is a world of difference between their flavours. Some kinds of fresh fruit, moreover, develop their full aroma only when cooked in syrup or wine. Nor should any strict distinction be drawn between salad and compote, because combinations of raw and stewed fruit, allied to interesting sauces, often make very clever desserts.

The eye also should be seduced by this colourful banquet. Scooped-out fruits like melons, pineapples or avocados can become bowls of fruit salad, or the fruit can be arranged in appetising patterns on the plates. Here there are useful tricks, like piping a line of jam to outline the sauce on the plate. But even the most ingenious arrangement must not disturb the harmony of the flavours.

Fruit Salad with Mango Purée

Salade de fruits à la purée de mangue

2 nectarines
2 tamarillos (tree tomatoes)
2 kiwi fruit
1 tablespoon lemon juice
2 tablespoons sugar syrup (20°)
1 tablespoon sieved strawberry jam
1 well-ripened mango
(weighing about 400 g/14 oz)
juice of $\frac{1}{2}$ lime · 2 teaspoons honey
75 g/3 oz redcurrants
lemon balm leaves for decoration

Blanch the nectarines briefly and peel off the skin, remove the stones and cut into wedges. Peel and slice the tamarillos and kiwi fruit. Arrange these in a serving dish in layers and pour over the lemon juice mixed with the sugar syrup. Leave it to macerate for 1 hour in the refrigerator, then spoon it onto plates and pipe a border of sieved strawberry jam around it. Purée

the flesh of the mango with the lime juice and honey in the blender, spoon it either over or around the fruit, sprinkle with redcurrants and decorate with lemon balm leaves
Serves 4.

Filled Melon

Melon farci

2 Galia or Ogen melons,
each weighing about 575 g/1¼ lb
75 g/3 oz sugar
juice and shredded rind of 1 orange
2 tablespoons Bénédictine

Cut the ripe melons in half zig-zag fashion. Remove the seeds with a spoon and collect the juice. Scoop out melon balls from the flesh, spoon out the remainder and put the juice in a small pan. Boil it for about 3 minutes with the sugar and the juice and grated rind of the orange. Fill the hollowed out melon-cups with the melon balls. Stir the liqueur into the cooled syrup and pour it over the melon. Serve ice-cold. The melon halves may also be served embedded in crushed ice.
Serves 4.

Italian Apricots

Abricots italiens

Blanch 575 g/1¼ lb fresh apricots for a moment and remove their skins, then halve and stone them. Bring to the boil 1 tablespoon honey with 75 g/3 oz sugar, and the juice and grated rind of 1 orange and ½ lemon and continue to cook lightly for 3 to 4 minutes. Add the apricots cut into wedges and 50 g/2 oz slivered almonds and let them infuse for 2 minutes. Finish the dish with 3 tablespoons Amaretto (almond liqueur) and leave to cool. Serve ice-cold with or without whipped cream.

Serves 4.

Fruits with Orange Sauce

Fruits à la sauce à l'orange

Cut melon balls from a honeydew melon, weighing about 800 g/1¾ lb. Blanch and peel 3 apricots, and cut them in wedges. Bring to the boil the juice of 2 and the grated rind of 1 orange with 60 g/2½ oz sugar and reduce by about one-third. Stir in 2 tablespoons dark rum and 2 tablespoons Cointreau. Put the fruit into the hot sauce and let it all get cold. Pipe a border of sieved strawberry jam onto the plate and arrange the well-chilled fruit and sauce inside. Sprinkle one or two fresh raspberries on top.

Serves 4.

Figs with Cox's Orange Pippin

Figues et Pommes

Boil a scant 150 ml/¼ pint dry white wine, 1 tablespoon lemon juice and 100 g/4 oz sugar steadily together for about 2 minutes. Remove from the heat and add 50 g/2 oz raisins. Peel 16 small green figs, halve them and macerate them for 2 to 3 hours in the cold liquid. Peel a large Cox's apple, cut it into stick shapes and arrange these with the figs on 4 plates. Chill. Over a low heat reduce the sauce a little with the raisins. Let it cool and divide it between the desserts.

Serves 4.

Mango with Tamarillo Sauce

Mangue à la sauce aux tamarillos

Peel 2 large, ripe mangoes and cut out the seeds. Slice the flesh and arrange it on 4 plates. Sprinkle with a few drops of lemon juice and chill. Peel and purée 4 ripe tamarillos and sieve them. Stir in 3 tablespoons sugar syrup (20°), a generous pinch of cinnamon, the juice of 1 lime and a dash of peppermint liqueur. Serve onto the plates with the mango slices, and add a tablespoon of yoghurt to each. Sprinkle with fresh mint leaves.

Serves 4.

Fruits with Passion Fruit Sauce

Fruits à la sauce aux fruits de la passion

Peel and slice horizontally 1 banana and 1 orange. Hull and halve 100 g/4 oz strawberries. Arrange the fruit on plates and put to chill. Spoon out the seeds and flesh of 3 passion fruit and bring to the boil with 2 tablespoons maple syrup and the juice of 1 lime. Sieve and add 50 g/2 oz fresh or frozen redcurrants and poach gently for 1 to 2 minutes. Add 2 tablespoons dark rum, chill this and pour it over. Decorate with mint leaves. Serves 4.

Grapefruit Dessert

Dessert aux pamplemousses

Peel 2 grapefruits and remove the membrane from the segments. Arrange in layers in a bowl, sprinkle with 2 tablespoons each sugar and white rum. Cover and leave to macerate for 2 to 3 hours. Pour off the surplus liquor, bring it to the boil, reduce to about 2 tablespoons and cool again. Arrange on 4 plates. Lightly whip 150 ml/¼ pint double or whipping cream and flavour it with the reduced macerating liquor and a hint of grated nutmeg. Serve with the grapefruit segments, decorated with halved strawberries and crushed nut brittle.

Serves 4.

Pears, Plums and Ginger

Poirs aux prunes et gingembre

Peel, halve and core 2 pears, and slice thinly. Mix 2 tablespoons lemon juice with 3 tablespoons pear *eau de vie* and 4 tablespoons sugar syrup (20°) and macerate the pears in it for 1 hour. Blanch and peel 16 plums and put them in a pan with 40 g/1½ oz preserved ginger cut into short sticks. Add the pear marinade, cook for about 4 to 5 minutes then cool. Pipe a fine border of apricot jam onto 4 plates, arrange the pears in the middle and the plums with the ginger and sauce on top. Decorate each with a pecan nut.

Serves 4.

Oranges with Cranberries

Oranges aux airelles rouges

Peel 4 oranges carefully, slice horizontally and arrange in a serving dish. Sprinkle with 40 to 75 g/1½ to 3 oz sugar and pour over 3 tablespoons dark rum. Cover and macerate for 4 to 6 hours. Then pour off the liquor into a pan, thin it with 3 tablespoons water and bring to the boil. Put 150 g/5 oz fresh cranberries (or redcurrants) into the pan and lightly poach them for 2 minutes. Add 40 g/1½ oz quartered walnuts and a dash of Pernod, pour the sauce, still hot, over the oranges and chill before serving.

Serves 4.

Tropical Fruit Salad

Salade exotique

Peel and slice 1 small cherimoya, 2 tree tomatoes, 2 kiwi fruit and half a small fresh pineapple. Peel and stone 20 lychees and distribute with the rest of the fruit among 6 plates. Stir together a sauce made from the juice of 1 lime, a pinch of cayenne pepper, a dash of Pernod and 3 tablespoons sugar syrup (20°) and pour over the fruit. Chill well. Peel 1 large, ripe mango or 2 small ones, take out the stone and purée the flesh. Only add sugar if necessary, and pour the mango sauce over or around the fruit.

Serves 6.

Fruit Salad with Yoghurt Sauce

Salade aux fruits à la sauce de yaourt

Put 4 cups of mixed fruits in a bowl: in this example they are water-melon balls, orange segments, apricots, bananas, strawberries, apples, grapes, pineapple and redcurrants. Add 100 ml/4 fl oz sugar syrup (20°), the juice of ½ lemon and 2 tablespoons Cointreau and let them macerate for 30 minutes. Stir together 100 ml/4 fl oz yoghurt with 2 tablespoons soured cream, the juice of ½ lemon, 3 tablespoons sugar syrup (20°) and 1 tablespoon brandy and pour it over the ice-cold fruit. Decorate with toasted, flaked almonds.

Serves 4.

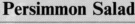

Composition with Nectarines

Composition aux nectarines

Poach the flesh (with the seeds) of 2 passion fruit in 3 tablespoons white wine and 50 g/2 oz sugar for 4 minutes and then sieve it. Add 2 tablespoons Cointreau and 75 g/3 oz wild strawberries and leave to cool. Blanch, skin and halve 2 well-ripened nectarines. Pipe a fine border of sieved strawberry jam onto 4 plates, place the halved nectarines inside and fill the cavities with wild strawberries. Pour over the sauce. Also give each plate a spoonful of kiwi fruit sauce and 2 sliced, preserved kumquats. Decorate with lemon balm.

Serves 4.

Persimmon Salad

Salade aux kakis

Slice 2 peeled limes very thinly. Peel and slice 4 ripe persimmons also and remove any seeds. Arrange on 4 or 6 plates, scatter 1 tablespoon chopped pistachio nuts over each serving and chill well. Bring 75 ml/2½ fl oz sugar syrup (20°) and 4 tablespoons Grand Marnier to a gentle boil, add 50 g/2 oz fresh blackberries, take them off the heat and chill. When ice-cold pour them over the persimmon salad.

Serves 4 to 6.

Flambéed Fruit Desserts

One could say that these desserts have a dubious reputation because their charm rests on and their quality is fixed and judged by the height of the cooking flames. But the controversial practice of flambéing can, if one knows what one is doing with alcohol, be wholly beneficial. This is logical, because spirits – and especially strongly flavoured liqueurs – while being reduced by it are also intensified by it: the alcohol is burnt away but the essential flavour remains to spice the fruit-based dessert. It should also be noted that a good number of exotic fruits are very well adapted to the process – bananas particularly, for which D. Sunil, under-chef at the Colombo Interconti Hotel has his own special recipe. He uses short sugar-bananas that have ripened in the bunch, but the following recipe has been modified to suit those we can buy here. His brown arrack, distilled from the nectar of the coconut palm, will also have to be replaced by white arrack.

Flambéed Bananas

Bananes flambées

3 ripe bananas
(weighing about 450 g/1 lb)
60 g/2½ oz butter · 75 g/3 oz brown sugar
juice of 1 lime · juice of 2 oranges
grated rind of 1 orange
3 tablespoons Grand Marnier
1 tablespoon arrack

Peel the bananas and cut into two lengthways. Melt 40 g/1½ oz of the butter in a pan and fry the bananas lightly and quickly on both sides over a high heat then remove and keep warm. Melt the remaining butter in the flambé pan and sprinkle in the sugar. Stir continuously to melt it and add the juices of the lime and oranges and the grated rind. Cook this sauce for some 2 to 3 minutes over a high heat. Add the Grand Marnier and the arrack, tilt the pan a little, set light to the alcohol in it and let it all burn. Add the lightly fried bananas and their juices, heat them in the sauce and serve piping hot.

A second method is to pour the alcohol over the bananas and then set light to it. This will give a stronger flavour but also turns them a darker brown. To prevent them becoming too dark it is sometimes necessary to put out the flames rather than let them die naturally. Serves 4 to 6.

Cardamom is a spice that is particularly compatible with banana. If you have a few pods to hand, remove the seeds and crush them, then add them to the sauce for this flambéed banana recipe.

Here is a variation with fresh strawberries: the same method and quantities apply, only the alcohol need be changed. The strawberries should be hulled, halved and fried very lightly and quickly in the melted butter. Reduce the orange sauce and flambé it with 2 tablespoons dark rum and 2 tablespoons Bénédictine. Then return the strawberries to the sauce and heat them through.

You can proceed in the same way with fresh apricots too: blanch them quickly, peel them and remove the stones. In this case however use almond liqueur (Amaretto) instead of Bénédictine.

Fresh Fruit with Chocolate Ice Cream

Fruits à la glace au chocolat

40 g/1½ oz butter
4 slices from a fresh pineapple
2–3 kiwi fruits
75 g/3 oz brown sugar
scant 125 ml/¼ pint
fresh pineapple juice
3 tablespoons dark rum
100 g/4 oz fresh strawberries
4 scoops chocolate ice cream
whipped cream for decoration

Melt the butter in a pan and fry the sliced pineapple and kiwi fruit lightly and quickly on both sides. Take them out and keep them warm. Melt the sugar with the rest of the liquid in the pan. Pour on the pineapple juice and then the rum. Tilt the pan and set the liquid alight. Let it burn out, put in the lightly fried fruit slices and the halved strawberries and heat them up in the liquid. Arrange on plates, put a scoop of chocolate ice cream on each and top with a rosette of whipped cream.
Serves 4.

Flambéed Cherries

Cerises flambées

75 g/3 oz brown sugar
scant 150 ml/¼ pint
light red wine (Beaujolais)
juice of ½ lemon
1 tablespoon redcurrant jelly
25 g/1 oz butter
rind of ½ lemon
250 g/9 oz sweet cherries
2 tablespoons kirsch

Melt the sugar in the pan. It should be a nice light brown. Dissolve it in the red wine and lemon juice and add the redcurrant jelly. Melt the butter in this mixture, add the lemon rind and reduce by boiling for some 2 to 3 minutes. Add the cherries (they can be stoned beforehand but in this event they will lose a lot of their juice and shape in the poaching). After 2 more minutes pour over the kirsch and set it alight. Let it completely burn out.
Serves 4.

Cherries flambéed in this way are excellent with vanilla ice cream. They also make a good hot filling for crêpes, in which case each portion should be accompanied by a spoonful of ice-cold whipped cream.

Peaches with Vanilla Ice Cream

Pêches à la glace à la vanille

500 ml/17 fl oz water
300 g/11 oz sugar
a very small piece of cinnamon stick
4 fresh, white peaches
200 g/7 oz fresh raspberries
75 ml/2½ fl oz red burgundy
3 tablespoons marc de Bourgogne
4 scoops vanilla ice cream
whipped cream and
chocolate leaves for decoration

Bring the water, 250 g/9 oz of the sugar and the cinnamon to the boil. Blanch the peaches and skin them. Add them to the sugar syrup, let them poach for 2 to 3 minutes, then take the pan off the heat. Purée and sieve the raspberries and bring them to the boil with the remaining sugar and the burgundy. After about 3 minutes add the marc de Bourgogne and set it alight. Let it burn out and immediately lift the peaches out of the sugar syrup and add them to the sauce. Warm them up again and arrange them on 4 plates with the sauce poured over. Give each plate a scoop of vanilla ice cream (or pipe it onto the plate) and decorate with whipped cream and chocolate leaves.
Serves 4.

SPECIAL DESSERTS

The classics and the moderns

The magnificent display of desserts opposite, a prodigious assortment of delicious-looking classic creations, might perhaps be more reminiscent to some of the groaning sideboards of Victorian seaside hotels, although in fact it does come from one of France's most fashionable hotel restaurants. Such desserts as these are as much a delight to the eye as they are to the palate, the result of many hours of patient work by master pastry chefs. Some of us may have been fortunate enough to have seen and enjoyed the artistry they display in the setting up and composing of a sideboard of desserts: something fresh and fruity, like a fruit salad or soft fruit in season, served in their own syrup or with a sorbet; something slight and slimming for those who, at the outset anyway, are resolved to watch their weight; perhaps a few jellies, fresh fruit flans and velvety *pots de crème*. And then there are the stars of the collection – the charlottes, gâteaux and babas, the ices, the Bavarian creams, the Riz à l'Imperatrice dreamed up to honour Eugénie, the dishes of exquisite petits fours, and so on. What bliss to be there to choose a spoonful from this, a sliver or a slice from that, and marshal them all on your plate. They conjure up and in some way recreate for our rather more mundane times those heady days of Victorian and Edwardian high society when desserts were created for no better – or no lesser – reason than to honour an empress, fête a famous diva or celebrate a king's birthday.

Some cooks feel that decoration is superfluous – a dessert is a dessert and needs no finery but its own deliciousness. But it is incomparably more inviting with a little ornament: a marzipan rose, a tiny pastry bow, a rosette of choux pastry or whipped cream. A collection of such desserts, each arranged and presented to look its best, makes a fine and generous impression. At the end of the last century culinary patriotism insisted that the great desserts, ceremoniously carried to the table, quite often portrayed historical events or famous figures of national importance – either of which might be the reason for the dinner in question: for example, on navy day there might be a ship in full sail running before the wind on billows of meringue and manned by sugarloaf sailors.

Then, for some time decorated desserts went out of fashion: it was considered unnecessary, and a dessert needed no adornment other than its own luscious flavour. But today we have rather come around to the view that a dessert is much improved for being well presented: the castellated moulds, the marzipan roses, the pastry barquettes, the gem-like petits fours all play their part in creating an irresistible array which will tempt even the most abstemious of us into trying at least one of these most perfect ways of ending a perfect meal.

A display of classic French patisserie at the Hotel Bristol in Paris. This lavish presentation scarcely corresponds to our idea of everyday desserts but one cannot fail to be impressed by its luxury and profusion.

Vanilla Bavarian Cream

Crème bavaroise à la vanille

6 egg yolks · 100 g/4 oz sugar
500 ml/17 fl oz milk · 1 vanilla pod
7 leaves gelatine or
20 g/¾ oz powdered gelatine
500 ml/17 fl oz whipped cream

The basic Bavarian cream is made like an English custard, the egg yolks being blended with the sugar, the milk boiled with the vanilla pod then blended with the egg yolks and all of it heated till it coats the spoon lightly. The gelatine is dissolved in this basic cream which is then cooled, over ice if possible. Meanwhile stiffly whip the cream and fold it into the mixture at the moment when it is beginning to set. Serves 6 to 8.

Bavarian cream with macaroons:
50 g/2 oz almond macaroons
2 tablespoons kirsch
1 tablespoon honey
1.5-litre/2¾-pint mould

Break up the macaroons, sprinkle them with kirsch and honey and give them time to soak in it. Fill the mould with two-thirds of the Bavarian cream, drop in the macaroons and top up with the rest of the cream. Leave to set for about 2 hours in the refrigerator, then turn out and serve with ice-cold coffee custard. Serves 6 to 8.

Bavarian cream with fruit salad:
Use half the basic recipe; bind with 2 leaves gelatine, or 15 g/½ oz powdered gelatine.

575 g/1¼ lb fresh fruit
(peaches, kiwi fruit, pears, and raspberries)
4 tablespoons sugar syrup (20°)
2 tablespoons dark rum
2 tablespoons maraschino liqueur
100 ml/4 fl oz double or whipping cream

Macerate the fruit salad for 30 minutes in the syrup and alcohol. Make the Bavarian cream and put half of it in a glass bowl. Arrange the fruit salad on top and pour the rest of the cream over. Stiffly whip the cream with a little sugar and decorate the Bavarian cream with it. Serves 6.

Bavarian cream with strawberry sauce:
225 g/8 oz fresh strawberries
3 tablespoons sugar syrup (20°)
2 tablespoons brandy
scant 150 ml/¼ pint whipping cream
a few strawberries for decoration

Make the same light Bavarian cream as before and spoon it into glasses. Make a purée of the strawberries and mix with the syrup and brandy. Pour this sauce onto the Bavarian cream and decorate with a rosette of whipped cream and half a strawberry.
Serves 4 to 6.

Pistachio Bavarian cream/Crème bavaroise aux pistaches. Caramellise 40 g/1½ oz shelled pistachio nuts with a generous pinch of salt and 25 g/1 oz icing sugar. Cool and break up small. Make an English custard from 3 egg yolks, 60 g/2½ oz sugar and 250 ml/8 fl oz milk and melt 4 leaves gelatine or 1 tablespoon powdered gelatine in it. Leave to cool and fold in 250 ml/8 fl oz whipped cream. Stir 60 g/2½ oz melted couverture and 2 tablespoons rum into half of the Bavarian cream and pour this into small moulds. Stir the caramellised pistachio nuts into the rest of the cream and make a second layer with this. Leave to set in the refrigerator. Turn it out, scatter chopped pistachio nuts on top and serve with strawberry sauce. Serves 6.

Orange Bavarian cream/Crème bavaroise à l'orange. Blend together 3 egg yolks, 50 g/2 oz sugar and the juice and grated rind of 1 orange till creamy and stir in 250 ml/8 fl oz scalded milk. Heat up the Bavarian cream until it thickens and dissolve 4 leaves of gelatine/1 tablespoon powdered gelatine in it. Liquefy 75 g/3 oz sugar to a pale brown, stir in 50 g/2 oz flaked almonds, pour the nut brittle onto an oiled baking tray and leave to get cold. Break it up small and stir it with 2 tablespoons of orange liqueur into the already thickening cream. Fold in a scant 150 ml/¼ pint whipped cream and fill into individual moulds. Leave to set, turn out and serve with chocolate sauce. This makes 6 servings, and will fill 6 100 ml/4 fl oz timbale moulds.

Strawberry Bavarian cream/Crème bavaroise aux fraises. Purée 100 g/4 oz strawberries and stir in 3 tablespoons sugar syrup and 2 tablespoons Cointreau. Make a syrup with 100 g/4 oz sugar and the juice and grated rind of 1 orange. Cool slightly. Blend with 3 egg yolks till creamy. Boil 250 ml/8 fl oz milk, stir it into the egg yolks and cook this custard until it coats the spoon lightly. Dissolve 15 g/½ oz gelatine in this. Let it cool and then fold in 150 ml/¼ pint whipped cream. Combine 100 ml/4 fl oz more whipped cream with the strawberry purée, line 6 small moulds with this and pipe the orange Bavarian cream inside. Chill, turn out and decorate with meringue flowers. Serve with rum-and-chocolate sauce. Serves 6.

Chocolate Bavarian cream/Crème bavaroise au chocolat. Make an English custard from 4 egg yolks, 100 g/4 oz sugar, 300 ml/½ pint milk and 1 vanilla pod. Melt 4 leaves gelatine or 1 tablespoon powdered gelatine in it. Stiffly whip 300 ml/½ pint cream with 25 g/1 oz sugar and fold it into the Bavarian cream, which should be cool but still fluid. Put one-third of it into small moulds and into the remaining two-thirds stir 1½ tablespoons Bénédictine and 75 g/3 oz melted chocolate. Pipe the chocolate Bavarian cream into the centre of the vanilla cream, which must still be soft. Chill, turn out and pipe liquid couverture over the top. Serve with apricot sauce. Serves 6.

Strawberry Charlotte

Charlotte aux fraises

For the sponge:
4 egg yolks · 50 g/2 oz sugar
generous pinch of salt
3 egg whites · 60 g/2½ oz flour
175 g/6 oz strawberry jam
3 tablespoons brandy

For the charlotte:
200 g/7 oz fresh strawberries
1 tablespoon vanilla sugar

4 egg yolks · 100 g/4 oz sugar
plus 1 tablespoon
250 ml/8 fl oz milk · ½ vanilla pod
4 leaves gelatine or
15 g/½ oz powdered gelatine
1 tablespoon brandy
250 ml/8 fl oz double or whipping cream
75 ml/2½ fl oz apricot glaze
1-litre/1¾-pint hemispherical mould

Make the sponge mixture as described on pages 62 to 63 and spread it into a baking tin about 22 cm/8 to 9 in square. Bake, turn it out at once onto a damp cloth and peel off

Line the mould with Swiss roll slices as closely as possible so as to leave a minimum of gaps between the slices. Trim those which protrude above the rim; the trimmings can be used for the covering layer after the mould has been filled.

the paper. Sieve the strawberry jam if necessary and blend it with 1 tablespoon of the brandy. Spread the sponge cake with this and roll it up. Let it get cold and cut into thin slices, about 5 mm/¼ in thick. Line the mould with the slices as closely as possible.

Hull and halve the fresh strawberries. Drain them well, lay them in a dish, sprinkle them with vanilla sugar and pour over 1 tablespoon brandy. Leave them to macerate in the refrigerator for at least 30 minutes. Cream the egg yolks and 100 g/4 oz sugar. Bring the milk to the boil with the vanilla pod and, as for an English custard, stir it into the egg yolks and heat it up again till the custard coats the spoon lightly. Dissolve the leaf gelatine in it, previously softened in cold water and squeezed dry, or the powdered gelatine, and stir in the last tablespoon of brandy. Cool the custard over ice until it starts to thicken. Meanwhile stiffly whip the cream with the remaining sugar and at the right moment, when the custard is beginning to set, carefully fold the cream into it. Fill the sponge-lined mould with about two-thirds of it and stir the strawberries into the rest.

Then fill the mould to the top with this mixture and cover with a layer of slices from the sponge roll or, if you have it, a round of sponge cake. Let the charlotte set for about 2 hours in the refrigerator, then turn it onto a serving dish and brush over with apricot glaze (hot apricot jam). Decorate with a strawberry dipped in melted chocolate and serve with chocolate sauce. Serves 6 to 8.

This charlotte is equally good when made with raspberries. You can follow the same method as described here exactly, with the exception that kirsch might make a good alternative flavouring to brandy. You might like to serve it with a fresh raspberry sauce, or the chocolate sauce suggested above.

Kiwi Fruit Charlotte

Charlotte aux kiwis

12 sponge finger biscuits
2 kiwi fruit
1 tablespoon honey
2 tablespoons kirsch
4 egg yolks
100 g/4 oz sugar
250 ml/8 fl oz milk
1 vanilla pod
4 leaves gelatine or
15 g/½ oz powdered gelatine
300 ml/½ pint double or whipping cream

for decoration:
1 kiwi fruit
1 maraschino cherry
scant 150 ml/¼ pint double
or whipping cream
1 tablespoon sugar
1 tablespoon broken nut brittle
a fluted 1-litre/1¾-pint mould

Sprinkle the mould base with sugar to prevent the charlotte from sticking when turned out and place sponge fingers in the corrugations. Peel and slice the kiwi fruit, lay them in a glass dish and pour over the honey mixed with the kirsch. Cover and let them macerate in the refrigerator for about 30 minutes. Cream the egg yolks and 75 g/3 oz of the sugar. Bring the milk and the vanilla pod to the boil and, as for an English custard, stir it into the egg yolks and cook till it coats the spoon. Dissolve the gelatine leaves, softened in cold water and well squeezed out, or the powdered gelatine, in the warm custard, then cool over iced water until it starts to thicken. Stiffly whip the cream with the remaining sugar, fold it into the custard and put about three-quarters of it into the prepared mould. Lay the sliced kiwi on top and fill with the rest of the custard. Chill until set thoroughly – it will take about 2 hours – and turn out onto a serving dish. Cover with sliced kiwi and a maraschino cherry. Pipe sweetened whip-ped cream around the edge and sprinkle over broken nut brittle.

Serves 6.

A fluted mould is ideal for a charlotte, as the finger biscuits will not slip out of position. It is even simpler if the biscuits were piped in a tapering shape in the first place so that they do not have to be cut to fit.

Coconut Mousse

Crème de coco

This is a truly exotic cream in which, if at all possible, fresh coconuts should be used, for they give an incomparably better-flavoured milk than can be made with desiccated coconut. And, to be really authentic, this mousse should be sweetened with coconut palm syrup, although sugar beet syrup is no bad substitute.

300 g/11 oz freshly grated coconut
(about 2 coconuts) or desiccated coconut
350 ml/12 fl oz milk
(to produce some 300 ml/½ pint
coconut milk)
4 egg yolks
75 ml 2½ fl oz palm syrup
or sugar-beet syrup
4 leaves gelatine or
1 tablespoon powdered gelatine
2 tablespoons dark rum
2 tablespoons fresh lime juice
3 egg whites
60 g/2½ oz sugar
250 ml/8 fl oz double or whipping cream
lime and chocolate shavings
for decoration

Bore holes in the 'eyes' of the coconuts, drain out the liquid and crack or saw them open. Grate the copra (coconut flesh) finely into a bowl. Bring the milk to the boil and pour it hot over the grated coconut. Mash it thoroughly, cover and leave it till lukewarm. Line a fine sieve with a linen cloth, tip in the grated coconut and liquid and press it well until the flesh is dry.

Beat the egg yolks with the palm or sugar beet syrup till they froth. Heat the coconut milk to just below boiling point and, stirring continuously, add it slowly to the egg yolk mixture. Heat this mixture slowly as for English custard until it has a light dropping consistency and coats the wooden spoon. Take it off the heat and dissolve in it the gelatine leaves, previously soaked in cold water and well squeezed out, or the powdered gelatine. Stir in the rum and lime juice and cool the custard to lukewarm. Whip the egg whites to a snow, beat in the sugar in a thin stream and fold the stiffly beaten snow into the custard. Finally fold in the whipped cream carefully with a wooden spoon. Pour the mousse into glasses and decorate each with chocolate shavings and a wedge of lime.

Serves about 6.

Mangosteen Mousse

Crème de mangostanes

150 g/5 oz mangosteen purée
(from about 6 fruits)
150 g/5 oz confectioner's custard
(page 58)
4 leaves gelatine or
15 g/½ oz powdered gelatine
1 teaspoon fresh lime juice
scant 150 ml/¼ pint double
or whipping cream
50 g/2 oz sugar
2 tablespoons cold chocolate sauce
4 almond biscuit paste leaves
(page 66)

Peel the mangosteens, take out the seeds and pass the fruit through a fine sieve. Pass the confectioner's custard through a fine sieve also and warm it up with the mangosteen purée, stirring all the time. Squeeze out the gelatine leaves, softened in cold water, and dissolve them, or the powdered gelatine, in the mixture. Add the lime juice and let the mixture get almost cold. Stiffly whip the chilled cream with the sugar and fold it into the mousse which should not be firm. Spoon it into a piping bag. Pipe it with a wide nozzle into glasses. Finally, pour cold chocolate sauce over and decorate each with a leaf biscuit. Serves 4.

Caribbean Ginger Mousse

200 ml/7 fl oz milk · 3 egg yolks
50 g/2 oz sugar
4 leaves gelatine or
15 g/½ oz powdered gelatine
75 g/3 oz diced preserved ginger in syrup
2 tablespoons ginger syrup
75 ml/2½ fl oz dark rum · 3 egg whites
350 ml/12 fl oz double or whipping cream

chocolate shavings

Scald the milk. Cream the egg yolks and sugar, slowly stir in the hot milk and then, as with an English custard, cook until it coats the spoon. Dissolve the well squeezed out leaves of gelatine or the powdered gelatine in the custard and pass it all through a fine sieve. Reserve half of the diced ginger for decoration and add the rest to the mixture. Heat up the ginger syrup and the rum together, set it alight and let it burn until the flame dies out. When it has cooled a little combine it with the custard and when this is nearly cold fold in first the stiffly beaten egg whites and immediately afterwards 250 ml/8 fl oz whipped cream. Spoon the ginger mousse into glasses and leave to set in the refrigerator. Decorate with the remaining whipped cream, the reserved diced ginger and chocolate shavings. Serves 6.

Maple Syrup Mousse

Crème au sirop d'érable

4 egg yolks, separated
50 g/2 oz brown sugar
250 g/9 oz maple syrup
6 leaves gelatine or
25 g/1 oz powdered gelatine
350 ml/12 fl oz double or whipping cream
juice of 1 orange and 1 lemon
40 g/1½ oz sugar
2 tablespoons orange liqueur

Cream the egg yolks and brown sugar till the sugar has almost dissolved. Pour in the maple syrup and heat the mixture, stirring all the time, until the custard is of a dropping consistency and – as in English custard – coats the wooden spoon, indicating that it is near to boiling point. Take it off the heat, dissolve the softened and well squeezed out leaves of gelatine or the powdered gelatine in it and let it get cold. Beat the egg whites to a stiff snow and fold into the custard, then fold in the whipped cream. With the star nozzle on a piping bag pipe it into glasses, chill and pour ice-cold orange sauce over. For this the orange and lemon juice is reduced by being boiled with the white sugar and then the liqueur is added. Decorate each glass with a chocolate flower. Serves 4 to 6.

Cornets with Bilberries

Cornets aux myrtilles

150 g/5 oz icing sugar
2 eggs
75 ml/2½ fl oz milk
250 g/9 oz flour
seeds of ½ vanilla pod
250 g/9 oz butter
oil for greasing the crêpe pan

250 ml/8 fl oz double or whipping cream
25 g/1 oz sugar
seeds of ½ vanilla pod
60 g/2½ oz crushed nut brittle

75 g/3 oz sugar
75 ml/2½ fl oz fresh redcurrant juice
2 tablespoons fresh lime juice
generous pinch of cinnamon
2 tablespoons rum
250 g/9 oz fresh bilberries

Sift the icing sugar into a bowl and beat it with the eggs till it froths. Then stir in the milk and the flour alternately, add the vanilla seeds and lastly the melted, but only slightly warmed, butter in a thin stream. Leave the batter to rest for a few minutes and make very thin 15 cm/6 in pancakes. Alternatively, the cornets can be spread thinly on a greased baking sheet and baked in the oven. As soon as they are done, wrap them around a wooden spoon handle about 3 cm/1 in thick and roll them up. Stiffly whip the cream with the sugar and vanilla seeds and fill the cornets from either end with the aid of a piping bag. Dip the ends in crushed nut brittle.

Cook the sugar with the redcurrant juice, lime juice and cinnamon for 2 to 3 minutes. Then add the rum, set it alight and let it burn out. Add the fresh bilberries to the sauce and leave to get cold.

Serves 12 to 15.

Snow Eggs

Oeufs à la neige

This is one of *the* classic desserts, of which many variations are to be found on menus the world over. The recipe below is, as it were, the original article which may be embellished with various extras. The delicate flavour is indeed compatible with chocolate, coffee, all fruits and fruit sauces and alcoholic flavourings as well.

6 egg whites
200 g/7 oz sugar
vanilla sauce (English custard)
made with 500 ml/17 fl oz milk
(see page 54)

Whip the egg whites to a stiff snow, adding the sugar as you do so in a thin stream. Fill a piping bag with this meringue mixture and, using a wide nozzle, pipe rosettes onto baking parchment that has been sprinkled with water. Have a shallow pan ready with 600 ml/1 pint boiling water in it and reduce the heat to just below boiling point. Dip a palette knife in water, lift the rosettes from the paper with it and slide them into the pan of water. Poach them for 3 to 4 minutes on either side. Lift them out with a slotted spoon, drain and place them on the cold vanilla sauce.

It is even easier to make this dish if the raw meringue is spooned directly into the water with a wet tablespoon.

Serves about 8.

Saint Honoré Puffs

Saint Honoré chiboust

This is a traditional French dessert, often also served as a cake, which should be eaten as fresh as possible, because the caramel-covered choux pastry quickly absorbs moisture from the *crème chiboust*.

350 g/12 oz puff pastry
choux pastry as in the recipe on
page 67
300 g/11 oz sugar
4 tablespoons water
1 teaspoon lemon juice

confectioner's custard made with
500 ml/17 fl oz milk
3 egg whites
60 g/2½ oz sugar

Roll out the puff pastry thinly and evenly (3 mm/⅛ in thick at the most) and stamp out 20 bases 7.5 cm/3 in in diameter. Lay them on a baking sheet and prick them with a fork to prevent bubbles forming in the baking. Prepare the choux paste as in the recipe on page 75 and pipe rings of it through a star nozzle onto the puff pastry bases. Pipe 20 small choux puffs from the rest of the paste in the bag onto the baking sheet. Bake them to a nice crisp brown in a hot oven (220 C, 425 F, gas 7). The small choux puffs will be ready after about 15 minutes, the rings will take 8 to 10 minutes longer. Meanwhile boil the sugar with the water and lemon juice to a pale caramel (160 C, 325 F). Dip the tops of the rings and the choux puffs in it. For the filling (*crème chiboust*) make a confectioner's custard (as on page 58 with 500 ml/17 fl oz milk and while still hot fold in the beaten egg whites (as described on page 59). Fill the puffs with it and place a small choux puff on top of each.

Serves 20.

Waffles with Strawberry Sauce

Gaufres à la sauce aux fraises

375 g/13 oz flour
25 g/1 oz fresh yeast · 50 g/2 oz sugar
500 ml/17 fl oz lukewarm milk
4 eggs
100 g/4 oz melted butter
generous pinch of salt
grated rind of ½ lemon
oil for greasing the waffle iron

1 tablespoon honey
100 g/4 oz sugar
3 tablespoons fresh lime juice
350 g/12 oz fresh strawberries
250 ml/8 fl oz double or whipping cream
seeds from ½ vanilla pod

Sift the flour into a bowl and make a well in the middle. Crumble the fresh yeast into it and blend it with 1 teaspoon sugar and 150 ml/¼ pint of the milk, drawing in a little of the flour. Cover the bowl and leave the yeast mixture to prove. Add the rest of the sugar and milk, the eggs, the melted butter, salt and grated lemon rind and beat all together with the rest of the flour until the batter has bubbles in it. Leave the batter to rise for 25 minutes. Heat the waffle iron and brush the inside with oil. For each waffle spread 3 tablespoons batter on the waffle iron and cook to a golden brown. It will take some 4 to 5 minutes depending on the temperature of the waffle iron. The cooled waffles may be dusted with icing sugar but need not be, since they contain a fair amount of sugar already. Bring the honey to the boil with 75 g/3 oz of the sugar and the lime juice and reduce to a thick syrup. Purée the strawberries, if necessary sieve them too, mix them with the syrup and let cool thoroughly. Serve with the waffles along with vanilla-flavoured whipped cream sweetened with the remaining sugar.
Serves 15 to 20.

Mont Blanc

Mousse aux marrons

500 g/18 oz chestnuts
generous pinch of salt
100 ml/4 fl oz milk
½ vanilla pod
100 ml/4 fl oz single cream
75 g/3 oz sugar
250 ml/8 fl oz double or whipping cream
1 tablespoon dark rum
whipped cream and a
maraschino cherry for decoration

To prepare the chestnuts, nick them on the round surface and roast them in the oven till they split open. While the chestnuts are still warm carefully remove the outer shell and the thin inner skin. Put the peeled chestnuts into a saucepan, add salt and enough water just to cover. Cook till soft – they will take about 45 to 50 minutes. Drain the chestnuts, mash them and push them through a fine sieve or, if possible, purée them in a blender or food processor. Bring the milk to the boil with the vanilla pod, then remove the pod and add the chestnut purée. Stirring all the time over high heat, cook to a thick mass. Add the single cream and 50 g/2 oz of the sugar and again bring to the boil. Leave to get cold. Whip the double cream stiffly with the remaining sugar, add the rum and stir it into the cold purée. Put the mixture through a potato ricer or the fine disc of a food mill. Decorate with whipped cream and a maraschino cherry.
Serves 6 to 8.

Ginger Mousse Meringue

Vacherin à la mousse de gingembre

12 meringue bases of
6 cm/2½ in diameter
60 g/2½ oz diced preserved ginger
in syrup
3 egg yolks · 75 g/3 oz sugar
250 ml/8 fl oz milk
½ vanilla pod
3 tablespoons ginger syrup
4 leaves gelatine or
15 g/½ oz powdered gelatine
2 egg whites
250 ml/8 fl oz double or whipping cream
40 g/1½ oz melted couverture
2 tablespoons brandy
12 meringue flowers of 7 cm/3 in diameter
cocoa powder for dusting

Make a collar of aluminium foil 5 cm/2 in high for each meringue base and fasten with sellotape. Cream the egg yolks and 50 g/2 oz of the sugar. Bring the milk to the boil with the vanilla pod and the ginger syrup and stir gradually into the egg yolks. Cook this mixture as for an English custard until it coats the spoon, keeping the heat just below boiling point. Dissolve in it the gelatine leaves, previously softened in cold water and squeezed out, or the powdered gelatine. Cool the custard over ice till it starts to thicken. Meanwhile whip the egg whites to a snow with the remaining sugar; stiffly whip the cream and stir in the chopped ginger. Fold carefully first the egg white snow and then the cream into the custard. Use half the mousse to form a first layer on top of the foil-collared meringue bases. Stir the liquid couverture and the brandy into the remainder and make a second layer with it. Leave in the refrigerator for at least an hour to set, peel off the aluminium foil, place a meringue flower on top and dust with sifted cocoa powder. Serve with orange sauce.
Serves 12.

Petits Pots de Crème

Petits pots de crème

This is the finest egg custard that can be imagined. It is prepared and cooked in the same way as the famous Cream Caramel (page 55) but it is more delicate and because it contains relatively little egg white cannot be turned out, not being sufficiently firm. It is a cream that can be given a variety of flavours with different ingredients. The example with vanilla serves as a basic recipe.

375 ml/13 fl oz milk
scant 150 ml/¼ pint cream
½ vanilla pod
1 egg
3 egg yolks
100 g/4 oz sugar
6 small ramekins or pots
holding about 100 ml/4 fl oz each

Bring the milk and cream to the boil with the vanilla pod cut open lengthways. Cream the egg, egg yolks and sugar well together but on no account allow it to foam, then stir in slowly the hot milk and cream. Pass it all through a fine sieve and skim any froth from the surface with a spoon. Fill up the soufflé dishes or other small pots if the cream is to be served on its own, or two-thirds full if with fruit. Put the pots in a water bath and poach for about 20 minutes in a moderate oven (180 C, 350 F, gas 4). The water should come up to about 1 cm/½ in below the rim of the dishes and must always be kept below boiling point. The creams are done when the surface feels elastic if lightly pressed with the finger. Take them out of the water bath and leave to cool.

Serves 6

Petits pots de crème with sour cherries:

basic recipe for petits pots with vanilla

100 ml/4 fl oz cherry juice
100 ml/4 fl oz light red wine
75 g/3 oz sugar
a small piece of cinnamon stick
1½ teaspoons cornflour
400 g/14 oz stewed sour cherries
100 ml/4 fl oz double or whipping cream
a little sugar and kirsch

Bring the cherry juice and red wine slowly to the boil with the sugar and cinnamon and bind the liquid with the cornflour previously moistened with a little water. Add the strained sour cherries, taking care not to crush them. Leave them to get cold and spoon them on top of the creams. Decorate the pots with sweetened whipped cream flavoured with kirsch.

1 **Divide the sour cherries between the pots.** The sour cherry compote, lightly thickened with cornflour, should be completely cold before it is spooned into the pots. These should be only two-thirds full of the vanilla cream which should also be quite cold.

2 **Decorate with whipped cream,** or pour some liquid cream over. The cream should be lightly sweetened, stiffly whipped and then flavoured with kirsch. Pipe a rosette onto each cream pot using a star nozzle. Liquid cream for this recipe should not be sweetened.

Chocolate cream pots with whipped cream or raspberry sauce. The basic method is altered a little in that the sugar is caramellised to a mid-brown with 1 tablespoon water in a saucepan. Add the milk, cream and vanilla pod to the pan and bring the caramel to the boil with them. Dissolve 1 teaspoon instant coffee and 50 g/2 oz plain chocolate in the flavoured milk, heat it up again and strain it through a fine sieve onto the beaten eggs. Cook the cream in a water bath and let the pots get completely cold before serving them with whipped cream or raspberry sauce. Decorate them with chocolate ornaments or baby meringues.

Chocolate Mousse

Mousse au chocolat

This is one of the most famous classic desserts, inimitable in flavour and simple in execution. It demands however the best ingredients, above all the best chocolate – which is plain chocolate, even though some recipes do specify milk chocolate. Its bitter-sweet taste is precisely what harmonises so perfectly with the creamy consistency of the mousse. There are innumerable variations in the method of preparing it, many of them calling for cream and butter, and ranging from a heavy, creamy consistency to the airiest chocolate thistledown lightened with egg white. The ideal chocolate mousse probably lies somewhere in between the two extremes – like Eva Klever's recipe, slightly sharp in flavour and very airy, although it can be kept for some hours.

Eva Klever's chocolate mousse:
200 g/7 oz plain chocolate
4 tablespoons strong mocha coffee
5 egg yolks
25 g/1 oz vanilla sugar
scant 150 ml/¼ pint double
or whipping cream
5 egg whites
50 g/2 oz sugar

Break up the chocolate and melt it over a water bath. Stir in the coffee. Beat the egg yolks and vanilla sugar till frothy and the sugar is completely dissolved. Stir them into the chocolate and take care that the mixture stays lukewarm because the addition next of lightly whipped cream will cool the mousse considerably. For this reason the egg whites should be beaten to a stiff snow with the sugar in advance, so that this can be folded into the mousse while it is still soft and loose in texture. Fill a large bowl or individual glasses and leave it to set in the refrigerator, where it should preferably be well covered with aluminium foil or cling film since it is liable to be affected by other flavours. Serve it with some whipped or liquid cream.

Serves 8.

A chocolate mousse may be varied in flavour: brandy or rum may be used, or a liqueur such as Bénédictine or Cointreau, or a fine kirsch. Grated orange rind too, boiled with a little juice and sugar, perfectly harmonises with the bitter taste of the chocolate.

Monsieur Piffet, pastry-chef at the Paris Intercontinental Hotel, with the help of an assistant folds the beaten egg white into the chocolate mousse for which he is famous. He substitutes cocoa powder for some of the chocolate, to give an extra-strongly flavoured mousse.

Everything required for making the mouse should be lined up ready, because success largely depends on the right temperature of the ingredients. Beat the strong coffee into the melted chocolate till it is shiny and satin-smooth. Now stir in the egg yolk and sugar mixture, beaten until frothy. The mixture should still be lukewarm.

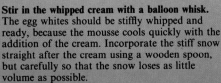

Stir in the whipped cream with a balloon whisk. The egg whites should be stiffly whipped and ready, because the mousse cools quickly with the addition of the cream. Incorporate the stiff snow straight after the cream using a wooden spoon, but carefully so that the snow loses as little volume as possible.

Baba or Savarin?

To enquire after the origin of baba and savarin, or ask what the difference between them may be, is a pointless exercise. The descriptions chop and change within international cookery literature as much as do the recipes themselves. The baba is of Russian origin and was an integral part of the sumptuous Easter feast. Its name is derived from *babuschka* (granny), presumably because the *babuschkas* were the ones who prepared these succulent moulded cakes. Like a good many other Russian specialities, the baba was incorporated into French classic cooking and given added refinement. Whether this traditional Russian dessert stood godfather at the invention of the savarin is not certain. In any case a yeasted-cake saturated with sugar syrup was dedicated to the French gastrosoph Brillat-Savarin and today ranks as one of the great international classic desserts.

An Adaptable Recipe

All recipes for babas and savarins have yeast in common, and a good soaking in sweetened and flavoured liquid after they are baked. Depending on the recipe they are sometimes made with a lot of butter, sometimes with a lot of eggs, often too with candied orange and lemon peel and raisins.

The following recipe is a happy compromise. The cake absorbs an equal volume of liquid and adapts itself well to any flavour. Once baked, savarins freeze excellently.

Yeast Dough for Baba or Savarin

Pâte à savarin

350 g/12 oz flour
15 g/½ oz fresh yeast
100 ml/4 fl oz lukewarm milk
150 g/5 oz butter
40 g/1½ oz sugar
½ teaspoon salt
½ teaspoon grated lemon rind
4 eggs

Sift the flour into a bowl, make a well in the middle, crumble the yeast into it and dissolve it with the milk. Draw a little flour over the yeast mixture. Cover the bowl with a cloth and leave in a warm place for 15 minutes to prove. Melt the butter and cool until lukewarm. Add the sugar, flavourings and eggs and stir all together briefly with a whisk or electric mixer. It must not be foamy. When the crust over the yeast begins to split add the egg mixture and knead the dough energetically, preferably by hand, until it is elastic. It must not be too firm. Let it rise again for 15 minutes. Grease the savarin moulds with butter, dust them with flour and half fill them with the dough. Cover again with a cloth and leave to rise again until double in size – about 10 to 15 minutes.

Baking time: large moulds 25 to 30 minutes in a moderately hot oven, at 200 C, 400 F, gas 6, individual moulds 12 to 18 minutes at the same temperature. This quantity is sufficient for 2 savarins of 15 cm/6 in diameter or 6 individual savarins of 9 cm/3½ in diameter.

Filling the individual moulds. Grease the moulds with butter and dust with flour. Pipe in the yeast dough with a piping bag, fitted with a wide nozzle. Take care only to half-fill the moulds, because the dough has still to rise and double itself.

The Syrup and the Glaze

These two things turn a simple yeast cake into a much appreciated delicacy.

An example with rum:
500 ml/17 fl oz water
300 g/11 oz sugar
100 ml/4 fl oz dark rum
100 ml/4 fl oz apricot glaze

Bring the water and sugar to the boil, cool to lukewarm, then add the rum. Lay a wire rack over a bowl and place the savarin on it. Ladle the syrup over it until it has absorbed as much as possible, basting it with the syrup in the bowl if necessary. Individual savarins may be dipped in the syrup, but take care when lifting them out, because they break easily. Brush the savarin lightly with hot apricot glaze and cool well. Spoon in compote, whipped cream, confectioner's custard or any other filling. The syrup and filling should each enhance the flavour of the other. Savarins can also be served hot with a filling of hot compote and a sabayon sauce. This quantity is sufficient for 2 savarins of about 15 cm/6 in diameter or 6 or so individual savarins.

Grape Savarin/Savarin aux raisins. Syrup: bring 250 ml/8 fl oz water, 75 g/3 oz sugar, 50 g/2 oz honey and the thinly peeled rind of an orange to the boil. Cool the syrup a little, remove the orange peel, and add 1 teaspoon lemon juice and 3 tablespoons brandy. Soak the savarin in this and lightly brush it with apricot glaze. Compote: peel 350 g/12 oz grapes. Boil together a scant 150 ml/¼ pint water, 75 g/3 oz sugar and ½ vanilla pod and reduce a little. Remove the vanilla pod, add the grapes and boil for a few more minutes. Add 3 tablespoons brandy and cool. Fill a large savarin with the grapes and a scant 150 ml/¼ pint slightly sweetened whipped cream. Decorate with chocolate curls.

Redcurrant savarin/Savarin aux groseilles. Syrup: bring 250 ml/8 fl oz water to the boil with 100 g/4 oz sugar and cool it just a little. Add 3 tablespoons white rum, heat it up again, soak the savarins – if possible still warm – in it and brush with a thin apricot glaze. Compote: bring a scant 150 ml/¼ pint red wine, 100 g/4 oz sugar and the juice of an orange gently to the boil and poach 350 g/12 oz redcurrants in it till soft. Do not let them disintegrate. Fill hot savarins with them and accompany with a hot white wine sabayon. This is enough for 10 to 15 small or 1 large savarin.

Cranberry Savarin/Savarin aux airelles rouges. Syrup: bring 250 ml/8 fl oz water to the boil with 75 g/3 oz sugar. Let it cool, and add 1 teaspoon Tia Maria liqueur. Steep the savarins in the syrup, then cover with a thin apricot glaze. Compote: bring 250 ml/8 fl oz water, 150 g/5 oz sugar, a little piece of cinnamon stick and 2 cloves to a steady boil and boil for a few minutes. Strain the liquid and add the juice of an orange and 400 g/14 oz fresh cranberries. Cook again until the berries begin to pop. Chill them well and fill the savarins with them, together with some vanilla-flavoured whipped cream. This is enough for 15 small or one large savarin.

Plum savarin/Savarin aux prunes. Syrup: bring 250 ml/8 fl oz water, 100 g/4 oz sugar, 1 clove and a strip of thinly peeled lemon rind gently to the boil. Take out the cloves and lemon peel, and add 3 tablespoons slivowitz (plum brandy). Soak the savarins and cover thinly with apricot glaze. Compote: bring a scant 150 ml/¼ pint each white wine and water, 100 g/4 oz sugar and 1 tablespoon honey just to boiling point; blanch, peel and stone 500 g/18 oz damsons or plums and cook till soft in this. Fill the savarins with the cooled compote. Decorate with whipped cream and chopped pistachio nuts. Enough for 10 to 15 small or 1 large savarin.

Blackberry savarin/Savarin aux baies de ronce. Syrup: bring 250 ml/8 fl oz water with 75 g/3 oz sugar to the boil. Cool it, add 3 tablespoons Cointreau and soak the savarins with the syrup. Flavour some apricot glaze with Cointreau and brush it on thinly. Compote: cook together 250 ml/8 fl oz red wine, the juice of an orange, a piece of cinnamon stick, ½ vanilla pod and 100 g/4 oz sugar for a few minutes and strain. Put in 400 g/14 oz blackberries and reduce the liquid to a syrup. Add 2 tablespoons Cointreau and when cold spoon it into the savarins. Decorate with whipped cream and toasted almond flakes. Enough for 10 to 15 small or 1 large savarin.

Mini-Meringues

Petites meringues

These are not exactly a dessert, but delightful titbits to go with the coffee. Two factors are critical: the meringues must be tiny and the filling must be adapted to their sweetness; thus the cream must be well-flavoured without being too sweet. Coffee and chocolate creams are good, but only with bitter chocolate. So are fruit creams made with strawberries, raspberries, etc., sharpened with lemon juice and laced with an *eau de vie* of the fruit. Meringues can be dusted with cocoa powder before baking, or coloured with it. When done, a glaze of couverture can be put on them or just onto the cream piped over them, which must first have been left to set in the refrigerator.

5 egg whites
200 g/7 oz icing sugar
4 whole eggs
200 g/7 oz sugar
½ vanilla pod
250 g/9 oz butter

Beat the egg whites and icing sugar warm and cold (see 'Meringues for Decoration', page 64) and with a piping bag pipe it through a plain or star-shaped nozzle onto a baking sheet lined with cooking parchment. Bake for about 3 hours in a very cool oven (120 C, 250 F, gas ½). For the cream, beat the whole eggs with the sugar in a water bath over barely simmering water and again beat until cold. Scrape out the inside of the vanilla pod and beat it with the butter until fluffy. Slowly add the egg mixture to it.

This is enough for 50 small meringues, and the butter cream to go with them.

Petits Fours

These diminutive, sweet frivolities are really pastries rather than a dessert, though they are frequently served on their own as the very last item on the menu. With a cup of good coffee, however, they could well stand as the dessert course if you so wished.

75 g/3 oz flour
5 eggs, separated
grated rind of ½ lemon
generous pinch of salt
5 egg whites
60 g/2½ oz sugar
50 g/2 oz cornflour

Beat the flour and egg yolks. Add the lemon rind and salt. Whip the egg whites to a snow, slowly trickle in the sugar and lastly fold the cornflour into the stiff snow with a wooden spoon. Beat a small amount of the snow briskly into the dough to lighten it a little, then carefully fold in the rest so that a firm sponge mixture is produced. With a piping bag pipe the mixture in shapes onto the baking sheet and bake to a nice pale brown. Leave the oven door slightly open so that the steam can escape. This will make 40 to 50 bases (or 20 to 25 petits fours).

Baking time: 8 to 12 minutes in a moderately hot oven (190 C, 375 F, gas 5).

For filling the petits fours a butter cream (see under mini meringues in the previous column) is as suitable as a confectioner's custard and it keeps somewhat longer. All creams must however be well-flavoured, so be generous with the chocolate, coffee or fruit purée to counteract the sweetness of the fondant icing. The icing itself can be laced with an appropriate liqueur.

1 **Pipe the sponge mixture onto baking parchment.** Line the baking sheet with the parchment and pipe the selected shapes through a large nozzle. This must be done fairly swiftly because the sponge mixture does not hold its shape for too long and there is a risk of it spreading out in the oven.

Filling 1:	chocolate cream with a little rum.
Icing 1:	fondant flavoured with a few drops of lime juice and rum.
Filling 2:	cream with strawberry purée and some drops of lemon juice.
Icing 2:	fondant with kirsch.
Filling 3:	coffee cream.
Icing 3:	fondant flavoured with Tia Maria.
Filling 4:	lemon cream.
Icing 4:	fondant with almond liqueur (Amaretto).

It looks good if the colour of the icing is chosen to suit the filling, for example yellow for a lemon filling. There are plenty of natural colours to use, such as saffron,

reduced cherry juice and so forth. A delicate decoration of the fondant itself can be piped over the icing or a special filigree effect achieved with chocolate (couverture). Crown it with a tiny piece of candied fruit or pistachio nut or a gold or silver sugar-plum.

2 **Hollow out the sponge cakes,** preferably with a pointed knife. Pare a thin slice off the underside to give the cakes a steady base. Fill them with cream (light butter cream or confectioner's custard), put them together in pairs and leave to cool.

3 **Insulate with apricot glaze.** It is an excellent idea, before putting on the fondant icing, to brush a thin coat of hot apricot glaze over the surface. This prevents the moisture from the icing being absorbed into the cake, which would take the shine off the icing and slightly spoil the finished effect.

4 **Ice with fondant.** Slightly warm the fondant in a *bain marie* over barely simmering water, flavour it and colour it if you wish, perhaps following the suggestions given above. It is important that the fondant should be of a creamy consistency. Dip the petits fours in it to coat both top and sides and place them on a wire rack to set.

Palm sugar both flavours and sweetens

Its English name is jaggery and it comes from a whole lot of different varieties of palm, the ordinary coconut palm included. But, for the connoisseur, it is the unprepossessing Kithul palm that yields the finest sugar. 'Malty' is a less than adequate description of its flavour: it is indeed both sugar and spice, its characteristic taste giving it an important place in the composition of a number of tropical desserts.

To obtain the sugar, the palm-flower, consisting of numerous pendant panicles, must first be tapped. In order to speed up secretion a wedge-shaped incision is made in the stalk and filled with a mixture of herbs and spices – such as salt and chillies – and then wrapped round with a bandage. From the cut blossom the nectar can be drawn off daily for up to six months and is immediately boiled into 'treacle' (syrup) because in that climate it would begin to ferment after 3 to 4 hours. This is a wholly desirable feature if the nectar is to be made into 'toddy' (an intoxicating drink with quite a pleasant taste) or distilled as arrack; but to be made into jaggery it must be unfermented and that no doubt is one reason why this tasty sugar is a cottage industry product only.

Collecting palm nectar: a truly acrobatic performance. Normally a group of 10 to 20 palms is linked by cables of coconut fibre. These serve as bridges for the collector, who empties the contents of the containers hanging on the flowers into his calabash, and lets his harvest down on a rope. Up to 5 litres/9 pints a day can be drawn off each palm, continuing for a period of 6 months in each year.

The milk-white nectar is poured out of the calabash. It is then boiled into 'treacle', the first phase in the manufacture of palm sugar. 5 litres/9 pints nectar are boiled down in about 4 hours to 1 litre/1¾ pints of syrup (treacle).

The syrup is thickened into jaggery over an open fire. It takes on its malty flavour and dark brown colour in 2 to 3 hours, and is then drawn off into half coconut shells which hold some 500 ml/18 fl oz each.

Vattalapam

Coconut cream mould

This is a refreshing, but filling, dessert from the tropics, that with only minor alterations is served all over South-East Asia, but in Sri Lanka it has become a national dish. We would normally have to replace the palm sugar with a mixture of soft brown sugar and syrup, but that makes hardly any difference to the quality of the dessert.

300 g/11 oz grated fresh coconut
(from about 2 nuts)
or desiccated coconut
400 ml/14 fl oz milk
175 g/6 oz palm sugar
(or 175 g/3 oz soft brown sugar
and 100 g/4 oz golden syrup)
4 tablespoons water · 4 eggs
¼ teaspoon ground cardamom
¼ teaspoon ground mace
generous pinch of ground cloves
100 g/4 oz cashew nuts
8 100-ml/4-fl oz timbale moulds

First prepare the coconut milk. Bore holes in the 'eyes' of the coconuts, drain out the liquid and crack open the shells. Remove the thin skin from the white flesh and grate it. Bring it to the boil with the milk and squeeze it out. Break up the palm sugar and heat it in the water till dissolved. Stir the eggs together with the coconut milk, add the palm sugar syrup and lastly the spices. Slice the cashew nuts and divide them between the lightly oiled individual moulds. Pour on the egg and coconut mixture, place the moulds in a water bath and cook for 1 hour in a moderate oven (160 to 170 C, 325 to 340 F, gas 3 to 4). Leave to get cold, chill and turn out. Serves 8.

1 **Pour the milk onto the grated coconut** and bring slowly to the boil. Let the milk rise up in the pan once and then cool it to lukewarm. If desiccated coconut is used the mixture should be boiled very gently for a further 1 to 2 minutes to draw out the flavour.

2 **Squeeze out the coconut milk.** Line a sieve with a linen cloth and tip the milk mixture into it. Gather up the corners and squeeze the grated coconut in the cloth as dry as possible with both hands.

3 **Pour the coconut milk onto the eggs** and stir thoroughly with a balloon whisk until the milk and eggs are thoroughly blended. But do not let it froth, or the cream will become too porous and cook unevenly. Add the spices to the mixture.

4 **Pour the dissolved palm sugar or the mixture of brown sugar and golden syrup into the egg mixture** and blend them together. The syrup should not be more than lukewarm. Scatter the sliced cashew nuts into the lightly oiled timbale moulds, pour on the mixture and stand the moulds in the water bath.

5 **The coconut and the palm sugar** (jaggery) give the *vattalappam* its unmistakable flavour, helped by the addition of the exotic spices, cardamom, mace and cloves. For this reason it is worth taking the trouble to find and grate fresh coconuts, which are incomparably stronger in flavour. Should you have no alternative but to use desiccated coconut it should be carefully examined to see that it is very fresh. The cashew nuts rise to the top of the mixture in the cooking and form, with the palm sugar, a mouth-watering crust. It is therefore as well to turn the coconut creams out and serve them with this side uppermost.

DESSERTS MADE WITH QUARK AND YOGHURT

Sweets for slimmers as well as traditional recipes

In the old days in the country, from springtime onwards there was nearly always a white jelly bag hanging over the kitchen range at a spot where the oven-plate was still just warm while in front the fire was smouldering under the pots. Underneath this bag, made of linen or muslin, stood an earthenware bowl into which from time to time a watery drop plopped as the whey drained out of the quark or curd cheese. In summer, after a sudden thunderstorm for example, the quark in the muslin bag was very apt to turn sour and would then taste rather bitter or even downright nasty. It was also extremely variable in quality, whether influenced by the cows and their feeding, or because it was difficult for you to divine with sufficient accuracy the exact moment to finish straining and pronounce the quark to be ripe. It sometimes exuded so much moisture that it was really only fit to use as cooking cheese.

The different German names for this one kind of cheese testify to its regional character and manifold uses. Since it was made from curdled milk, it was both a clever conversion of a waste product and a cheap source of valuable protein. Furthermore, it was good for all, from the very young to the very old, and a glance at any old cookbook will show a wide variety of recipes for it: creams and baked desserts, dumplings and pastries, cakes and pancakes, fritters and fillings. Quark mixes in well almost everywhere, because almost anything can be mixed with it.

Today it is one of the few basic foodstuffs which have benefited from being developed by the dairy industry. Nowadays a homogenous, creamy dairy product comes out of a hermetically sealed package: its texture is smooth, it has the true, slightly sour flavour and needs only a little effort with the balloon whisk and some lemon peel, egg yolks and perhaps a little flavouring to make it into a light and delectable dessert. It is nevertheless too homogenous and too moist to be suitable for all kinds of cooking. If it is to be kneaded into puff pastry, for example, or a bun loaf, or stirred into the dough for a quark Gugelhupf, then it must, as of old, be hung in a bag to get rid of some of its whey, otherwise the dough will curdle. But for all other purposes its creaminess is an advantage.

Quark, and the whole related yoghurt family, are back in fashion thanks to the modern tendency towards healthy eating. Low-fat yoghurts combine so well with fruit and a little sugar that they are the ideal low-calorie desserts. However, yoghurt itself and the dishes that can be made with it, have become known and appreciated in Europe to the extent that tourists visiting India and Bulgaria are more than prepared to enjoy the many ways in which it is served in the cooking of those countries and, generally speaking, that of Eastern Europe, Asia and the Far East. More good ideas come from Central and North America, where, for one example, the very popular combination of yoghurt with tropical fruits has both flavour and character. Add to this the various creations which you will find in the following chapter, developed with an eye to lightness as well as culinary excellence, and you will have a very good idea of what can be made of these simple ingredients if they are handled with skill.

Yoghurt and tropical fruits often make extremely good partners, and nowhere is this better understood than in India and Sri Lanka, where such desserts are ideal for the hot climate. The yoghurt there is either home-made or bought in the bazaar, in which case the graceful, unglazed earthenware pots are used as disposable containers, just like our plastic ones here.

Cannoli

Stuffed lardy-snaps

125 g/4½ oz flour · 60 g/2½ oz sugar
generous pinch of salt
1 egg yolk · 25 g/1 oz lard
6 tablespoons Marsala
2 tablespoons milk
a little egg white
225 g/8 oz ricotta or quark
2 teaspoons Amaretto, or to taste
oil for deep frying
25 g/1 oz diced candied lemon peel
25 g/1 oz chopped glacé cherries
icing sugar for dusting

Sift the flour onto a work surface, make a well in the middle and put in 15 g/½ oz of the sugar, salt, half the egg yolk and the lard. Knead all together a little, add the Marsala and milk and knead to a smooth, soft dough. Let it stand for 30 minutes, shape it into a roll and slice this into 10 equal-sized pieces. Roll these out into discs of roughly 12 cm/4½ in diameter, bend them around well-greased cream horn moulds and stick them together with a little egg white. Deep-fry them in oil at 180 C, 350 F till light brown then slip them off the moulds. Beat the ricotta or quark with the sugar, the rest of the egg yolk and the liqueur till foamy and add the chopped glacé fruit. Stuff the cannoli with this mixture and dust them with icing sugar. Makes 20.

Ricotta, unmatured ewe's milk cheese, has properties which are ideal for sweet desserts, i.e. creaminess and a low acid content. But cannoli can also be filled with quark or cottage cheese. And the cream filling can take any flavouring and any kind of candied fruit. At Valenti's in Palermo, where cannoli is a speciality, they also add chopped chocolate to the filling.

Quark Dumplings

Quenelles au fromage blanc

5 stale bread rolls
200 g/7 oz quark
50 g/2 oz sugar
generous pinch of salt
125 g/4½ oz butter
6 tablespoons double cream
4 eggs
100 g/4 oz flour

Remove the crusts from the rolls with a grater and cut them into very small cubes. Prepare the dough as described below, shape it into 20 dumplings and put them in boiling water. Lower the heat and simmer very gently for some 12 to 15 minutes. Lift out, place a portion on each plate and serve with fried breadcrumbs and a hot plum compote. Serves 6.

Blend the diced bread with the quark. Add the sugar, salt and melted butter. Stir the cream into the eggs and combine them with the quark mixture. Lastly fold in the sifted flour. Leave the dough to rest for about 30 minutes and then form it into small dumplings.

Slit the dumplings open at once when they come out of the boiling water. Then they will not collapse. Serve them with *Polonaise* – the buttery fried breadcrumbs – and *Zwetschkenröster* or hot damson compote: two really typical Austrian accompaniments which are described on pages 145 and 140 in the chapter on Austrian specialities.

Yoghurt and Tropical Fruits

Yaourt et fruits tropiques

It is no news that our domestic fruits, and soft fruits in particular, complement yoghurt deliciously. Really ripe fruits call for no special skill: when mixed with yoghurt and perhaps sweetened with a little sugar or a spoonful of honey they are a complete dessert in themselves. The same method can also be applied to tropical fruits and in no way are we its inventors, for in many tropical regions such combinations have been enjoyed for centuries. In Indian cooking there is an especially wide variety of yoghurt desserts, where bananas, mangoes, coconuts and other fruits are mixed with yoghurt and jaggery, the sugar obtained from the palm.

Yoghurt Banana Cream:

This yoghurt cream made with coconut milk can also be made with the same quantity of well-ripened mangoes or tamarillos (tree tomatoes).

150 g/5 oz freshly grated coconut
150 ml/¼ pint milk
150 g/5 oz soft brown sugar
250 g/8 oz mashed banana
350 ml/12 fl oz plain yoghurt
juice of 1 lime · 3 egg whites
100 g/4 oz sugar
extra freshly grated coconut

Make the coconut milk from the grated coconut and milk (see page 118) but bring the sugar to the boil immediately with the milk. Blend the banana flesh with the squeezed-out coconut milk and the yoghurt cream and add the lime juice. Serve chilled with snow dumplings: to make these, stiffly beat the egg whites, trickle in the white sugar and roll little spoonfuls of it in freshly grated coconut. Drop into barely simmering water, and cook for 2 to 3 minutes.

Yoghurt with exotic fruits:

60 g/2½ oz icing sugar
175 ml/6 fl oz plain yoghurt
75 ml/2½ oz fresh guava purée
2 tablespoons fresh lime juice
2 ripe bananas, thinly sliced
2 tablespoons lemon juice
2 tablespoons rum

Stir the icing sugar into the yoghurt. Pass the guava purée through a sieve and add to the yoghurt, together with the lime juice. Macerate the sliced bananas for 30 minutes in the lemon juice and rum. Drain, and stir them into the yoghurt mixture.

Yoghurt Creams

Crèmes de yaourt

Yoghurt and peach dessert:
1 to 2 mashed peaches
(about 100 g/4 oz)
175 ml/6 fl oz plain yoghurt
40 g/1½ oz icing sugar
juice of ½ lime
juice of ½ orange
4 leaves gelatine or
1 tablespoon powdered gelatine
scant 150 ml/¼ pint double
or whipping cream
6 small moulds
of 100 to 200 ml/4 to 7 fl oz capacity
For decoration:
whipped cream and 6 meringue flowers

Blanch the peaches briefly in hot water, peel off the skin, halve them and remove the stones. Purée them in the blender with the yoghurt and icing sugar. Heat up the lime and orange juices, dissolve the softened and squeezed-out leaves of gelatine, or powdered gelatine, in it and stir it, still warm, into the peach and yoghurt mixture. Chill for 5 minutes. Whip the cream stiffly and carefully fold it in. Divide the mixture between the small moulds or individual bowls and leave to set for 2 to 3 hours in the refrigerator. Before serving dip the moulds up to the rim quickly in hot water and turn them out onto plates. Decorate the dessert with cream and meringue blossoms dusted with cocoa. Serve a raspberry sauce with it. Serves 6.

Lime cream with fruits:
75 g/3 oz sugar
75 ml/2½ fl oz fresh lime juice
3 leaves gelatine or
1 tablespoon powdered gelatine
175 ml/6 fl oz plain yoghurt
scant 150 ml/¼ pint double
or whipping cream
350 g/12 oz fresh fruits
cut into small pieces
(pineapple, apricots, raspberries)
2 tablespoons Himbeergeist
(raspberry liqueur)
whipped cream and
slices of lime for decoration

Make a pale caramel with the sugar and about 1 tablespoon of the lime juice in a saucepan, then liquefy it with the rest of the juice. Dissolve the softened and squeezed out gelatine or the powdered gelatine in the warm mixture, add the yoghurt, let it cool and, just before it sets, incorporate the whipped cream. Put the fruit in a glass dish, sprinkle it with the liqueur and pour the yoghurt mixture over it. Decorate with whipped cream and wafer-thin slices of lime. Serves 6.

Cherry Yoghurt Dessert

Crème de yaourt aux cerises

100 g/4 oz sweet cherries
50 g/2 oz icing sugar
175 ml/6 fl oz yoghurt
4 leaves gelatine or
1 tablespoon powdered gelatine
2 tablespoons red wine
1 tablespoon cherry brandy
scant 150 ml/¼ pint whipping cream
6 100-ml/4-fl oz moulds

Stone the washed cherries and purée them. Blend the purée with the sugar and yoghurt. Squeeze out the softened gelatine, and dissolve it, or the powdered gelatine, completely in the heated red wine then stir it into the yoghurt and cherry mixture with the cherry brandy. Fold in the whipped cream. Serve unmoulded, with orange sauce. Serves 6.

Orange Yoghurt Cream

Crème de yaourt à l'orange

3 oranges · 50 g/2 oz sugar
4 leaves gelatine or
1 tablespoon powdered gelatine
50 g/2 oz almond paste
175 ml/6 fl oz plain yoghurt
scant 150 ml/¼ pint whipping cream
6 sponge cake or shortcrust pastry bases

Bring the juice and grated rind of the oranges to the boil with the sugar. Dissolve the gelatine in it and beat the almond paste with the liquid till fluffy. Stir in the yoghurt, let it cool a little and then fold in the whipped cream. Fill 6 small moulds. Leave to set, then arrange the creams on the bases and decorate each with a slice of orange and a cherry. Serves 6.

Strawberry Yoghurt Dessert

Crème de yaourt aux fraises

150 g/6 oz strawberries
1½ tablespoons orange juice
50 g/2 oz sugar
4 leaves gelatine or
1 tablespoon powdered gelatine
175 ml/6 fl oz plain yoghurt
2 tablespoons rum
scant 150 ml/¼ pint whipping cream
6 individual moulds
6 strawberries for decoration

Purée the strawberries and bring this gently to the boil with the orange juice and the sugar. Dissolve the softened and well squeezed-out leaf gelatine or the powdered gelatine in it. Let it cool a little, stir in the yoghurt and the rum and fold in the whipped cream. Put 2 half strawberries in each mould and fill with the mixture. Chill. Serve unmoulded with apricot purée. Serves 6.

Cream Cheese Desserts with Fruits

Fromage blanc aux fruits

These ideal partners make refreshing summery sweets. The cheese mixture is an airy cream that can be stirred into various fruit purées, or enriched with a little fruit juice or liqueur and served with stewed or fresh fruits in small glass bowls or in edible containers such as the chocolate cups described on page 76.

For the cheese mixture:
200 g/7 oz cream cheese
75 g/3 oz icing sugar
juice of 2 limes
50 ml/2 fl oz double or whipping cream

Beat the fresh cream cheese with the icing sugar and lime juice till fluffy. Fold in the stiffly whipped cream. Pipe the mixture through a piping bag, using a broad nozzle to make rings on small plates or in chocolate cups or around meringue bases. Fill these with macerated fresh summer fruits or with compote.

Grape filling:
75 g/3 oz sugar
3 tablespoons white wine
100 g/4 oz peeled grapes
50 g/2 oz fresh redcurrants
1 tablespoon brandy

Cook the sugar and wine together to reduce it a little, put the grapes and redcurrants in it and leave them to poach for 4 to 5 minutes. Stir in the brandy. Chill before serving.

Bilberry filling:
100 ml/4 fl oz sugar syrup
2 tablespoons rum
150 g/6 oz fresh bilberries

Bring the sugar syrup to a gentle boil, add the rum and leave the bilberries to macerate in this liquid for 4 to 5 minutes. Chill before using and scatter some toasted flaked almonds over them. Serves 4 to 6.

Cheese mousse with wild strawberries/Mousse au fromage blanc aux fraises de bois. Put 200 g/7 oz cottage cheese into a bowl. Pick out 150 g/5 oz ripe wild strawberries and scatter them on top. Sift 25 g/1 oz icing sugar over and sprinkle in 2 tablespoons Cointreau. Cover it and leave in the refrigerator for at least 30 minutes. Heat 2 tablespoons each lemon and orange juice and dissolve 2 leaves of softened and well squeezed out leaf gelatine or 1 tablespoon powdered gelatine in it. Stir this while still warm into the cottage cheese mixture. Stiffly whip a scant 150 ml/¼ pint cream and fold it in. Serve the mousse out onto plates, decorate with a few wild strawberries and a meringue rosette and serve with some chocolate sauce. Serves 6.

Passover cheese blintzes. Make a batter from 100 g/4 oz flour, 2 eggs, 100 ml/¼ pint each milk and water, a generous pinch of salt and 1 tablespoon melted butter. Leave it to stand for 15 minutes. Following the method on page 155 fry thin crêpes of about 15 cm/6 in diameter in butter. Blend 400 g/14 oz cottage cheese with 1 egg yolk, a generous pinch of salt, 40 g/1½ oz sugar and a generous pinch of cinnamon. Spread a strip of this cheese mixture across each crêpe and fold it up. Have some melted butter in the pan and fry the blintzes on both sides in it until the cheese is beginning to melt. Serve with cranberry compote. This quantity is sufficient to fill 12 blintzes.

Fruit salad with cottage cheese/Fromage blanc à la salade de fruits. Bring 75 g/3 oz cranberries, 75 g/3 oz raspberries and 4 tablespoons orange juice gently to the boil with 60 g/2½ oz sugar and continue boiling for 5 to 6 minutes so that it reduces a little. Pass the mixture through a fine sieve and stir in 2 tablespoons brandy. Leave to get cold. Peel 1 ogen melon (about 450 g/1 lb weight) and 3 kiwi fruit and cut them in slices. Arrange them on 6 small plates. Stir 25 g/1 oz icing sugar into 200 g/7 oz cottage cheese and spoon it over the fruit. Chill well till ready to serve, then pour over a fruit sauce (here, raspberry is used) and scatter with quartered walnuts. Serves 6.

Cream cheese with strawberries. Purée 150 g/5 oz strawberries, pass through a fine sieve and bring the purée briefly to the boil with 60 g/2½ oz sugar and 2 tablespoons lime juice. Dissolve 2 leaves of gelatine or 15 g/½ oz powdered gelatine, in the hot strawberry purée. Add 1 tablespoon dark rum and let it cool a little. Blend 150 g/5 oz fresh cream cheese and stir the strawberry mixture in slowly. Whip 150 ml/¼ pint cream stiffly and fold it into the strawberry cheese. Pipe it through a piping bag with a star nozzle into little cups made from almond biscuit paste, decorate with slices of strawberry and lime and serve with rum and chocolate sauce. Serves 6.

127

SOUFFLES AND CLAFOUTIS

Light and airy creations

Since its heyday, around the turn of the century, the soufflé has fallen into some obscurity rather in the same way as the hot pudding. If in the latter's case it was the unconscious desire for lighter dishes (and not just easier ones) that led to the popularity of quite new ingredients and methods, in the case of the soufflé it was clearly just one, albeit nerve-shattering risk that caused it. Triumph or tragedy hangs on the one anxious question: will it really rise like a cloud above the horizon of the dish? And will it go on floating or be blown to pieces by a sudden cold draught, and collapse?

Larousse Gastronomique refers to two basic kinds of sweet soufflé, one cream based, the other fruit based. Then comes the first gentle warning: a soufflé must be cooked in a moderate oven so that the heat can penetrate right to the middle of it. And then, in italics, follows the main point: *'once cooked and glazed the soufflé must be served without delay'*. Anyone who does not take just a little fright at these words has certainly never cooked with one of those wood or coal ovens, temperamental as maiden aunts, which in the old days were to be found in every kitchen. It required great skill to coax out of them the correct heat for something as fragile as a soufflé, one which would neither by its fierceness cause the egg whites to harden on the outside (and surround the inside with armour-plating so that it could not rise), nor allow the tiny air bubbles to fizzle out for want of enough heat to maintain their pressure. This was a feat which we, even with our perfectly regulated ovens, would rarely attempt at home today, had we not (of course) this book to hand. If, however, we wish now and then to settle for peace of mind at our dinner table rather than run the risk of failing to scale the heights of the hot soufflé, we can make a cold soufflé (which *Larousse* likens more to a mousse) that can be prepared and served without drama or suspense. Here fruit purées or cream custards, after being thickened by beating over a water bath are whisked to a foam away from the heat of the range, then, stiffened with dissolved gelatine and – when half-set – they are transformed by means of beaten egg white or whipped cream into those cloud-like confections which stay fluffy and can never collapse. Nor do they have to be rushed into the oven at the last moment, helped on their way (we hope) by our prayers, but can be made the day before and kept cool. And in the end they really will melt in the mouth just like a real soufflé.

Except for the beating and folding in of the egg whites, which must be incorporated at the last moment or else they will lose precious volume, a soufflé can be prepared ahead, thereby making the cook's task that much easier. On the morning of a dinner party therefore, you can prepare the soufflé dish, choose and prepare the base mixture, setting aside the egg whites in a covered container. Then, all you have to ensure is that they and your beating bowl and whisk are immaculate and at room temperature, and your oven has been preheated. In this way the perfect soufflé need take you away from your guests just for the few minutes it takes to beat and fold in the egg whites and, at the end, remove your masterpiece from the oven to the table.

Lemon soufflé: made according to the basic recipe on the next two pages, but only 200 ml/7 fl oz milk is used and the vanilla, naturally, omitted. After it has been boiled with the blended flour, 3 tablespoons lemon juice and the grated rind of a lemon are stirred in and the soufflé finished as in the basic recipe, dusted with sifted icing sugar, and served straight away.

Vanilla Soufflé

Soufflé à la vanille

If the Germans have a word for it, it ought to be *Auflauf*, meaning a baked sweet that 'runs up', while the French verb *souffler* means to 'puff' or 'puff up'. But the two are not quite the same: for one thing, a soufflé is expected to be something lighter and airier than an *Auflauf*. Just because these soufflés are so delicate and fragile the baking of them is believed to be fraught with difficulty. But quite wrongly so, because a sound basic soufflé recipe is perfectly practicable if the rules are observed. It makes no difference whether the soufflé is cooked in a water bath (in the oven) or baked in the usual way. It is no more difficult than many other desserts provided that the basic principles are observed. Milk, egg yolks and flavourings are bound with flour or cornflour (or both) and beaten egg white combined with sugar lightens and stabilises the whole. Liqueurs or fruit flavourings can be added but the principles remain the same. As with other basic dessert recipes, the vanilla soufflé lends itself best to variations because its delicate flavour seldom conflicts, and in any case the vanilla can easily be replaced by another flavour.

The following recipe is a compromise based on wide experience. It isn't the lightest of soufflés perhaps, but a well-tried recipe that succeeds perfectly.

250 ml/8 fl oz milk
½ vanilla pod
50 g/2 oz butter
50 g/2 oz flour
5 egg whites
4 egg yolks
75 g/3 oz sugar
a soufflé dish of 18 cm/7 in diameter
and 1.25-litre/2¼-pint capacity
butter for greasing
sugar for dusting
icing sugar for decoration

The adjoining step-by-step pictures explain the process in detail and show the necessary equipment, which every serious cook can surely muster – with the exception, perhaps, of the soufflé dish which can hardly be done without. The typical soufflé dish is made of earthenware, porcelain or ovenproof glass and is usually fluted on the outside but must be smooth and absolutely vertical on the inside so that the soufflé can rise evenly as it cooks.

1 Prepare the soufflé dish. It should be greased with melted, nearly cold butter thinly and evenly. Dust it with sugar inside and turn and tilt it, using both hands, until the bottom and sides are thoroughly coated. Tip out what is left of the sugar.

2 Bring the milk to the boil. Measure it and pour it into a saucepan. Cut the vanilla pod in half lengthways, put it in the milk and bring it once slowly to the boil. Take out the vanilla pod and return any seeds that are still adhering to the pod to the milk.

6 Add the egg yolks. Tip the milk mixture into a bowl and let it cool a little so that it is just lukewarm. Add one egg white and then the egg yolks one at a time, beating the mixture long enough to bring it to a smooth, creamy consistency.

7 Tip the sugar onto the 4 egg whites. Contrary to the usual rule for whipping egg whites, in this recipe the whole of the sugar is added at once to the egg whites. The result will be less volume but it will give a firmer snow and one that will stand up better.

10 Pour in the soufflé mixture to come about 1 cm/½ in below the rim of the dish; stand it in a water bath at a temperature of 80 C, 190 F. The water must reach to at least half way up the sides of the dish. Cook it in a moderately hot oven (200 C, 400 F, gas 6) for about 40 minutes.

11 Dredge the soufflé with icing sugar when it comes out of the oven and serve it at once. Even the most perfect soufflé will collapse but it should nevertheless still stand as high as the mixture was when first poured in. This shows that it has been correctly cooked.

3 **Bind with a *beurre manié*:** work the softened butter and the flour together, shape it into a roll and divide into small portions. Stir them one by one into the boiling milk until they have thickened and bound the liquid to a smooth and even consistency.

4 **Stir in one of the egg whites.** Turn off the heat and stir an egg white into the still hot mixture. The unbeaten egg white acts as an additional stabiliser to the soufflé by lightly coagulating. It also helps to keep it moist after it is baked and to prevent it from collapsing.

5 **Beat the soufflé mixture until smooth.** To ensure that the egg white is evenly distributed all through the mixture must be beaten quickly and briskly, and great care must be taken all the time to remove and reincorporate any that sticks to the side of the saucepan and so prevent lumps forming.

8 **A stiffer, yet creamier, egg white snow.** If using an electric hand-mixer, begin at a low speed, which can be increased as the snow thickens. Give it a final stir with a balloon whisk.

12 **Air and foam under a crisp brown crust.** This is how a soufflé should look when cut with a fine serving spoon. Accompanied by a fruit sauce it is one of the lightest desserts and will adapt itself to an uncommonly wide variety of ingredient combinations.

9 **Incorporating the egg whites.** The German 'technical' term for this crucial operation is *melieren*, from the French verb *mêler*, to mix or mingle. First stir in about a quarter of the whipped egg whites in order to make the mixture lighter and more receptive to the rest of the snow which should next be folded in carefully with a wooden spoon. This is where the more flexibly textured egg snow helps by blending easily and rapidly with the soufflé mixture, and thus prevents it collapsing.

Hazelnut Soufflé

Soufflé aux avelines

a scant 150 ml/¼ pint milk
¼ vanilla pod
generous pinch of ground cinnamon
50 g/2 oz butter
50 g/2 oz flour
5 egg whites
4 egg yolks
75 g/3 oz toasted chopped hazelnuts
75 g/3 oz sugar
8 small soufflé moulds
butter for greasing
sugar for dusting
2 tablespoons crushed nut brittle
or chopped nuts
icing sugar for decoration

The soufflé is prepared as in the basic recipe on pages 130–1. The chopped hazelnuts should be stirred in before the egg white snow is incorporated. Pour the mixture into the prepared individual dishes and bake in a water bath for about 20 minutes in a moderately hot oven (200 C, 400 F, gas 6). Serves 8.

A tip: soufflés, like sponge cakes, can be tested by piercing them with a skewer or thin knife to see if they are done. If none of the mixture is sticking to the skewer when withdrawn, the soufflé is cooked through.

Soufflé Rothschild

Soufflé aux fruits

200 ml/7 fl oz milk
½ vanilla pod
50 g/2 oz butter
50 g/2 oz flour
5 egg whites
4 tablespoons Grand Marnier
4 egg yolks
75 g/3 oz sugar
8 to 10 small soufflé dishes
butter for greasing
sugar for dusting
4 sponge fingers
100 g/4 oz chopped crystallised fruits
icing sugar for decoration

Prepare the mixture as explained in the basic recipe and stir in half the liqueur before the egg yolks. Scatter the bottoms of the dishes with the broken-up sponge fingers and the candied fruits, and then sprinkle them with the remaining Grand Marnier. Pour over the soufflé mixture and bake them in a water bath for about 20 to 25 minutes in a moderately hot oven (200 C, 400 F, gas 6).
Serves 8 to 10.

Chocolate Soufflé

Soufflé au chocolat

75 g/3 oz plain chocolate
250 ml/8 fl oz milk
25 g/1 oz cocoa powder
50 g/2 oz butter
50 g/2 oz flour
5 egg whites
4 egg yolks
75 g/3 oz sugar
8 to 10 small soufflé dishes
(or 1 large 18 cm/7 in diameter dish)
butter for greasing
sugar for dusting
8 to 10 sponge fingers
2 tablespoons Bénédictine
2 tablespoons sugar syrup (20°)
icing sugar for decoration

Break up the chocolate into small pieces and bring it gently to the boil with the milk and the cocoa powder. Then mix the soufflé exactly as in the basic recipe, put a layer of broken sponge fingers into the prepared dishes, sprinkle with the liqueur and syrup and pour the chocolate mixture on top. Bake in a water bath for about 20 minutes in a moderately hot oven (200 C, 400 F, gas 6).
Serves 8 to 10.

Cointreau Soufflé

Soufflé au Cointreau

This is a recipe of Jean-Paul Piffet's which combines a cornflour-based liaison in the form of confectioner's custard with added flour. It is a soufflé that is not cooked in a water bath but baked in the regular manner in the oven and is especially light and airy.

1 (18 cm/7 in) soufflé dish, of
1.25-litre/2¼-pint capacity
melted butter for greasing
flour for dusting
8 sponge fingers
4 tablespoons Cointreau
2 tablespoons sugar syrup (20°)
250 ml/8 fl oz milk
½ vanilla pod
25 g/1 oz cornflour
100 g/4 oz sugar
generous pinch of salt
6 egg yolks
25 g/1 oz flour
4 egg whites

Brush the soufflé dish with melted butter and dust with flour. Place in it a layer of the sponge fingers soaked in 2 tablespoons of the Cointreau and the syrup. Make the confectioner's custard first: as usual, bring the milk just to the boil with the vanilla pod, moisten the cornflour with a little of the milk, half the sugar, the salt and 2 of the egg yolks and then bind the rest of the milk with this mixture. Let the custard cool a little, then stir in the rest of the egg yolks one at a time, and finally the sifted flour. The mixture must be briskly beaten to ensure that no lumps remain. Bring this to the boil, stirring all the time, until it is smoothly bound with the flour. Remove it from the heat, stir in the rest of the Cointreau and leave to cool. Whip the egg whites to a snow, slowly trickling in the rest of the sugar. Stir one-third of the egg snow into the soufflé mixture and then fold in the rest carefully with a wooden spoon. Spoon it into the prepared soufflé dish and bake for 25 minutes in a moderately hot oven (200 C, 400 F, gas 6). If necessary protect the surface with aluminium foil.
Serves 4.

1 **Stir the egg yolks into the confectioner's custard,** preferably one at a time, and then the sifted flour. Bring this mixture to the boil, stirring constantly till the flour and custard combine. Add the Cointreau and stir till the mixture is smooth again.

2 **Pour in the soufflé mixture.** The bottom of the soufflé dish has been lined with the sponge fingers, moistened with a mixture of Cointreau and sugar syrup. The soufflé mixture is poured over them and the top levelled with a spatula.

3 **A souffle method that guarantees success** provided that the rules are observed. The combination of confectioner's custard with additional flour as extra binding makes this recipe very reliable. At the same time it is exceptionally light and airy and will keep its shape for a comparatively long time. It is also adaptable to, for example, Bénédictine or other liqueurs. Adding some compote or candied fruit to the moistened sponge fingers makes it extra good.

Black and White Soufflé

Soufflé blanc et noir

50 g/2 oz plain chocolate
ingredients for the vanilla soufflé
on pages 130–1
6 sponge fingers
2 tablespoons dark rum
2 tablespoons sugar syrup (20°)
an 18 cm/7 in soufflé dish

Melt the chocolate in a double boiler. Stir the unbeaten egg white into the milk mixture, incorporate the liquid chocolate into half of the mixture and proceed to combine equal amounts of egg yolk and beaten egg white with both halves. Line the bottom of the soufflé dish with sponge fingers sprinkled with the rum and syrup, and fill up with the soufflé mixtures. Bake in a water bath in a moderately hot oven (200 C, 400 F, gas 6) for about 40 minutes. Serves 6 to 8.

Gingerbread Sponge Pudding

Soufflé au pain d'épices

100 g/4 oz butter · 100 g/4 oz sugar
6 eggs, separated
100 g/4 oz gingerbread
50 g/2 oz cake crumbs
generous pinch of ground cinnamon
generous pinch of ground cloves
25 g/1 oz chopped candied orange peel
25 g/1 oz chopped candied lemon peel
50 g/2 oz currants
grated rind of ½ lemon
6 to 8 7.5-cm/3-in individual moulds
butter for greasing · sugar for dusting

Beat the butter and half of the sugar together till fluffy and add the egg yolks one by one. Crumble the gingerbread finely and add half of it, together with half of the cake crumbs, to the egg yolk and butter mixture. Stir well, and add the spices, candied peel, currants and grated lemon rind. Whip the egg whites to a snow, trickling in the rest of the sugar slowly, and fold it with the rest of the crumbled gingerbread and cake crumbs carefully into the mixture. Pipe the finished gingerbread mixture with a piping bag and a wide nozzle into the buttered and sugared dishes and smooth the tops. Bake in a water bath for 25 to 30 minutes in a moderate oven (180 C, 350 F, gas 4).

Serves 6 to 8.

1 **First pour the chocolate mixture into the prepared soufflé dish.** Smooth it with a spatula without touching the sides of the dish. Then make a second layer with the vanilla mixture and again carefully smooth the top with the spatula.

2 **This soufflé looks extra good in a glass dish** showing the two contrasting layers. It goes well with a chocolate sauce laced with rum or brandy, or with puréed fresh wild strawberries.

This is an airy sponge, or soufflé even, that can be served either in the dishes or turned out and can equally well be made in a large-size (18 cm/7 in diameter) mould. A red wine sauce goes well with it: bring 250 ml/8 fl oz light red wine to the boil with 150 g/5 oz puréed and sieved raspberries, 75 g/3 oz sugar and a piece of cinnamon stick. Boil gently for about 2 minutes, then remove the cinnamon stick and bind the sauce with 25 g/1 oz potato flour. This sponge can be served hot or cold and can be given a really sophisticated touch by the addition of 2 tablespoons Framboise (raspberry liqueur) to the mixture after it has been taken off the heat.

Clafoutis

Call it a raised sweet or call it a tart – it is in either case a typical, simple country dish that goes to show that the success of a dish depends on the best ingredients – which in this case are fresh, ripe fruits. The clafoutis hails reputedly from the Limousin area of France but is enjoyed all over that country when the sweet, dark cherries are ripe. They are the favourite fruit for this dessert, but late plums, greengages from the Bordeaux region, mirabelles – and apples too in winter – can all be used. The mixture is principally a plain sponge but it can be lightened with beaten egg white, or given added flavouring to match the chosen fruit; this of course can be accentuated with the help of the corresponding fruit liqueur – a glass of kirsch with cherries for example, Calvados with apples, and so on. But it is not these refinements that make a good clafoutis, but simply and solely the perfection of fresh, ripe, seasonal fruits.

Cherry Clafoutis

Clafoutis aux cerises

4 eggs
100 g/4 oz sugar
1 vanilla pod
generous pinch of salt
1 tablespoon dark rum
100 g/4 oz flour
350 ml/12 fl oz milk
400 g/14 oz stoned cherries
an oval ovenproof dish
about 32 cm/13 in long
butter for greasing
icing sugar for decoration

Beat the eggs and sugar until frothy. Add the seeds of the vanilla pod, the salt and rum. Then stir in the flour with a balloon whisk and finally the milk.

Grease the ovenproof dish with softened butter, put in the stoned cherries. Top with the sponge batter. Bake for 40 to 45 minutes in a moderate oven (180 C, 350 F, gas 4), but to make sure test it like a sponge cake with a wooden cocktail stick to see whether any of the batter still clings to it. Dredge with icing sugar at once, and serve hot.

Serves about 8.

AUSTRIAN SPECIALITIES

Famous pastries from a famous tradition

All recipes set down in Austrian cookbooks or handed down in Austrian families come from cities and the countryside all over the former Austro-Hungarian empire. The foreign origin of certain ingredients lives on in their Austrian names, so that for example the redcurrant is called *ibisel* after the Italian *ribes*, and the list of *Mehlspeisen* – the popular name in Austria for anything that can be made with flour and sugar – sounds like a folk song from Bohemia, Hungary or Slovakia: for example, *Liwanzen* and *Pogatscherln*, *Dukatenbuchteln* and *Poganzen*, *Potizen* and *Kolatschen*, *Wuchteln*, *Beugel* and *Muskatzin Pudding* – while those which roughly translate as Cushion Corners, Rabbits' Ears, Wasps' Nests, Locksmith Lads, Wood Shavings and Baked Mice sound more like a child's treasury of comic verse. Many of these confections originated from farmhouse kitchens and what went into the mixture was all grown or raised on farms along the Danube plain, in the neighbouring vineyards or in the mountains; simple foodstuffs went into them, just flour and cream, eggs, lard and very sweet, well-ripened fruits of the apple or apricot tree. Raisins and sugar bought from the grocer were signs of real affluence, but white wine and red, from the vineyards at hand, were commonplace ingredients.

The great Austrian pastry-making tradition had all evolved through a slow, centuries-long process of assimilation. The Italian boiled pudding or *bodino* became the Austrian *Dunstkoch*. Spanish spiced cake from the days of Charles V improved and enriched the native *Kletzenbrote*. The Hungarian *Palatschinken* continued to be what it had always been, a pancake, but acquired a worthy cousin, the *Kaiserschmarren*, made with a richer paste and often containing as much butter and sugar as a sponge cake. When made at home this is fried on top of the stove and as soon as the batter sets is torn into small pieces then cooked in butter, frequently turned so that it gets well saturated with it as it cooks, and lastly dusted with icing sugar.

The secret of all these Austrian sweets lies in first-class ingredients and in the patient skill of the cook. Yeast cookery means a life consistently but happily spent in the kitchen, with occasional breaks for a gossip and a cup of coffee from the business of kneading, rolling out and baking. A generation ago in Austria soup would have been served before the main course, without exception. Now the soup is often omitted, but the sweet course never, for it is as much a part of the everyday meal as the cup of black coffee that follows. But which of us, Austrian or otherwise, could resist the sophisticated delights of her cuisine, and above all that from Vienna? Chocolate puddings made with nuts and almonds (the direct ancestors of the famous *sachertorte*), fruit cakes of rich, crumbly texture, fritters and twists, and the strudel itself, are living symbols of the deliciousness we have come to expect from the fine Austrian culinary tradition.

Apple strudel is universally known and liked throughout the world. It's a real 'do-it-yourself' dessert, demanding little more than everyday ingredients, yet exacting in the manner of its preparation. Only those who take the trouble to roll out their pastry paper-thin will be rewarded with those crispy leaves enfolding that sweet and succulent filling.

Apple strudel

Apfelstrudel

Apple strudel, to most people synonymous with Austrian patisserie, is essentially a simple and straightforward dessert but, as with so many great specialities, the art lies in the execution and not in any exact or subtly contrived recipe. An Austrian pastry-cook would smile pityingly if he were required to measure anything. With him it is a matter of instinct rather than calculation and actually it is not easy to give an exact recipe for strudel pastry, because it depends on the flour, on how much liquid it will absorb; and that again will make all the difference to the consistency of the dough. The following recipe should be taken as a basic guide; the rest is up to instinct and experience. Everything depends, if the dough is later to 'pull out' satisfactorily, on its firmness – or rather its suppleness. But it all looks more difficult than it really is.

300 g/11 oz flour · 1 egg yolk
15 g/½ oz salt · 2½ tablespoons oil
120 to 150 ml/about ¼ pint water
3 kg/6 lb apples
250 g/9 oz soft breadcrumbs
200 g/7 oz butter
150 g/5 oz butter, melted
300 g/11 oz sugar
25 g/1 oz ground cinnamon
100 g/4 oz raisins
75 g/3 oz chopped walnuts
100 g/4 oz butter

If the strudel is to be for a large party this recipe will give enough for about 20 portions. For family use the quantities may of course be halved or quartered.

Sift the flour onto a work surface, make a well in the middle and put in the egg yolk and salt. Then pour in the oil. What follows is handwork in the most literal sense of the word. Strudel pastry may be worked in a bowl with the dough hook of an electric hand mixer but after that it must still be worked through again by hand: first, to ensure that it is really smooth and elastic and, secondly, it is only the feel of the pastry that will tell you when the correct degree of firmness has been reached. Blend the ingredients with one hand and then little by little add the water until the pastry is of the right consistency. Dip the hand that has pastry adhering to it in flour and rub it off with it, then, using both hands, knead the pastry thoroughly until it is nice and smooth. Form it into a round lump, put it on a floured work surface or baking sheet

---

The perfect apple for strudel

Which is really the best apple for a strudel is something the experts cannot agree on. Many, for example, use Golden Delicious for preference, others favour Cox's Orange or Boskop. But Austrian housewives just ask for 'strudlers', meaning apples for strudel, and these are usually not very good eating apples. Whichever kind you use, it should in any case be a strongly flavoured apple, a little on the tart side.

---

and rub some oil over the top so that the pastry, which must now rest for at least 30 minutes, cannot develop a skin.

Peel and core the apples and slice them thinly. Fry the breadcrumbs in the butter until light brown and let them get cold.

Cover a table with a linen cloth measuring about 120 × 70 cm/48 × 30 in and dust it evenly all over with flour. Lay the pastry on it, at the same time pulling it into a long strip. If the pastry is right this will happen almost of itself, as it will hang due to its own weight. The pastry is now rolled out length and widthways with a rolling pin, and then begins the 'long haul'. Take the pastry with the flat backs of both hands from underneath and stretch it from the middle outwards. Continue this all around the table until the pastry overlaps the entire cloth: it must be thin enough to allow a newspaper to be read through it. Any remaining thick edge that is difficult to handle may be trimmed off. Now brush two-thirds of the pastry with about half the melted, but not more than lukewarm, butter. This is to stop it sticking to itself and preserve its leaf-like quality. Sprinkle the fried breadcrumbs over the remaining third and on top spread over the apple slices, sugar, cinnamon, raisins and walnuts. If the apples are very sour more sugar may be added.

Now the strudel must be rolled up by lifting and moving the cloth, and you must take care to hold it together all the time so that it makes a compact roll. Lay the roll in a buttered baking tin and brush the top with the rest of the melted butter. Bake it for about 30 minutes in a hot oven (220 C, 425 F, gas 7), cut it up while still hot and, finally, dust it with icing sugar.

An Apple strudel should be served fresh and hot. Only then can its fine flavour be fully appreciated, the crisp wrapping contrasting deliciously with the moist filling inside.
Apple strudel may be frozen after baking so that it is always possible to have some on hand, which only needs warming up when the need arises. It loses none of the flavour of a freshly-baked one, but it will not look quite as good, because the surface becomes brittle after the second time in the oven and some leaves of pastry may break off.

Semolina Strudel

Strudel à la semoule

150 g/5 oz butter
generous pinch of salt
5 eggs, separated
200 g/7 oz wheat semolina
250 ml/8 fl oz soured cream
50 g/2 oz raisins
60 g/2½ oz sugar
strudel pastry as in the recipe
for Apple strudel on page 138
250 g/9 oz butter, melted
150 g/5 oz breadcrumbs

Beat half of the butter with the salt until fluffy and add the egg yolks one by one. To this foamy mixture add the semolina a little at a time and then stir in the soured cream. Add the raisins, whip the egg whites to a snow with 40 g/1½ oz of the sugar and fold carefully into the semolina mixture. Brush the fully-stretched strudel pastry with the melted butter. Spread a layer, finger thick, of the semolina mixture over two-thirds of the pastry and then roll it up. Press down with the handle of a wooden spoon to divide the roll into portions 10 cm/4 in long and then separate them with a knife. Roll them in a floured cloth and put them into simmering, salted water. The water temperature must be kept just below boiling. Cook the strudels on both sides for 8 to 10 minutes. Fry the breadcrumbs in the remaining butter in a pan until light brown and stir in the remaining sugar. Lift out the finished strudels with a slotted spoon, let them drain for a moment and then scatter the breadcrumbs over thickly. Serve them with plum compote.
    Serves 15.

Plum compote is traditionally served with semolina strudel, and goes with it better than anything else. Bring 250 g/9 oz sugar to the boil in a scant 150 ml/¼ pint water with a piece of cinnamon stick, a clove and the juice and thinly peeled rind of a lemon. Add 450 g/1 lb ripe plums, halved and stoned, and cook the compote until the fruit is quite soft and losing its skin. This compote, another Austrian traditional dish, can be served either hot or cold with semolina strudel.

Salzburg Dumplings

Noques salzbourgeoises

There are several ways of preparing this famous sweet, properly known as *Salzburger Nockerln*. One not very simple, but traditional, way is to cook them on top of the stove, turn them over (which calls for a certain dexterity) and finish them in the oven. Perhaps that explains why the simpler method, in which the *nockerln* are entirely baked in the oven, is more popular.

6 eggs, separated
75 g/3 oz sugar
25 g/1 oz flour
seeds from ½ vanilla pod
40 g/1½ oz butter for greasing
icing sugar for dusting
an oval ovenproof dish,
33 cm/13 in long

In a large bowl whip the egg whites to a snow, trickling in the sugar as you do so. Slip the egg yolks in at the side of the bowl and blend them with a little of the beaten egg white without them touching the main part of it. Next, sprinkle the flour and the vanilla seeds over the entire surface of the bowl and incorporate them with a balloon whisk. This should be done as quickly as possible in order not to lose volume. Melt the butter in the baking dish, scoop up 6 *nockerln* with a dough-scraper, arrange them in the dish and bake for some 2 to 4 minutes in a hot oven (220 C, 425 F, gas 7) until a good light brown colour. Sift icing sugar over the dumplings and serve quickly.
    Serves 4 to 6.

Viennese Soufflé

Soufflé viennois

2 tablespoons butter
6 slices white bread
100 g/4 oz cranberry jelly
100 ml/4 fl oz hot mulled red wine
4 eggs, separated
50 g/2 oz icing sugar
40 g/1½ oz flour
an oval ovenproof dish,
33 cm/13 in long

Heat the butter in a pan and fry the sliced bread until golden brown on both sides. The slices can be used while still hot for the recipe illustrated opposite. Serves 6 to 8.

1 **Whip the egg whites to a snow,** trickling in the sugar. Slide the egg yolks in at the side of the bowl. Taking in a little of the beaten egg whites, beat them with a balloon whisk till the mixture is smooth. Do not disturb the rest of the egg white snow.

2 **Tip the flour over the beaten egg whites** and add the vanilla seeds. Both the flour and the vanilla seeds should be evenly distributed over the surface, so that they can be incorporated as quickly as possible. This is most easily done with a sieve.

3 **Stir the ingredients with a balloon whisk.** This should be done very lightly so that the beaten egg whites lose as little as possible of their volume. The best way to do it is to make circular sweeps with the whisk around the edge of the bowl until all the ingredients combine into a smooth mixture.

4 **Place large dumplings of the mixture into the buttered baking dish.** This can be done most easily with a spatula or a fish-slice. Take care that the dumplings hold their shape: they should form tall pyramids with the divisions clearly defined.

5 **Hannes Ehrenreiter of the Vienna Interconti Hotel** is a master of this airy dessert. Under a delicate, light brown crust the dumplings should be soft and creamy. That is why they collapse so quickly and must therefore be served at once.

1 **Spread the white bread, previously fried in the butter, with cranberry jelly** and lay the slices in a baking dish so that the bottom is completely covered. Gradually pour over the hot mulled wine so that all the bread becomes saturated.

2 **Arrange the dumpling mixture on the fried bread.** Beat the egg whites to a snow with the sugar then, as for Salzburg dumplings, blend the egg yolks with a little of it, sift over the flour and combine all with a balloon whisk. Scoop up this mixture with the dough scraper and place on the fried bread.

3 **Dust the Viennese soufflé with sifted icing sugar.** Bake it first in a moderate oven (180 C, 350 F, gas 4) until the top is golden brown. This will take some 8 to 10 minutes but check at intervals after 4 minutes to see that it does not brown too much.

Liwanzen go well with various fillings and especially with *Topfen*, as quark is called in Austria, also hot or cold fruit compotes and of course *Powidl*, that popular Austrian speciality which we simply call plum purée. *Liwanzen* are traditionally fried in special pans with rounded hollows 7 to 8 cm/about 3 inches in diameter. But it is also possible to use egg poaching rings, or to make the dough a little firmer, cut it into rounds and fry them in a normal pan.

Liwanzen

Gâteaux bohémiens

400 g/14 oz flour · 25 g/1 oz fresh yeast
300 ml/½ pint milk · ½ oz butter
25 g/1 oz sugar · ¼ teaspoon salt
grated rind of ½ lemon · 2 eggs

Sift the flour into a bowl, make a well in the middle, crumble the yeast in it and dissolve it with the lukewarm milk. Draw the flour over the top and leave this batter to prove for about 15 minutes until the top shows large cracks. Melt 25 g/1 oz of the butter and blend it with the sugar, salt, lemon rind and eggs. Add this mixture to the yeast batter and stir all into a thick, heavy yeast dough. Cover, and leave in a warm place for 30 minutes to 1 hour to rise. Grease the *liwanzen* pans with the rest of the butter and 1 tablespoon oil and ladle in the yeast dough (if you have no *liwanzen* pans, use egg poaching rings instead, about 7.5 to 13 cm/3 to 5 in diameter). Brown for about 3 minutes on both sides and serve hot, just dusted with sugar, or in pairs sandwiched with a filling as illustrated. This recipe makes 15 to 20 *liwanzen*.

Cherry filling:
1 425-g/15-oz can black
cherries in juice
1 tablespoon cornflour
1 tablespoon kirsch
2 tablespoons caster sugar
scant 150 ml/¼ pint double
or whipping cream

Drain the cherries, saving the juice, and stone them if necessary.

Blend the cornflour with a little juice. Heat the remainder of the juice and pour over the cornflour mixture.

pour back into the pan, add the kirsch and cherries and reheat until thick. Fill pairs of *liwanzen* with this mixture, sift caster sugar over and serve with whipped cream. Serves 4.

Quark filling:
250 g/9 oz quark · 1 egg yolk
juice and grated rind of 1 lemon
50 g/2 oz sugar
chopped walnuts for decoration

Cream together 200 g/7 oz of the quark, the egg yolk, lemon juice and grated rind, and sugar. Fill the *liwanzen* and decorate with the rest of the quark, put through a potato ricer, and some chopped walnuts. Serves 4.

Plum purée filling:
grated rind of ½ lemon
generous pinch of cinnamon
100 ml/4 fl oz plum purée

Stir the lemon rind and cinnamon into the plum purée, fill the *liwanzen* with it and dust the tops with icing sugar. Serves 4.

Ducat Yeast Cakes with Vanilla Sauce

Nouilles au four

These are called 'ducats' because they are as small and neat as a gold coin, unlike ordinary noodle cakes which are thought to be of Bohemian origin. The latter variety are very much bigger, weighing about 50 g/2 oz, and are often filled with quark or plum purée and are familiar in southern Germany as '*Rohr*', that is to say oven noodles. When freshly baked they too are an excellent dessert, one only per person being served, perhaps with vanilla or chocolate sauce.

300 g/10 oz flour
15 g/½ oz fresh yeast
100 ml/4 fl oz milk
25 g/1 oz butter
50 g/2 oz caster sugar
pinch of salt
grated rind of ½ lemon
1 egg
50 g/2 oz butter, melted
a baking tin, about
20 × 30 cm/8 × 12 in

Sift the flour into a bowl, make a well in the centre and crumble the yeast into it. Dissolve it with the lukewarm milk, and cover with a layer of the flour. After 15 minutes in a warm place the *Dampfl* (as the Austrians call the yeast batter) will show cracks – a sign that it has proved enough. Melt the butter and cream it with the sugar, salt, grated lemon rind and egg. Add it to the yeast batter and knead all into a smooth, dry yeast dough that comes away easily from the side of the bowl. If necessary add a little milk or water according to whether it is too soft or too stiff. Cover and leave for another 15 minutes to rise and, as is shown in the step-by-step pictures, continue by cutting it into noodle cakes. Cover these with a cloth once more and leave to rise until they have nearly doubled in size. Paint the tops with melted butter and bake in a moderately hot oven (200 C, 400 F, gas 6). After 15 minutes paint the tops again with butter and finish cooking them at a somewhat lower temperature (about 180 C, 350 F, gas 4). This will take another 15 minutes or so, and at the end of the cooking time the cakes should look done, that is really nice and crisp and a light brown. Turn them out of the baking tin.

This recipe makes about 25 to 30 ducat cakes.

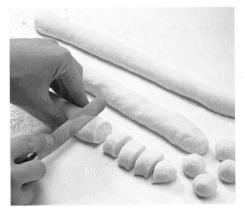

1 '**Polishing' the yeast dough is** the pastry cook's term for rolling the dough into seamless balls. First it is rolled into cylinders of about 2 cm/¾ in diameter and cut into pieces 3 cm/1 in wide. These are then rolled between the palms of the hands and given a smooth 'polish' on the work surface.

2 **Cutting out the ducat cakes is** a simpler way of making them an equal size, provided that the dough is rolled out to an even thickness (about 1.5 cm/½ in). Use a pastry cutter of about 2.5 cm/1 in diameter and lay the pieces on a floured board.

3 **Put the ducat cakes in the baking tin.** Butter it first, and also dip the sides of the ducat cakes in melted butter before arranging them close together in the tin. This not only enriches them but ensures also that they will then come apart easily after baking. Brush the tops with butter as well.

4 **The delicate, buttery crust** is the delicious secret of the warm ducat cakes, and they go best with a cold vanilla sauce. But it must be a real one, an English custard, made according to the recipe on page 54. They are also very good, although rather richer, with hot chocolate sauce.

Yeast Dumplings

Quenelles à la levure

The yeast dumpling family probably also comes from Bohemia. These airy dumplings are made with yeast, or *Germ* as it is called in Austria – hence their name, *Germknödel* – and are usually served with a filling and sprinkled with poppy seeds or breadcrumbs. The fillings range from plum purée with poppy seeds to fresh fruits such as damsons, apricots or apples. But what matters most is that they should always be sprinkled with fresh, melted butter.

500 g/18 oz flour
25 g/1 oz fresh yeast
200 ml/7 fl oz milk
75 g/3 oz butter
60 g/2½ oz sugar
½ teaspoon salt
grated rind of ½ lemon
2 eggs
300 ml/½ pint plum purée
150 g/5 oz butter, melted
100 g/4 oz poppy seeds
50 g/2 oz icing sugar
an oval ovenproof dish

Sift the flour into a bowl, make a well in the middle and crumble the yeast into it. Dissolve it with the lukewarm milk and draw some of the flour over this yeast batter. Leave it to prove for 15 minutes until the surface shows distinct cracks. Beat the butter and cream it with the sugar, salt, lemon rind and eggs. Add to the yeast batter and knead all to a smooth, dry and supple yeast dough which should be covered and left again to rise for another 15 minutes. Lift out the dough onto a floured work surface, roll it out 1.5 cm/about ½ in thick and cut it into 7 cm/3 in squares. Place a spoonful of plum purée on each. Fold the dough over the filling and roll the dumplings into shape with the palms of the hands. Lay them on a floured board, cover them with a cloth and leave to rise again until they have nearly doubled in size. Half-fill a large pan with salted water, bring it to a gentle boil and put in the dumplings. Put a lid on the pan, but do not cover it completely: the water should simmer rather than boil. After 10 minutes take off the lid and tap each dumpling on the side with the handle of a wooden spoon to make it turn over. After another 5 minutes lift them out with a slotted spoon and prick them immediately with a long skewer in two or three places to stop them collapsing. Next lay them in an ovenproof dish brushed with melted butter and leave them in a cool oven (140 C, 275 F, gas 1) with the door open until all the dumplings are done. Finally, sprinkle with melted butter and scatter over a mixture of poppy seeds and icing sugar.

This makes 20 dumplings.

Specialities made with Potatoes

In the Austrian kitchen sweet dishes made from potato pastry are especially popular and have even won themselves an international reputation. Once again, as with a good many other Viennese specialities, the home of the plum and the apricot dumpling is probably Bohemia. They are sometimes made with choux pastry but are everywhere more popularly made with potato pastry.

Plum or Apricot Dumplings

Quenelles aux prunes/aux abricots

1 kg/2¼ lb potatoes
250 g/9 oz butter, softened
100 g/4 oz semolina
25 g/1 oz salt
1 egg, plus 2 egg yolks
200 g/7 oz self-raising flour
200 g/7 oz soft breadcrumbs
icing sugar for dusting

There are two ways of making a good potato pastry. One is to boil the potatoes the day before and then peel and mash them. If this is done, about 450 g/1 lb flour will be needed for 1 kg/2¼ lb potatoes in the

Powidl Purses

Pomponettes farcies de confiture de pruneaux

potato pastry
(as for plum dumplings)
250 ml/8 fl oz plum purée
½ teaspoon ground cinnamon
2 tablespoons rum
1 egg yolk
150 g/5 oz butter
200 g/7 oz soft breadcrumbs
icing sugar for dusting

Roll out the potato pastry about 5 mm/¼ in thick on a floured work surface and cut out about 10-cm/4-in diameter rounds with a serrated pastry cutter. Stir the plum purée with the cinnamon and rum and put a spoonful on each round. Brush the edges with egg yolk, fold them over to form purses and press well together with thumb and forefinger so that none of the filling can escape in the cooking. Cook these in boiling salted water as you would the dumplings and

1 **Cut open the baked potatoes while they are still warm** and spoon out the pulp. Press this through a potato ricer and leave it to cool on the work surface. Then make a well in the centre for the remaining ingredients.

2 **Put the remaining ingredients in the well.** Using your hands, and working from the centre outwards, thoroughly combine first the butter, then the semolina, salt, egg and egg yolk with some of the potato. Finally, sift the flour over the mixture and knead it in.

3 **Roll out the dough to about 5 mm/¼ in thick.** Place a stoned plum on each square (if you like you can fill the cavity in each plum with a piece of lump sugar). Fold each dough square together and roll it into a ball using the palms of your hands.

above recipe. But if the potatoes are baked in the oven they will contain much less moisture and only need about 200 g/7 oz flour. Also the pastry will not be so tough and will taste better.

Spoon the baked potatoes out of their skins and put them through a potato ricer onto a work surface. Make a well in the middle and put in 100 g/4 oz of the softened butter, the semolina, salt, egg and egg yolks. Work the ingredients together with the hand and sift the flour over. Knead it all into a smooth dough (if necessary increasing the

quantity of flour) and chill for 15 minutes. Roll it out 5 mm/¼ in thick onto a floured board. Cut into squares and wrap a plum or apricot in each. Lower the dumplings into boiling salted water and as it comes back to the boil reduce the heat so that they just lightly boil and rise to the surface. Take them out with a slotted spoon after 15 minutes, refresh them in cold water and roll them in the breadcrumbs, fried in the remaining butter.

Fried breadcrumbs – correctly known as *Polonaise* – are used with various hot sweets

in Austria and give a special quality to potato pastry or yeast dough in particular. The butter is melted in a pan (but not browned) and the crumbs added and fried to a good crisp brown while being stirred continuously. If they become too dry more butter may be added. Dust the dumplings with icing sugar before serving.

This recipe makes about 25 dumplings.

refresh in cold water. Roll them at once in fried breadcrumbs and sift icing sugar over.

This recipe makes about 20 purses.

As for potato pastry dumplings, different fillings may be used. Apricot jam laced with apricot brandy makes a very good one for example. Only hot melted butter should be poured over them.

PUDDINGS

– not just an English speciality

The German comic name for an Englishman is 'Jack Pudding', because the English are credited with having invented the genuine boiled pudding. In fact, the name 'pudding' is given to a considerably greater number of sweet dishes than are in fact true puddings: apple dumplings and baked crumbles, bread and butter pudding, for example. And plums baked on sponge cake and strawberry sponge roll are both called 'sponge puddings', so the concept of pudding seems to defy precise definition, in England and elsewhere. But there is no doubt that the right way to boil a pudding was discovered in mediaeval England: dough is rolled out, filled, clapped together and placed on a well-buttered and floured cloth. This is then tied up, a long spoon pushed through under the knot and the pudding carefully lowered into boiling water. Then it is left to simmer gently and for a considerable length of time.

British folklorists have identified innumerable variations on this method of cooking, most of which show how ingeniously Irish and Scottish and English peasants solved the problem of the long cooking time by exercising the utmost economy in fuel consumption. The pot or kettle would be sunk in the ground and covered with embers, packed around with hot stones or stood one on top of the other, as in a charcoal-kiln. What ultimately came out was described by French and German cooks, as polite as they were distrustful, as 'very heavy fare, which is therefore usually served with a strong wine or brandy sauce'. And English Christmas pudding, which can take a whole day to cook and is often made at one Christmas and kept till the next, is still a very heavy dish. But in the Victorian age Britain too adopted the lighter pudding which on the continent is boiled in a water bath in a closed metal mould whereas the British still prefer a cloth folded around the pudding mould and tied with string, the fold at the top opening when the pudding begins to rise.

The *puddings chauds* – cabinet puddings, white and brown bread puddings, Viennese, chocolate, chestnut or rice pudding are, within the context of the classic menu, *entremets de douceur* and accordingly constituted the substantial hot dish before the actual dessert and at about the turn of the century they began to merge with it. Then cold or iced puddings came into fashion. As this century advanced the menu shrank but the pudding course did not get any less delicious though it gradually took on quite a new role. Today, with our ovens which guarantee a perfectly even heat, we are accustomed to cooking the most delicate of classic fluffy puddings without the protection of a water bath, sometimes in small individual moulds which are then turned out onto warm dessert plates right away.

Christmas pudding, also known as plum pudding, is traditionally eaten on Christmas Day in Britain and Ireland. It is perhaps the quintessential 'pudding', being the richest of all. Old as it is, however, the Christmas pudding did not in fact assume its more-or-less present form until the end of the seventeenth century. Fascinatingly, it seems to have started life as a humbler, more savoury dish – more of a porridge with added dried fruits and spices. It must, in its way, have tasted like a warmed-up version of today's breakfast favourite, muesli. Nowadays, made with fine fruits and spices, well flavoured with stout and whisky or rum, and left to mature, it is a most impressive affair. And, of course, the whole ceremony of its serving makes it even more memorable. Brandy or rum butter is the usual accompaniment, but others find whipped cream a lighter alternative.

Finally, remember that every steamed pudding should have its sauce, both the colour and the flavour of which must complement it: white with brown, for example, the red of fruit with the gold of crumbs, cool and creamy with crisp, or sweet with bland.

The pudding is a traditional dessert in many countries, though sometimes under a quite different name – in Austria, for example, it is called a *kuch*. As a close relative of the German *Auflauf*, and of the soufflé, it tends to elude precise definition. Even if puddings are not at the moment among the Top Ten in the desserts league, these spongy creations – moistened with fruit sauces or wine – should not be overlooked.

1 **Melted butter and flour, known internationally as a *roux*,** is the foundation of this basic pudding. Melt the butter in a saucepan, add the flour and cook together for 2 minutes or so. Heat up the milk in a pan with the vanilla pod and just bring it to the boil, then blend it into the *roux*.

2 **Add the egg yolks.** Turn the mixture into a bowl and stir in first 2 of the egg whites. Then add the yolks one at a time, beating the mixture until smooth each time. Next whip the rest of the egg whites, with the sugar, to a stiff snow.

3 **Fold in the beaten egg whites.** Take about one-third of this and stir it well into the yolk mixture with a balloon whisk. Then fold in the rest with a wooden spoon. Do not stir it and take great care that the mixture loses as little volume as possible.

4 **Fill the moulds from a piping bag.** First butter the moulds and dust them out with sugar. They are very easy to fill using a piping bag and a large nozzle, but the mixture should only come three-quarters of the way up the moulds because it rises considerably in the cooking.

Saxony Pudding should really be classed as a raised pudding, and is one with a long tradition. It is also the basis for several other varieties of pudding. It may also be served with vanilla or caramel sauce. It is usually made in individual moulds although large moulds of 1, 1.5 or 2 litre/1¾, 2¾ or 3½ pint capacity are also used.

Hazelnut pudding is a variation of Saxony pudding and is based on that recipe. 100 g/4 oz ground and toasted hazelnuts are simply added to the mixture at the end. Here too of course there is a wide choice of different sauces to please both the palate and the eye.

Saxony Pudding

*Pouding à la saxonne
à la sauce aux framboises*

100 g/4 oz butter
100 g/4 oz flour
250 ml/8 fl oz milk
1 vanilla pod
10 egg whites
6 egg yolks
100 g/4 oz sugar
butter for greasing
sugar for dusting
10 250-ml/8-fl oz moulds

For the raspberry sauce:
450 g/1 lb frozen raspberries
(to yield 400 ml/14 fl oz purée)
100 g/4 oz icing sugar,
or to taste

Heat the butter in a long-handled saucepan, carefully stir in the flour and cook them gently together for 12 minutes to make a white *roux*. In another pan heat the milk together with the vanilla pod. Let it boil up once and remove the vanilla pod. Blend this hot milk into the *roux* over the heat. Tip the mixture into a bowl and thoroughly stir in 2 of the egg whites. Incorporate the egg yolks one at a time, beating the mixture until smooth between each added yolk. Whip the 8 remaining egg whites to a snow with the sugar and stir about a third of it into the yolk mixture with a balloon whisk. Fold in the rest carefully with a wooden spoon. Spoon the mixture into the moulds, previously brushed with melted butter and dusted with sugar. Fill them only three-quarters full, for the pudding will rise considerably during the cooking. Cook them in a water bath for 25 to 30 minutes in a moderate oven (180 C, 350 F, gas 4).

Serves 10.

To make the sauce, purée the raspberries in a blender or food processor then push through a fine sieve, and finally sweeten it with icing sugar.

Hazelnut Pudding

*Pouding aux noisettes
à la sauce au chocolat*

This is a variation of Saxony pudding with hazelnuts. The ingredients, quantities and method are the same, but 100 g/4 oz ground, roasted hazelnuts are added at the end. They must be folded, rather than stirred, in – so that none of the volume is lost. Hazelnut pudding is served with chocolate sauce.

Spiced Pudding

Pouding aux épices

150 g/5 oz butter
175 g/6 oz sugar
generous pinch of ground cinnamon
generous pinch of ground cloves
15 g/½ oz cocoa powder
½ tablespoon flour
75 g/3 oz ground almonds
5 eggs, separated
100 g/4 oz soft breadcrumbs
100 g/4 oz crumbled gingerbread
3 tablespoons red wine
1 tablespoon rum
25 g/1 oz chopped candied lemon peel
25 g/1 oz chopped candied orange peel
grated rind of ½ lemon
100-ml/4-fl oz timbale moulds
butter for greasing
sugar for dusting

Beat the butter and 50 g/2 oz of the sugar together till fluffy. Add the spices, cocoa powder and flour. Stir in half the almonds and the egg yolks. Beat the egg whites to a snow with the rest of the sugar and fold it into the mixture. Moisten the breadcrumbs and gingerbread in the red wine and rum. Combine the rest of the almonds with the candied peel and grated lemon rind and, together with the moistened crumbs, fold them into the mixture. Butter the timbale moulds and dust them with sugar. Fill them with the mixture and bake for 25 to 30 minutes in a water bath in a moderate oven (180 C, 350 F, gas 4).

Serves 15.

To make a red wine sauce to go with this spiced pudding, bring 250 ml/8 fl oz each red wine and raspberry syrup and a piece of cinnamon stick to the boil. Moisten 25 g/1 oz cornflour with a little water and bind the sauce with it. Stir in 15 g/½ oz slivered almonds and 1 tablespoon thinly shredded candied lemon peel.

Chocolate Pudding

Pouding au chocolat

In the Austrian cuisine, with all its wealth of baked desserts, this one, famous under its original name *Mohr im Hemd* (loosely translatable as 'Othello in his nightgown') ranks among the best. The Austrians still call this sort of pudding a *Koch* or a *Dunstkoch*, names which imply boiling or steaming, because they are cooked in a water bath, and they are as popular with the professional as they are with the home cook. Variations on this one theme are legion: some have a lot of chocolate, some less but instead contain cocoa powder, and some even substitute hazelnuts for the almonds.

100 g/4 oz dark plain chocolate
6 eggs, separated
seeds of ½ vanilla pod
100 g/4 oz sugar
100 g/4 oz chopped almonds
50 g/2 oz soft breadcrumbs
a tall, fluted 1.25-litre/2¼-pint
pudding mould
butter for greasing
sugar for dusting

Melt the chocolate in a double boiler, then beat it with the egg yolks, the vanilla seeds and half the sugar until it is foamy. Mix the almonds with the breadcrumbs. Beat the egg whites with the rest of the sugar to a stiff snow. Blend about a quarter of this snow into the egg yolk mixture and then carefully fold in the rest of the egg white along with the nut and crumb mixture. Fill the mould, previously greased with butter and dusted with caster sugar, with this mixture and stand it in a water bath (the water should reach to about 2.5 cm/1 in below the rim of the mould) and bake for 35 to 40 minutes in a moderate oven (160 to 180 C, 325 to 350 F, gas 3 to 4). The water must be kept just under boiling point. Test with a wooden cocktail stick to ensure the pudding is cooked. It may be served with lightly whipped cream or with hot chocolate sauce, or both.

Serves 10 to 12.

Wine Gugelhupf

Gouglof au vin

In Austria, with scant respect for the cloth, they call this *Besoffener Capuziner* which might be translated as 'Friar Tipsy'. It is a genuine sponge pudding, light, airy and very receptive to mulled wine. The addition of this turns it into a dessert in which it is hard to decide which tastes better, the pudding or the sauce.

4 eggs, separated
175 g/6 oz sugar
grated rind of ½ lemon
150 g/5 oz fine breadcrumbs
a 1-litre/1¾-pint *gugelhupf* mould
butter for greasing
breadcrumbs

Beat the egg yolks until frothy with half the sugar and the grated lemon rind. Whip the egg whites to a snow, trickling in the rest of the sugar slowly. Stir about a quarter of the beaten egg whites into the yolk mixture and fold in the rest carefully with a wooden spoon, together with the breadcrumbs. Butter the *gugelhupf* mould, sprinkle the inside with breadcrumbs and fill it with the sponge mixture, smoothing the surface evenly. Bake it for 30 to 35 minutes to a good light brown in a moderate oven (180 C, 350 F, gas 4). It is wise to test whether it is really cooked through by inserting a wooden cocktail stick – if it comes out clean, the sponge is cooked. Leave it for a few minutes to cool, then turn it out onto a shallow serving dish.

750 ml/1¼ pints light white wine
200 g/7 oz sugar · juice of ½ lemon
juice of ½ orange · pared rind of 1 lemon
½ cinnamon stick · 2 cloves
2 tablespoons orange liqueur
250 ml/8 fl oz whipped cream (optional)

Bring the wine gently to the boil with the sugar, lemon and orange juices, the lemon rind cut in a long spiral strip, cinnamon and cloves, and let it mull for 2 to 3 minutes. Add the orange liqueur. Place the *gugelhupf* in a serving dish and baste it with the hot, spiced wine until it has absorbed as much as possible. The *gugelhupf* should then be chilled in the refrigerator and turned out for serving. Whipped cream tastes very good with it but should be served individually on each portion.

Serves 4 to 6.

Christmas or Plum Pudding

This is perhaps the richest pudding of all and should be served in small helpings. Though not the customary accompaniment, we think some freshly whipped cream rounds it off well, harmonising perfectly with the malted, fruity taste of the pudding.

100 g/4 oz fresh beef suet
100 g/4 oz breadcrumbs
175 g/6 oz currants
175 g/6 oz raisins
100 g/4 oz soft brown sugar
50 g/2 oz chopped almonds
50 g/2 oz chopped diced
candied lemon peel
100 g/4 oz quartered glacé cherries
grated rind of 1 lemon
3 eggs
2 tablespoons whisky
a little stout or beer, if necessary
oil for greasing the pudding basin
1 900-ml/1½-pint pudding basin
or mould

Prepare the suet as described below and mix it with the breadcrumbs. Mix the currants and raisins with the sugar, chopped almonds, diced candied peel and pieces of glacé cherry. Add the suet and breadcrumbs and lastly the lemon rind, eggs and the whisky. Oil the pudding basin, put in the mixture and press it down well. Cover with greaseproof paper and tie on a cloth or cover with the mould's lid.

Serves 10 to 12.

2 Put the dried fruit, currants and raisins into a bowl and add the sugar, chopped almonds, candied peel and glacé cherries. Then stir in the grated suet, mixed with the breadcrumbs.

3 Bind with the eggs, which have been lightly blended with the whisky and grated lemon peel. Stir it all into a stiff mixture with a wooden spoon, adding a little stout or beer if it is necessary to make it creamier. Press the mixture down into the oiled pudding basin.

4 Cover with lightly oiled greaseproof paper. English pudding basins have a thick rim under which a cloth may be firmly fastened with string and the corners lifted up and tied together at the top.

5 Put the pudding into a water bath. A small metal rack or large pastry cutter must be laid on the bottom of the pan so that the basin does not directly touch it. This ensures even cooking. The cooking time is 8 to 9 hours.

1 Prepare the suet, taking great care to remove all pieces of membrane. The suet must be as white as possible, and dry. It can now be grated coarsely, or put through the medium disc of the mincer.

6 Christmas pudding is a true 'storecupboard dessert' that can only improve with keeping. It is invariably simmered for 8 to 9 hours in the water bath, even though it is probably cooked through after 2 hours. The prolonged cooking causes the assorted ingredients to combine into an unmistakable flavour and, so to speak, embalm the pudding. In its basin, which can be sealed with wax paper, it will keep for months. In Britain it is generally decorated with holly, flamed with brandy and thus ceremoniously carried to the table. Brandy or rum butter is the indispensable English accompaniment although some may prefer whipped cream as a lighter alternative.

EGG-BASED DESSERTS

From delicate crêpes to soufflé omelettes

The pancake, which the Germans call *Pfannkuchen* or *Eierkuchen* and French call a *crêpe*, is one of Europe's oldest and most basic foods. It is made from what could be found on every farm blessed with one milking cow and just one laying hen, yet it turns up in fairy stories in every language and has become *the* dish of the feasts before Ash Wednesday precisely because there was no way then of keeping eggs, butter and milk fresh for the 40 days of Lenten fast before Easter and the Resurrection, during which time abstinence from them was uncompromisingly adhered to. So, come Shrove Tuesday, the housewives gathered everything that remained in their larder into a bowl and mixed a rich and appetising batter, to the delight above all of the children: and that was the origin of the thick, rich pancake that, in the classic tale, jumped out of its basket and onto the child and flew flippety-flap over the hills and dales with the fox and the wolf following after.

Even in the leanest times there were pancakes on Candlemas Day, the day when all candles were blessed – and still are – for use at home and in church during the following year. In many countries it became the custom to organise lantern processions with the candles that had just been blessed; in Paris women and children used to walk through their city and across the river Seine, candles in hand, singing hymns as they went, and at the end of it were given hot, fresh crêpes, made out of batter prepared in the early morning. All sorts of fortune-telling games were bound up with these Candlemas pancakes. Thus, if the lady of the house could toss the first crêpe so neatly that it landed back in the pan, she would never be short of money in the following year. Or else the first crêpe was given to the chickens, so that they would lay well throughout the summer, or perhaps thrown into a tree behind the house for the birds, so that they would show their gratitude by always giving warning if a wolf was about. So too in Britain Shrove Tuesday is never complete without pancakes and the day is called Pancake Tuesday simply because, as on the Continent, the stocks of eggs and milk are made into pancakes. In London the Pancake Bell used to be rung at 10 o'clock on that morning to summon the parishioners to confession.

Now that fine pancakes have been elevated to the realms of haute cuisine they tend to be referred to as *crêpes*; they are bathed in liqueurs and fruit syrups, and wrapped around ambrosial fillings. But despite all their decoration and elaboration they, more than any other dessert, recall the simple, even humble, beginnings of all festive fare and the times when you were lucky enough – and celebrated your good fortune – in being able to eat your fill of pancakes.

A special dish, whether flamed or not.
Crêpes Suzette: rub all over the rind of a washed orange with 4 lumps of sugar, then crush them. Melt 40 g/1½ oz butter in a pan and dissolve in it the crushed sugar lumps and 60 g/2½ oz more sugar. Moisten with 100 ml/4 fl oz fresh orange juice and reduce this sauce a little. Dip 6 to 8 crêpes in the sauce, fold them in half then in half again and place in the pan. Pour over 3 tablespoons orange liqueur and 2 tablespoons marc de champagne or cognac. Now flame the crêpes, or simply let them poach in the sauce for a minute or two over low heat.

Apricot Crêpes

Pannequets aux abricots

100 g/4 oz fresh apricots
100 g/4 oz apricot jam
2 tablespoons Galliano · 25 g/1 oz butter
75 g/3 oz chopped walnuts
2 apricots for decoration

Blanch the apricots, peel and stone them and cut the flesh into pieces. Bring the apricot jam to the boil, add the apricot pieces and let them poach for 1 to 2 minutes. Remove from the heat and stir in the liqueur. Fill 8 crêpes with this mixture, spread them with softened butter and put them for a few minutes under a hot grill. Scatter over the chopped walnuts, dust with icing sugar and decorate each serving with half an apricot. Serves 4.

'Sissi' Crêpes

Pannequets 'Sissi'

100 g/4 oz almond paste
2 tablespoons sugar syrup (30°)
2 tablespoons lemon juice
1 tablespoon kirsch · 25 g/1 oz butter
4 tablespoons strawberry sauce
4 tablespoons Advocaat
4 scoops vanilla ice cream
whipped cream for decoration

Beat the almond paste with the sugar syrup, lemon juice and kirsch until fluffy. Fill 4 crêpes with this mixture, roll them up, spread them with softened butter and put in a pan in a moderately hot oven (200 C, 400 F, gas 6) for 5 minutes. Put them on small plates, pour over the strawberry sauce and liqueur and serve with vanilla ice cream and whipped cream. Serves 4.

Chocolate Crêpes

Pannequets au chocolat

100 g/4 oz cherry jam
75 g/3 oz softened butter
scant 150 ml/¼ pint water
75 g/3 oz sugar · 25 g/1 oz cocoa powder
2 tablespoons rum
100 g/4 oz plain chocolate, chopped
4 tablespoons whipped cream

Fill 8 crêpes with the jam and roll them up. Spread them with half of the softened butter and heat them for 5 to 6 minutes in a moderately hot oven (200 C, 400 F, gas 6). Bring the water, sugar, the remaining butter and cocoa to the boil, take the pan off the heat – and stir in the rum and chocolate. If necessary thin the sauce with single cream. Pour the hot sauce over the crêpes and top each serving with a tablespoon of whipped cream. Serves 4.

Crêpe Batter

Pâte aux pannequets

200 g/7 oz flour
250 ml/8 fl oz milk
scant 150 ml/¼ pint single cream
3 eggs
generous pinch of salt
1 tablespoon sugar
2 tablespoons oil
butter for frying

Sift the flour into a bowl. Add the milk, cream, eggs, salt, sugar and oil and beat all together to a smooth, thin batter. Leave it to rest for about 1 hour, then beat once again and cook the crêpes as illustrated below. They should be made as thin as possible.

This recipe makes about 20 crêpes of 15 cm/6 in diameter.

Kaiserschmarren

Omelette rissolée

50 g/2 oz flour · 2 eggs separated
scant 150 ml/¼ pint milk
generous pinch of salt
1 tablespoon sugar
50 g/2 oz raisins · 25 g/1 oz butter

Beat the sifted flour with the milk, egg yolks and salt to a smooth batter. Beat the egg whites to a snow with the sugar and fold it into the batter along with the raisins. Heat the butter in a large ovenproof pan (30 cm/12 in diameter), pour in the batter and tilt the pan so that it spreads evenly. Heat it for a moment and then put the pan in a moderately hot oven (190 C, 375 F, gas 5) for 8 to 10 minutes to finish cooking. Tear it into pieces with the aid of 2 forks.
Serves 3 to 4.

Kaiserschmarren must be served straight from the oven. Arrange it on a serving dish and dust thickly with icing sugar. In Austria plum compote is traditionally served with it, but it goes equally well with any sharp stewed fruit or, as in this case, with apples poached in white wine.

Crêpes

This batter is a basic recipe that may either be cooked in a conventional pan or on the special crêpe iron shown here. The liquid – in this case milk and water – may be varied. When made entirely with water the crêpes can be really thin, and if beer or cider is used the action of the yeast will produce a delightfully airy texture.

200 g/7 oz flour
350 ml/12 fl oz milk
scant 150 ml/¼ pint water
¼ teaspoon salt
2 tablespoons sugar
5 eggs
2 egg yolks
50 g/2 oz butter, clarified
extra butter for greasing the pan

Make a batter from the ingredients as described in the adjoining pictures and leave it to rest for at least 1 hour, to give the flour plenty of time to swell in the liquid. Because it settles at the bottom, it must be beaten through the liquid again before use and this process must be repeated often while the crêpes are being made. Layer the cooked crêpes one on top of another and keep them warm between two plates in a moderate oven (160 C, 325 F, gas 3) until the last crêpe comes out of the pan.

This recipe makes about 35 crêpes of 15 cm/6 in diameter.

Prepare the crêpe batter. Sift the flour into a bowl and stir in the combined milk and water. Add salt and sugar, beat in the eggs and yolks and finally the melted clarified butter. Beat the batter well till smooth. To cook the crêpes, first melt butter in the pan and pour the surplus back into a saucepan. This will leave enough to cook one crêpe. Tilt the pan a little, pour in some batter and swirl it around the pan to spread evenly and paper-thin over the bottom. Turn it with a broad-bladed knife or a spatula or, when you have mastered the knack, toss it elegantly in the air.

The special crêpe iron guarantees paper-thin results. The convex pan shown here is for use over the gas flame, but an electrically heated one is available. Pour the batter into a suitably sized vessel and quickly dip the hot iron into it, Take it out and turn it over. It will be thinly coated with batter. Place it over the gas burner where it should be cooked on the one side only, but unfortunately this does not have a good effect on the flavour.

Crêpes with Sour Cherries

Crêpes aux griottes

Drain a 350 g/12 oz jar of stoned sour cherries and reserve the liquid. Moisten 25 g/1 oz cornflour with some cherry juice and bring the rest of the juice to the boil with a small piece of cinnamon stick and 50 g/2 oz sugar, stirring all the time, until the sugar has dissolved. Bind it with the moistened cornflour. Stir in the cherries and leave to cool. Cover half of each crêpe with the cherry compote, fold the other half over and serve dusted with icing sugar. If you wish you can accentuate the flavour of the cherry compote with 2 tablespoons kirsch. Serves 4.

Parisian Crêpes

Crêpes parisiennes

Make a filling as described on page 59 from confectioner's custard made with 250 ml/8 fl oz milk and 2 egg whites beaten to a snow with 50 g/2 oz sugar, and lace it with 1 tablespoon rum. Spread the custard over 6 crêpes and add 3 to 4 miniature macaroons to each. Fold them up into rectangular packages. Whip 3 egg whites with 60 g/2½ oz sugar to a snow and with a piping bag and medium nozzle pipe it decoratively on top of the crêpes. Lightly dust with icing sugar and brown under a very hot (240 C, 475 F) grill. Serve with strawberry sauce and miniature macaroons. Serves 6.

Crêpes with Kiwi Fruit and Zabaione

Crêpes aux kiwis et sabayon

Peel and slice 4 kiwi-fruit. Melt 1 tablespoon butter in a pan and lightly fry the fruit in it. Sift 1 tablespoon icing sugar over and sprinkle with 1 tablespoon brandy. Turn the kiwi slices, fry them quickly on the other side and cover one half of each of the 4 hot crêpes with them. Fold over, and serve with a hot zabaione made with 2 egg yolks beaten to a froth in a water bath with 4 tablespoons Marsala and 2 tablespoons sugar. Serves 4.

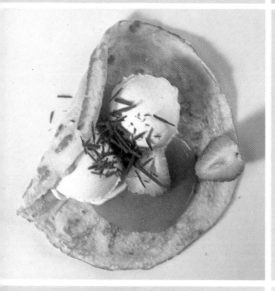

Crêpes with Vanilla Ice Cream

Crêpes à la glace à la vanille

Bring 4 tablespoons sugar syrup to the boil with 2 teaspoons lemon juice and 2 tablespoons rum. Stir in 150 g/5 oz puréed fresh strawberries and cook for about 2 minutes. Place 2 small scoops of vanilla ice cream on each crêpe, pour over the warm strawberry sauce and sprinkle with 1 tablespoon chocolate shavings. Decorate them with 2 half strawberries each.
Serves 4.

Normandy Crêpes

Crêpes à la normande

Heat the juice of a lemon in a pan and melt 25 g/1 oz butter in it. Peel and quarter 250 g/9 oz apples and then cut into slices. Poach them in the lemon butter with 1 tablespoon raisins, 1 tablespoon toasted almonds, laced with 2 tablespoons calvados and leave to cool. Melt 1 teaspoon sugar in a pan, turn the crêpes separately in it and loosen them from the pan again with a little butter. For the sauce melt 1 teaspoon sugar with 1 of butter and blend in the apple cooking liquid and 2 tablespoons Marsala. Cover half of each crêpe with the apple slices, fold them over and pour on the sauce. Serves 4.

Black Forest Crêpes

Crêpes à la Forêt-Noir

Beat 50 g/2 oz butter till creamy. Whip 1 egg white with 40 g/1½ oz sugar to a stiff snow and fold it into the butter. Flavour it with 2 tablespoons kirsch. Coarsely chop 100 g/4 oz bottled sour cherries and stir them in also. Spoon some of this cream into the centre of each of the 4 crêpes, fold up the sides to make small packages and quickly heat them under a hot grill. Decorate each with chocolate straws and a sour cherry. Serves 4.

Crêpes with Chocolate Cream

Crêpes à la crème au chocolat

Beat 50 g/2 oz butter till creamy. Whip 1 egg white with 40 g/1½ oz sugar to a stiff snow and fold it in. Melt 25 g/1 oz plain chocolate in a double boiler and stir it into the cream with 2 tablespoons rum. Pipe this from a piping bag fitted with a round nozzle onto 8 crêpes, making 2 long stripes across the middle of each. Fold the crêpes and pour over each 1 tablespoon chocolate sauce. Sprinkle with chopped pistachio nuts and serve. They can be decorated as well if you wish with whipped cream. Serves 4.

Crêpes with Redcurrants

Crêpes aux groseilles

Wash 150 g/5 oz fresh redcurrants and drain them. Bring 75 g/3 oz sugar, a scant 150 ml/¼ pint red wine and a small piece of cinnamon stick to the boil and reduce for 3 to 4 minutes. Put in the redcurrants and let them poach in it for 2 minutes before removing them with a slotted spoon. Moisten 15 g/½ oz cornflour with a little red wine, bind the sauce with it and heat up the redcurrants in the sauce. Make purses of 4 crêpes by folding them in half, then in half again, and fill them with the redcurrant compote. Serve sprinkled with icing sugar. Serves 4.

Crêpes with Maple Syrup and Wild Strawberries

Crêpes au sirop d'érable

Wash 100 g/4 oz wild strawberries and drain them in a sieve. Heat 100 g/4 oz maple syrup over a low heat. Put in the strawberries and warm them up but do not let them boil. Divide the strawberries and syrup between 4 crêpes and top each one with a spoonful of lightly whipped cream. Serve at once. Maple syrup also goes very well with fresh wild raspberries or bilberries.

Serves 4.

Macaroon Crêpes

Crêpes aux macarons

Spread 4 crêpes thinly with redcurrant jelly and fold into an oblong shape. Lay them on the plates with the open side underneath. Beat 100 g/4 oz almond paste with 50 g/2 oz sugar, a little grated lemon rind and 2 egg whites until creamy and pipe a lattice onto the crêpes with it using a piping bag and a round nozzle. Sift 2 tablespoons icing sugar over and brown under a hot grill. Decorate each with a small bunch of redcurrants.

Serves 4.

Chocolate Crêpes

Crêpes au chocolat aux fruits

The crêpes are made with the same batter as above but with the addition of 25 g/1 oz cocoa powder and 1 extra tablespoon sugar. Cut 100 g/4 oz fresh pineapple into small pieces, peel and slice 2 nectarines. Melt 1 tablespoon butter in a pan and quickly fry the fruit in it. Sift 1 tablespoon icing sugar onto them and cook until they glaze. Take them out and keep them warm. Divide 60 g/2½ oz fresh raspberries between the crêpes, with the warmed fruit. Pour mango sauce over, fold the crêpes and serve them dusted with icing sugar. Serves 4.

Soufflé Crêpes

Soufflé-Crêpes

Heat 15 g/½ oz butter in a saucepan, stir in 25 g/1 oz flour and cook together for 2 minutes to make a *roux*. Pour in a scant 150 ml/¼ pint milk and add the grated rind of ½ lemon. Bring it to the boil, stir in 1 egg yolk and take it off the heat. Flavour it with 1 teaspoon lemon juice. Stiffly whip 2 egg whites with 50 g/2 oz sugar and fold it in. Spread the soufflé mixture about 1.5 cm/½ in thick onto half of each crêpe, fold over and sprinkle with icing sugar. Put the crêpes into a moderate oven (180 C, 350 F, gas 4) for 10 minutes. Dust them with icing sugar and decorate each with a slice of lemon. Serves 4.

Soufflé Omelette

Omelette Soufflée

100 g/4 oz sugar
3 egg yolks
seeds from ½ vanilla pod
grated rind of ½ lemon
5 egg whites
1 teaspoon potato flour or
powdered instant mashed potato
butter for greasing the serving dish
sugar to sprinkle over

First separate the egg yolks carefully, scrape out the seeds from the vanilla pod and grate the lemon peel. Now blend 25 g/1 oz of the sugar and the egg yolks slowly together, add the vanilla seeds and lemon rind and beat well until the mixture is frothy. Whip the egg whites with the remaining sugar to a snow and stir the potato flour into it carefully with a balloon whisk. Fold this into the egg yolk mixture with a wooden spoon. Melt a little butter, brush the surface of a metal serving dish, then sprinkle with some sugar. Put about three-quarters of the soufflé mixture onto the dish with a dough scraper and smooth it with a spatula, shaping it to look like a boat. In the top make a hollow 7.5 cm/3 in deep and draw ripples along the sides with a decorating comb. Put the rest of the soufflé mixture into a piping bag fitted with a star-shaped nozzle and pipe a border of rosettes around the top and bottom edges.

Bake for 10 to 12 minutes in a moderately hot oven (200 C, 400 F, gas 6). Serves 4.

1 **Melt a little butter and let it cool.** Use a pastry brush to paint the surface of the dish with butter, then sprinkle with sugar. About three-quarters of the soufflé mixture is now piled onto the dish, using a dough scraper.

The soufflé omelette is a classic, traditional dessert. It is very light, being made almost entirely of eggs and sugar, but at the same time it is very satisfying. This quantity is plenty for 4 people, especially if the dessert is served with fruit as well: sour cherries, peeled and cooked with sugar and cinnamon, are particularly good with it. The boat shape with the deep cleft is traditional and enables the mixture to cook evenly. The metal or silver dish acts as an extra heat conductor for the bottom of the soufflé, which on a porcelain dish would not cook through evenly.

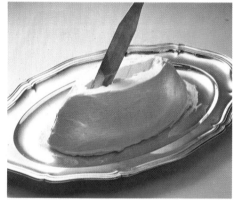

2 **Shape up the soufflé mixture.** With the help of a spatula the mixture is formed into a tall shape, suitable to the shape of the serving dish and the theme chosen – in this case a boat. A cleft 7.5 cm/3 in deep is then made in the top, lengthways.

3 **Decorate the omelette.** Score ripples along the sides with a decorating comb, preferably one not made of plastic. Then put the rest of the soufflé mixture into a piping bag fitted with a star nozzle and pipe a border of rosettes around the top and bottom edges.

Dessert Omelette with Fruit

Omelette aux fruits

3 egg yolks
grated rind of $\frac{1}{2}$ lemon
seeds from $\frac{1}{2}$ vanilla pod
6 egg whites
100 g/4 oz sugar
40 g/1$\frac{1}{2}$ oz flour
40 g/1$\frac{1}{2}$ oz butter, melted
25 g/1 oz butter for frying
2 tablespoons apricot jam
1 tablespoon orange liqueur
fruits for decoration

Blend the egg yolks, lemon rind and vanilla seeds well together. Whip the egg whites with the sugar till stiff and fold them carefully into the egg yolk mixture. Now sift the flour over, fold it into the mixture, then slowly add the hot melted butter. Melt the butter for frying in a skillet and put in the omelette mixture. Smooth the top over with a palette knife – or a dough scraper. Do not put the pan straight into the oven but place it on the heat for a minute or two to set the sponge a little and then bake it for 10 minutes in a moderately hot oven (200 C, 400 F, gas 6). Meanwhile mix the apricot jam with the orange liqueur. When the omelette is cooked but still in the pan, spread half of it with the liqueur mixture. Fold it over and slide it onto a serving dish. Fill it with fruits such as cherries, kiwi and mandarin oranges. Serves 4.

1 **Fold the beaten egg whites carefully into the egg yolk mixture.** First stir the egg yolks well with the lemon rind and vanilla seeds. Then whip the egg whites and sugar till they are really stiff and fold into the yolk mixture with a wooden spoon. Sift the flour over, blend all together and finally add the hot butter.

2 **Smooth out the omelette mixture in the pan.** When the omelette mixture is ready melt the butter in a heavy metal pan and put it in. Smooth over the surface with a palette knife. Heat the pan on the stove for a minute or two so that the omelette can begin to set, then slide it into the oven.

3 **Fold up the finished omelette while still in the pan. When the omelette is a good golden brown** quickly spread the mixed liqueur and jam on it in the pan and fold it over with the palette knife. Only then slide it onto a plate or serving dish, and decorate.

Dessert omelette with fruit is a type of omelette similar to the traditional Omelette Stéphanie which has the classic filling of wild strawberries, pineapple and a tender variety of pear such as, for example, Alexander Lucas, a late-ripening fruit. Dessert omelette can of course be filled in all sorts of ways. 'Viennese style' means with a jam filling; other fillings much to be recommended are those made from thickened fruit compotes, for example morello cherries or raspberries. A dessert omelette served with a chocolate cream filling based on confectioner's custard with melted plain chocolate goes down extremely well too.

ḤOME-MADE ICES

Some basic rules to follow

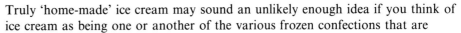

Truly 'home-made' ice cream may sound an unlikely enough idea if you think of ice cream as being one or another of the various frozen confections that are commercially produced nowadays. But then this chapter would really have no point, or at best could only discuss how and with what these convenience products should be served, were it not for the existence of an ice cream which everyone can make and which tastes extremely good as well.

Iced fruits and desserts made with ice – that is, frozen water – were the greatest luxuries which it was possible to give the gourmets of the ancient world. The most astonishing stories have come down to us from the days of the Greek and Roman empires, and beyond: how Alexander the Great on his wide-ranging military campaigns as far as India is said to have brought back snow with him from the glaciers and mixed it with fruit pulp and wine to refresh his thirsty troops; or how Hippocras, the celebrated Greek physician, used to prescribe cracked ice as a medicine to stimulate the body's vital secretions. In Rome the emperor Nero had snow from the Alps brought to him by courier and his cook mingled crushed ice with honey, rose water, fruits and tree-resin to make the dessert set firm. One can only guess how well these icy cargoes would have stood up to the journey.

Closer to our own times, during the last century in Hungary jars of frozen whipped cream used to be let down to the bottom of a well and in Germany large country houses would have an ice cellar – reminiscent of the English ice-house – a specially walled-in and insulated place which in winter was filled up with blocks of ice, sawn out of frozen ponds or streams, over which even at the height of summer the tender soft fruits could be stored on layers of leaves or straw. They came to the table lightly frosted – a delicacy as it were chilled by nature herself, and accompanied, if the times were good, by vanilla-flavoured whipped cream, a dish already halfway to being an ice cream as we know it today.

Today, large restaurant and hotel kitchens are equipped with highly sophisticated machines which can make quantities of ice cream in a matter of minutes, as you can see on page 171. For the home cook, there are small machines which can be bought quite cheaply and will make – at a rather more leisurely pace, but nonetheless very well – about 8 servings of ice cream. Electrically operated, these will fit into the freezer, and sometimes the ice-making compartment of a large fridge.

Should you have no form of ice cream machine, you can still make it by turning the unfrozen mixture into a shallow container in the freezer. As it freezes, stir it from time to time to break up the crystals which form. This will improve the finished texture.

Ice cream is a dessert with a long tradition that only relatively recently became widely popular. For centuries it was a dessert for the well-to-do. Even the hand-operated ice cream making machines that made their appearance around the turn of the century and made ices much simpler to prepare did not bring them a massive following. It was the arrival of factory produced ice cream which achieved the breakthrough that has since made it the world's biggest selling dessert. The United States of America now leads the field with an annual consumption of 24 litres/5 gallons per head.

Freshly made or from the freezer?

This question is no longer an easy one to answer, because no other group of desserts has been so successfully mastered by the food industry as ice cream. The reasons for this are many, but to the postwar generation ice cream is synonymous with a few big brand names and for older cooks it holds more memories of laborious churning away at the machine than of enjoying the frozen dessert that came out of it. Italian exponents of the art of ice cream making have also helped to make our own home-made efforts seem quite unnecessary.

The fact that shrewd housewives, keen amateurs and professionals alike make the most sophisticated parfaits for themselves but prefer to fetch a plain vanilla ice cream from the freezer is certainly a triumph for the ice cream industry. But it also points to a deficiency on the part of the otherwise extremely active manufacturers of kitchen gadgetry. Cooks who want to make the finest vanilla ice cream have only two satisfactory options: one is the old ice cream machine, powered by hand and packed around with cracked fishmonger's ice, which is now virtually unobtainable except perhaps from a local supplier; the other is an electric ice cream machine, an ice cream maker which will freeze small amounts not only of sorbets but also of other ices to an excellent standard. The advanced version of this shown on page 171, which will make the finest ice cream in a matter of minutes, is not a household gadget and belongs rather to the battery of the professional

Ice Creams

We mean by this the home-made variety, the very sound of whose ingredients makes the mouth water. They are of a standard quality to which the name 'ice cream' is legally applied, and the regulations concerning the making of iced desserts, besides being binding on the commercial sector, are also quite important to us consumers as well. Thus the unfrozen ice cream mixture should not be stored long and ices, once frozen, should really be consumed straight away. Under no circumstances should ice creams be refrozen after being thawed or their texture will be ruined.

Recipes for ice creams exist in abundance but once again the basic vanilla custard base acts as a sort of universal recipe that can be varied in all directions. Thus one custard with the addition of different flavourings will yield several kinds of ice cream, changing into a chocolate, coffee, hazelnut, pis-

tachio or strawberry ice as required. When using ingredients such as chocolate, nougat, nut brittle or caramel, which contain sugar, it is as well to decrease the amount of sugar in the recipe accordingly and then, if the same basic custard is to be used for a vanilla ice cream, increase the sugar to the correct proportion.

But fresh ice cream need not necessarily be made with this basic custard. All kinds of fruit ices, made from puréed fruits mixed either with cream or with wine or water, are very suitable material although in these cases the dividing line between ice cream and sorbet is very fine and the only difference lies in how firmly such ices are frozen. A quite contemporary note is however struck by the varieties of ice cream with yoghurt, especially the fruit ices because with its slightly acid taste yoghurt is an ideal partner for fruit purées and goes particularly well with the juices of citrus fruits. Also a yoghurt ice will do no harm at all to the waistline if made without whipped cream, perhaps substituting beaten egg white, and going easy on the sugar.

Vanilla Ice Cream

Glace à la vanille

7 egg yolks
200 g/7 oz sugar
500 ml/17 fl oz milk
250 ml/8 fl oz cream
1 vanilla pod

Proceed exactly as for the English custard on page 54: cream the egg yolks with the sugar in a bowl but do not allow them to froth. Scald the milk with the cream and the split vanilla pod, then remove the pod and scrape the seeds into the milk. Bring this to the boil again and, while stirring, blend it with the egg yolks. Pour the mixture into the top of a double boiler over a low heat and stir continuously with a wooden spoon until the custard flows heavily from the spoon. It must on no account boil. Pour it through a fine sieve and cool it over iced water, stirring occasionally. Tip the cold custard into the ice cream machine and freeze it, selecting the degree of firmness preferred, whether soft or a little less so. These quantities are enough to make 1 litre/1¾ pints ice cream, equivalent to 16 portions if a 50 ml/2 fl oz scoop is used.

Chocolate Rum Ice Cream

Glace au chocolat et au rhum

Melt 100 g/4 oz plain chocolate in a double boiler. Slowly add a scant 150 ml/¼ pint basic ice cream custard, stirring all the time with a balloon whisk, and finally add 2 tablespoons dark rum. Let the mixture cool a little and stir it into another 375 ml/13 fl oz basic ice cream custard. For this recipe the custard should be made with one-third less sugar. Freeze to creamy in the ice cream machine and serve with an Italian zabaione (page 73). Fruits in rum with whipped cream or vanilla sauce are also excellent with it.
Serves 8.

Hazelnut Ice Cream

Glace aux noisettes

Toast 100 g/4 oz hazelnuts on a baking sheet in a moderate oven (180 C, 350 F, gas 4) for about 15 minutes until the skins become flaky. Leave them to cool, lay them on a cloth and rub the skins off with it. Grind the nuts finely and stir them into 500 ml 17 fl oz basic ice cream custard. Freeze in the ice cream machine. Scoop out and decorate each serving with, for example, a meringue flower crowned by a hazelnut. Hot chocolate sauce (page 72) laced with a shot of rum partners it perfectly.
Serves 8.

Chocolate Flake Ice Cream

Glace au chocolat

Stir 2 tablespoons each Cointreau and dark rum into 500 ml/17 fl oz basic ice cream custard. Melt 100 g/4 oz plain chocolate in a double boiler. Put the custard into the ice cream machine and freeze it for 2 to 3 minutes. Pour the lukewarm chocolate into the revolving machine, when it will at once harden into small flakes. Finish freezing and scoop out. To each serving add a whipped cream rosette and some raspberry sauce.

Serves 8.

Lemon Yoghurt Ice Cream

Glace au citron et au yaourt

Macerate a small bunch of lemon balm (about 25 g/1 oz) in 50 ml/2 fl oz dry white wine for 1 to 2 hours. Strain it, add 100 g/4 oz sugar and boil it for about 2 minutes. Cool and stir in 1 tablespoon lemon juice and 175 ml/6 fl oz low-fat plain yoghurt. Stiffly whip a scant 150 ml/¼ pint cream and fold it in. Freeze to a creamy-soft texture and serve with blackberries and a caramel sauce. For the sauce cook 100 g/4 oz sugar with 1 tablespoon water to a light brown caramel and liquefy it with 150 ml/¼ pint water. Reduce it again to the desired strength. Serves 8.

Walnut Brittle Ice Cream

Glace aux noix

Make a light brown caramel in a small saucepan with 100 g/4 oz sugar and 1 tablespoon water. Add 60 g/2½ oz coarsely chopped walnuts and 25 g/1 oz ground almonds. Spread out this walnut brittle on an oiled baking sheet and leave it to get cold. Pound it finely. Freeze 500 ml/17 fl oz basic ice cream custard (if possible using one-third less sugar) in the ice cream machine, adding in the nut brittle only when it starts to become creamy to avoid dissolving the caramel and to keep it crisp. Serve with redcurrant sauce, slightly sweetened with honey if you wish. Serves 8.

Strawberry Yoghurt Ice Cream

Glace aux fraises et au yaourt

Stir 100 g/4 oz icing sugar into 350 ml/12 fl oz low-fat plain yoghurt, blend in 4 tablespoons lemon juice and 300 g/11 oz freshly puréed strawberries and flavour with 2 tablespoons Grand Marnier. Stiffly whip a scant 150 ml/¼ pint cream and blend it in with a balloon whisk. Freeze till creamy in the ice cream machine and serve with orange sauce.

Serves 8.

Pistachio Ice Cream

Glace aux pistaches

Finely chop 75 g/3 oz shelled pistachios and stir them into 500 ml/17 fl oz basic ice cream custard. Flavour it with 1 tablespoon almond liqueur (Amaretto or maraschino). Freeze it in the ice cream machine. A plum sauce or plum compote goes very well with it. For the sauce make a purée of 250 g/8 oz fresh, ripe plums and boil it steadily for 4 to 5 minutes with 60 g/2½ oz sugar, a generous pinch of cinnamon and 1 teaspoon lemon juice. It can be served either hot or cold.

Serves 8.

Pineapple Ice Cream

Glace à l'ananas

Purée 150 g/5 oz ripe pineapple and boil it with 150 g/5 oz sugar for 2 to 3 minutes to reduce it. Dice a further 150 g/5 oz pineapple and cook it in the purée over a low heat for 6 to 8 minutes. Cool, stir into 500 ml/17 fl oz basic ice cream custard (preferably made with one-third less sugar) and freeze it in the ice cream machine till creamy. Decorate each portion with a whipped cream rosette and a tablespoon of chocolate sauce, laced with rum.

Serves 8.

Peach Ice Cream Dessert

Glace aux pêches

250 ml/8 fl oz peach purée
350 g/12 oz low-fat plain yoghurt
100 g/4 oz icing sugar
2 tablespoons fresh lime juice
1 tablespoon kirsch
scant 150 ml/¼ pint double or
whipping cream

Combine the peach purée with the yoghurt, icing sugar, lime juice, kirsch and whipped cream and freeze until creamy. Glaze some petits fours (prepared as on page 116) with kirsch-flavoured fondant. Leave to dry, then cut them in half horizontally and fill them with the ice cream, piped from a piping bag with a star nozzle. Serve with chocolate sauce and peach slices. Serves 8.

Blackberry Ice Cream Dessert

Glace aux baies de ronce

75 g/3 oz sugar
1½ tablespoons Curaçao
300 g/11 oz blackberry purée
175 ml/6 fl oz low-fat plain yoghurt
generous pinch of cinnamon
scant 150 ml/¼ pint double or
whipping cream

Boil the sugar with 2 tablespoons water for 1 minute, add the Curaçao and stir into the blackberry purée. Stir in the yoghurt and cinnamon and finally fold in the whipped cream. Freeze till creamy. Cut in two horizontally some petits fours glazed with rum fondant (prepared as on page 116) and fill them with the ice cream, piped through a piping bag fitted with a star nozzle. Serve with apricot sauce and black-berries. Serves 8.

Vanilla Ice Cream Dessert

Glace à la vanille aux petits fours

Vanilla ice cream (half the recipe on
page 162)
2 tablespoons sugar syrup (30°)
2 tablespoons cognac

Prepare the vanilla ice cream as on page 162 and freeze until creamy. Glaze the petits fours as on page 116 with fondant flavoured only with lemon juice. When they are set cut them in half horizontally and moisten the sponge with the sugar syrup and cognac mixed. Using a small ice cream scoop set 2 scoops of the vanilla ice cream on each of the oval-shaped petits fours. Accompany with a sauce made from fresh wild strawberries as described on page 71. Serves about 8.

Ices and Fruits

Each of these complements the other perfectly. One only has to think of the enormous variety of custard ice cream and fruit combinations that appear in sundae glasses to realise this. But the container too can be edible, like the small cups or flowers made of almond biscuit paste on page 66 or the chocolate cups (page 76) which have the additional advantage that they can be stored for a considerable time. The meringue baskets illustrated here are especially elegant and their flavour suits ices and fruits of every kind. Sweet meringue harmonises well with the chocolate glaze too.

To make the meringue cups you will need hemispherical moulds which can be made out of thick aluminium foil. This must be fitted in a double or triple layer over a model and the projecting edges cut off. The foil should be lightly oiled so that the meringue cup can later be easily detached. After lifting the foil cups off the model place them on a wire rack covered with kitchen paper and put this on a baking sheet. If they were placed directly on the baking sheet too much heat would be generated under them.

Recipe for meringue cups:

8 egg whites
250 g/9 oz caster sugar
200 g/7 oz icing sugar
25 g/1 oz cornflour

Beat the egg whites, slowly trickling in the caster sugar. When they are a good stiff snow fold in with a wooden spoon the icing sugar blended with the cornflour.

Fill a piping bag with the meringue mixture and, with a round nozzle, pipe it spirally into the hemispherical moulds, beginning at the bottom. For large meringue cups a border of meringue balls can be piped onto kitchen paper as well, to be placed in position later. Put the cups to dry rather than bake in a very cool oven 110–120 C, 225–250 F, gas $\frac{1}{4}$–$\frac{1}{2}$), preferably overnight, with the oven door slightly ajar.

When thoroughly cool, fill them with melted plain chocolate, pour it straight out again and let them drain on a wire rack. Once the chocolate has set small meringue cups should have their edges dipped in melted chocolate again. They can now be filled with a scoop of ice cream and some fruit without the meringue going soft.

This recipe makes 4 meringue cups of 9 to 10 cm/about 4 in diameter or a larger one of about 15 cm/6 in diameter.

FROZEN FRUITS

Sorbets, granitas and spooms

This is a most refreshing subject, but owing to the many and often confusing terms associated with it not by any means an easy one to master; nor are its techniques by any means uniform. A sorbet used to be widely regarded as an iced drink and prepared accordingly. But, whatever we may care to call them today, the fact remains that fruit ices represent the oldest of all methods of preparing iced food. Fruit juice poured over cracked ice, or just snow, is itself already a complete iced dessert. That is the basic recipe for the Persian *sharbat* – hence our name for it, sorbet – as also for *frio frio*, that thirst-quencher popular all over the Caribbean, where little cardboard bags of crushed ice are peddled in the streets. With only a shot of fruit syrup poured over it, it's ready to eat (or rather, drink) the better-class traders offering a choice of two or three colours. Very noticeable differences of flavour, however, are not guaranteed.

History does not appear to record the origin of the fruit ice, be it ice with fruit or ice with the juices obtained from them, but it would seem that its development took a parallel course in each of several different cultures. We do know the ancestry of sorbet, from the Persian *sharbat*. *Sharbat*, *sherbet*, or the French *sorbet*: it is not only the word that has changed. Over the centuries innumerable different recipes have been created and the Italian and the French cuisines in particular have produced some of the most imaginative. A study of the relevant literature will show that up to the present century the sorbet was understood to be an iced drink of Eastern origin consisting of fruit juice or fruit served with syrup, cracked ice and often with small pieces of fruit in it as well. For a long time it had been served at banquets as a refreshing interlude before the main course.

More recently this custom has regained popularity, but the sorbets have transferred themselves from a drink into a light fruit ice of creamy texture, in which the 'fruit' may well take the form of champagne. To a greater extent the sorbet in its many shapes and forms has taken over the rôle of the sweet course. In the *nouvelle cuisine* with its emphasis on light meals it has become the classic dessert – and rightly so because its composition enables it to be a low-calorie dish that is relatively simple to make and yet lends itself more than any other dessert to innumerable variations – a circumstance which can also unfortunately lead to gastronomic solecisms.

A sorbet is variable not only in the composition of the frozen mixture but also in the manner in which it is served. It can be combined with all sorts of sauces and liqueurs, with everyday soft fruit or with exotics. Even vegetables like tomatoes and cucumbers are used in it by many exponents of the *nouvelle cuisine* school.

The consistency of a sorbet can also be varied, from a semi-fluid state when it is served in glasses to firm portions served on plates or in bowls.

Granita or granolata, punch and spoom are names for certain sorbet variations. Their formulae are as diverse as the ways in which they are frozen. Thus a granita is frozen crystal-clear as far as possible and is especially cool and refreshing, while a spoom – which has sweetened beaten egg white (meringue) folded into it – is like a fragrant, frothy dream.

A tip: it pays to put serving glasses, bowls or plates in the refrigerator or freezer in advance so that these delicacies do not melt away too rapidly.

Champagne granita with fruits
Granité au champagne aux fruits

Choose a shallow, freezer-proof dish and dust it all over inside with sugar. Pour in two-thirds of a bottle of champagne and freeze it. Then scrape the ice out with a spoon and fill some glasses with the ice together with fresh berries. Finally pour on the rest of the champagne, well chilled.

Granita

What the Italians call *granita* and the French call *granité* is surely the nearest thing to the original sorbet, the Persian *sharbat*. It is made with sharp-tasting fruit juice, wine or champagne and little added sweetening. Because of the low sugar content small crystals form in the freezing, hence its name. Whether you prefer a coarse or a somewhat finer texture, a granita should always give an impression of crushed ice.

Burgundy Granita

Granité au vin de bourgogne

175 g/6 oz sugar, plus 2 tablespoons
2 tablespoons water
juice of 1 lime and 1 orange
small bunch lemon balm leaves
1 bottle good Burgundy
250 ml/8 fl oz double or
whipping cream
fresh fruit, e.g. blackberries

Gently boil 175 g/6 oz of the sugar with the water, lime juice, orange juice and lemon balm leaves for 2 to 3 minutes. Leave to get cold, strain and then add to the Burgundy. Stir through well, pour it into as flat a freezerproof container as possible and put it into the freezer. When the liquid starts to freeze at the edges, stir it thoroughly with a spoon and repeat this process more or less frequently according to the fineness of the granulation desired. Then scrape off the frozen liquid, spoon it into tall glasses and decorate with whipped cream sweetened with the remaining sugar, and fresh fruit. Serves 10 to 12.

The granulation is variable. Depending on the sugar content it is possible to let the granita freeze without stirring and then simply scrape it up with a spoon. It freezes most quickly around the edge of the container, and so can be taken first from here. Alternatively, crystals forming at the edge can be repeatedly stirred into the still fluid middle part.

Peppermint Granita

Granité à la menthe

60 g/2½ oz icing sugar
1 bottle dry champagne
juice of 1 lemon
1 tablespoon chopped
fresh peppermint leaves
crème de menthe

Dust a shallow, flat-bottomed container, such as a watertight Swiss roll tin, with icing sugar. Combine the champagne with the lemon juice and peppermint leaves and pour it onto the layer of icing sugar. Let it freeze. When ready, shave off the ice with a spoon, spoon it into glasses and pour 2 tablespoons crème de menthe liqueur over each. Serves 8 to 10.

Sharbat-e-Riwas

Rhubarb granita

575 g/1¼ lb fresh rhubarb
a strip of lemon peel
375 ml/13 fl oz water
500 g/18 oz sugar

Peel the rhubarb and cut into roughly 2.5-cm/1-in pieces. Bring to the boil, with the lemon peel and water, over a fierce heat in a large pan (not copper or tin). Reduce the heat, cover the pan and cook the rhubarb till really soft (10 to 15 minutes). Let it cool a little and pass it through a fine sieve. Make this purée up to 500 ml/17 fl oz with water, add the sugar and boil steadily over a good heat. Do not cover the pan. Test it after 5 minutes: a drop of the syrup in iced water should at once congeal. Let it get cold and serve with crushed ice.

A true Persian *sharbat* is made by simply pouring syrup over finely crushed ice, with which fruits such as cherries or melon balls can also be mixed. Adding mineral water turns the dessert into a long drink.

A Tropical Refresher

This is a king-coconut granitá, made from what we might call the 'drinking coconut', since in many tropical countries it is the best refresher that can be imagined. Its liquid is more aromatic than that of ordinary coconuts, and there is more of it, hidden under the thick shell which is a most efficient insulator and keeps this delicious drink pleasantly cool in the hottest weather.

2 king coconuts (yielding about
900 ml/1½ pints liquid)
50 g/2 oz icing sugar
juice of 1 lime
juice of 1 lemon
3 tablespoons dark rum
2 ripe mangoes
50 g/2 oz soft brown sugar
4 tablespoons wild strawberry sauce

Combine the coconut liquid, icing sugar, lime and lemon juices and rum and put in a shallow freezerproof container into the freezer. When ice starts to form around the edges stir it into the middle with a spoon and repeat several times until the ice crystals have reached the desired granular texture. Spoon them into glasses or the emptied coconut shells and serve with pieces of mango and wild strawberry sauce. The mangoes should first be peeled, cut into small pieces, sprinkled with the brown sugar and left for an hour in the refrigerator to macerate.

Of course this recipe can be made with ordinary coconut liquid, but then it should have 100 ml/4 fl oz coconut milk squeezed from the copra added to it in order to strengthen the flavour. The granitá may be served either in the two empty coconut shells or in glasses which make distribution easier.

Serves about 8.

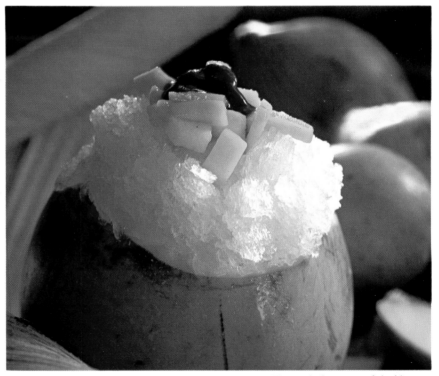

King-coconut granita, a most subtly flavoured tropical drink. The gentle fragrance of the king-coconut and a breath of the finest, dark West Indian rum partner each other perfectly in this granita. Together, spooned into the thick, protective coconut shell they can do without extra ingredients. However, the variation shown here, despite an admittedly foreign accent, can be highly recommended. The chunks of ripe mango are first dipped in soft brown sugar and then topped with some sauce made from fresh, wild strawberries.

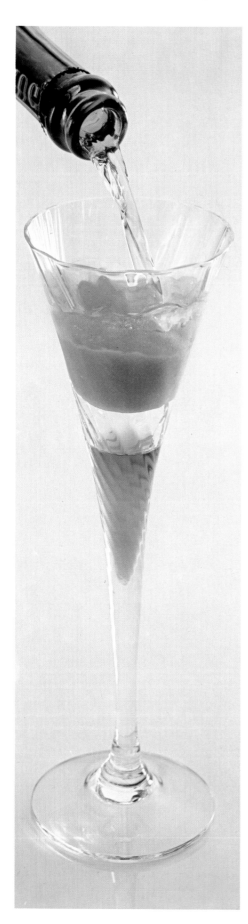

Sorbet As You Like It

To some this may mean a light ice dessert, to others an ice-cold drink. It can be made in whatever consistency you wish, but this will be determined partly by the sugar content and partly by the freezing time, and also by whether the sorbet is stirred manually while freezing or an electric ice cream machine used. These ideal ice cream machines are in fact what makes possible those creamy yet light sorbets so esteemed by the practitioners of the *nouvelle cuisine*. Alternatively, you can settle for the old-fashioned hand-operated ice cream churn surrounded by chipped ice, salt and saltpetre.

For a long time sorbets were, in principle, made only from strained fruit juices, wine or champagne. The modern cook is a little more flexible, and now these frozen specialities may also be made with puréed fruits. But these must be fresh and here an electric blender saves a great deal of trouble. Whether or not to strain out the remaining seeds and fragments of skin is a matter of taste.

How sweet should a sorbet be?

About 15° Baumé on the saccharometer. This is a medium density, which will ensure a light, creamy texture. The 15° provides a good guide but is no guarantee of quality and sorbets that are thinner, and thus not so sweet, may well taste better, depending on what fruits or sauces are served with them. The sugar content can also occasionally be higher if, for example, a glass containing a fruit sorbet is filled up with a very dry champagne. In other recipes sweetened beaten egg whites or whipped cream are added. Thus a strict rule would not make for better quality or the success of new, imaginative recipes. Basically you can only be wrong if the sorbet does not taste right.

A final tip: it is best to add sugar in liquid form, i.e. as syrup, which combines easily with the other ingredients. This is also the opportunity to bring spices to the boil at the same time, which brings out their full aroma. If time is short and no sugar syrup is available, icing sugar, which is relatively quick-dissolving, can be used instead.

Nectarine sorbet with champagne. The sorbet in this recipe can be transformed into almost a fluid and is then a delicious treat for special occasions. Put 2 teaspoons Amaretto into a tall champagne glass, add a scoop of nectarine sorbet and fill up with champagne.

A final check with the saccharometer. Not only the sugar content of the syrup but also the sugar density of the sorbet mixture as a whole can be measured with the saccharometer. It will take into account also the sugar components of the other ingredients such as fruit juice, fruit purée or wine. When fruit purée has been used, as in the left-hand picture, it may happen that the instrument will stick in the thick mixture and give a wrong reading. To give a correct reading it should be able to swing to and fro in the liquid, as in the right-hand picture which shows a thin mixture of fruit juices.

Nectarine Sorbet

Sorbet aux nectarines

According to the choice of sauces and fruits or added liqueurs many variations on this recipe are possible.

200 g/7 oz sugar
½ cinnamon stick
2 bitter almonds
2 tablespoons water
juice of 1 lime
575 g/1¼ lb nectarines (to yield
500 ml/17 fl oz fruit purée)

1 **Prepare the sugar syrup.** Bring the sugar and flavourings to the boil with the water to bring out their maximum flavour. Then let the syrup get cold and strain it. Stir the lime juice into the nectarine purée and mix all with the cold syrup.

An electric ice cream machine is the answer when it is a question of making a perfect sorbet. These very advanced, rather expensive, electric machines work quickly and will produce any degree of consistency from a semi fluid to a really firm fruit ice. Depending on the make of machine and the consistency desired freezing will take from 5 to 45 minutes. They are remarkably simple to operate: when the sorbet mixture is ready it is poured into the bowl of the machine, the timer adjusted and the machine switched on. At the end of the time the machine switches itself off automatically and the ice can be taken out. Cooks who like to make this kind of dessert at home often will certainly want this kind of gadget. The ice cream machine can have a capacity of 1 litre/1¾pints. This corresponds to the quantity required for about 8 to 10 servings. It is a great saver of time and work.

2 Freeze the sorbet mixture. Fill as large a vessel as possible with the mixture and put it into the freezer. When a layer of ice forms after about 30 minutes turn over the whole contents with a balloon whisk or electric hand mixer and return it to the freezer.

3 It must be repeatedly and thoroughly stirred. The consistency of the sorbet depends on how often this is done. The more it is stirred, the smoother it will be. Of course it will also take longer to freeze: that is, the more often it is stirred, the longer it will take to reach the desired firmness.

Nectarine sorbet with vanilla cream and redcurrant sauce. If the sorbet described on this page is to be combined with a fruit sauce it should be allowed to freeze fairly firmly: it has to be formed into individual portions easily and still retain a creamy lightness. Melt plain chocolate and make as many lattice decorations as you need. For the sauce, reduce redcurrant juice and sugar together, flavoured with a little cinnamon and lemon peel. Cool it. Flavour the cream with the seeds from a vanilla pod and whip it stiffly. Place a scoop of nectarine sorbet on the plate, put a spoonful of whipped cream next to it and pour fruit sauce around. Place a chocolate lattice on top.

Kiwi Sorbet

Sorbet aux kiwis

150 g/5 oz sugar
250 ml/8 fl oz water
450 g/1 lb kiwi fruit (about 5 or 6)
1 egg white
juice of 1 lemon
250 ml/8 fl oz white wine

Bring the sugar and water quickly to the boil and leave to get cold. Peel the kiwis and purée them in the blender. Pass half or all of the purée through a sieve so that there are not too many seeds in the sorbet. Whip the egg white, and fold it into the well-mixed fruit purée, lemon juice, white wine and sugar syrup. Freeze to a creamy consistency, and fill it into glasses with a spoon or a piping bag.
Serves 8 to 10.

Another variation with champagne: prepare the sorbet as above but instead of freezing it until creamy pour it into a shallow freezerproof container and let it get stiff in the freezer. Then scrape it out with a spoon, like a granita, serve it in glasses and pour champagne over.

Grapefruit Sorbet

Sorbet aux pamplemousses

175 g/6 oz sugar
2 tablespoons water
200 ml/7 fl oz pink grapefruit juice
(2 to 3 fruits)
juice of 1 lemon
250 ml/8 fl oz medium dry white wine
75 ml/2½ fl oz Campari
2 egg whites
lemon balm leaves for decoration

Boil the sugar and water to make a syrup and leave to get cold. Mix the grapefruit juice and lemon juice, strain them and add the wine, then combine them with the Campari and sugar syrup. Beat the egg whites half stiff and stir them energetically into the mixture with a balloon whisk. Freeze it so that it keeps fluffy by turning it over often or by making it in an ice cream machine. At the end decorate it with lemon balm leaves.
Serves 8 to 10.

The above made with wine: use 500 ml/17 fl oz instead of 250 ml/8 fl oz white wine and omit the egg whites. Then freeze like a granita in a shallow freezerproof container and scrape it into glasses.

Sour Cherry Sorbet

Sorbet aux griottes

175 g/6 oz sugar, plus 1 tablespoon
300 ml/½ pint water
1 piece cinnamon stick
500 g/18 oz fresh sour cherries
juice of ½ lemon
200 ml/7 fl oz whipped cream
seeds of ¼ vanilla pod
fresh cherries for decoration

Bring 175 g/6 oz of the sugar, the water and cinnamon quickly to the boil and leave to get cold. Take out the cinnamon. Stone the cherries and purée them in the blender, stir in the lemon juice, mix with the sugar syrup and freeze to a creamy consistency. Flavour the cream with the remaining sugar and vanilla seeds and whip it until thick, not too stiff. Put the sorbet into glasses with a spoon or through a piping bag, slip some whipped cream down the side and decorate with cherries.
Serves 8 to 10.

This is a semi-fluid variation: prepare the sorbet as above adding 250 ml/8 fl oz good Burgundy. Freeze only lightly and while still semi-fluid put into glasses. Top with whipped cream.

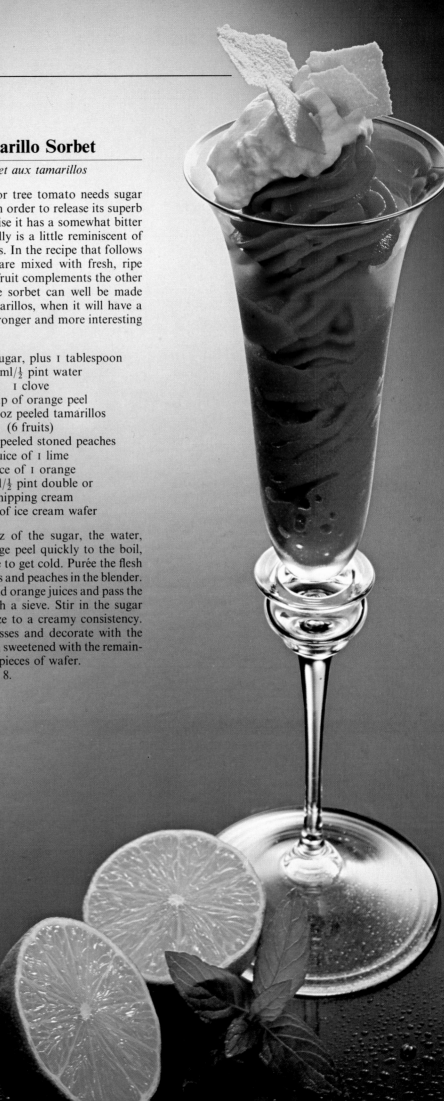

Tamarillo Sorbet

Sorbet aux tamarillos

The tamarillo or tree tomato needs sugar and fruit acid in order to release its superb aroma. Otherwise it has a somewhat bitter taste which really is a little reminiscent of unripe tomatoes. In the recipe that follows the tamarillos are mixed with fresh, ripe peaches. Each fruit complements the other ideally. But the sorbet can well be made solely with tamarillos, when it will have a considerably stronger and more interesting flavour.

150 g/5 oz sugar, plus 1 tablespoon
300 ml/½ pint water
1 clove
1 strip of orange peel
350 g/12 oz peeled tamarillos
(6 fruits)
250 g/8 oz peeled stoned peaches
juice of 1 lime
juice of 1 orange
300 ml/½ pint double or
whipping cream
pieces of ice cream wafer

Bring 150 g/5 oz of the sugar, the water, clove and orange peel quickly to the boil, strain and leave to get cold. Purée the flesh of the tamarillos and peaches in the blender. Add the lime and orange juices and pass the mixture through a sieve. Stir in the sugar syrup and freeze to a creamy consistency. Spoon into glasses and decorate with the whipped cream, sweetened with the remaining sugar, and pieces of wafer.
  Serves about 8.

Orange Sorbet

Sorbet aux oranges

150 g/6 oz sugar
150 ml/¼ pint water
rind of ½ orange
250 ml/8 fl oz freshly squeezed
orange juice
juice of 1 lime
250 ml/8 fl oz white wine
3 tablespoons Pernod
1 egg white
8 tablespoons sloe gin
slices of lime for decoration

Bring the sugar with the water and orange rind quickly to the boil, let it cool and strain it onto the orange juice. Add the lime juice, white wine and Pernod. Whip the egg white half stiff and fold it into the mixture with a balloon whisk. Freeze it to a smooth consistency. Put 1 tablespoon sloe gin into each glass first and then a scoop of sorbet. Decorate with a thin slice of lime.
  Serves about 8.

Two Sorbets with Exotic Fruits

In some respects the future is already here, or will be soon in our kitchens. It may take a little longer yet, but tropical fruits such as the bael and woodapple will undoubtedly before long become familiar in gastronomic circles here. In Sri Lanka these delicacies are marketed as sweetened preserves of the highest quality. And the prospect of all sorts of creations, combining mysterious fruits to delight our palates, arouses great expectations in us. These exotic curiosities present themselves as a completely new experience, whose flavour resembles that of none of the fruits we know: something really original and strange.

Mango Sorbet

Sorbet aux mangu

250 ml/8 fl oz mango purée
juice of $\frac{1}{2}$ lime
scant 150 ml/$\frac{1}{4}$ pint dry white wine
scant 150 ml/$\frac{1}{4}$ pint mineral water
1 egg white · 50 g/2 oz sugar

Mix the mango purée with the lime juice, white wine and mineral water. Whip the egg white to a snow, trickling in the sugar. When the sugar has thoroughly dissolved in it, fold the egg white into the mango mixture and freeze all to a creamy consistency.
Serves 6 to 8.

Woodapple Sorbet

Sorbet aux woodapples

75 g/3 oz sugar
1 clove
scant 150 ml/$\frac{1}{4}$ pint water
250 ml/8 fl oz woodapple cream
150 ml/$\frac{1}{4}$ pint plain yoghurt
juice of 1 lime
generous pinch of cinnamon
4 tablespoons sauternes
150 ml/$\frac{1}{4}$ pint crème de menthe liqueur
and peppermint leaves for decoration

Bring the sugar and clove to the boil in the water, leave the syrup to get cold and discard the clove. Blend the woodapple cream and yoghurt together. Mix it well with the syrup, lime juice and cinnamon. Next thoroughly beat in the yoghurt and the wine. Freeze the whole mixture to a creamy consistency. Pour about 2 tablespoons crème de menthe over each portion and decorate it with peppermint leaves.
Serves about 6 to 8.

Mangosteen Sorbet

Sorbet aux mangostanes

Mangosteens are among the finest and most noble fruits that tropical lands have to offer. They are unsurpassed in combination with dry champagne. Serve a fresh wild strawberry sauce with the sorbet, and you would think these fruits were specially created for one another.

150 g/5 oz prepared mangosteens
(about 5 to 6 fruits)
scant 150 ml/¼ pint dry champagne
1 egg white
50 g/2 oz sugar
6 slices of lime

Peel the mangosteens, chop the flesh and push it through a fine sieve. Stir the champagne into the purée. Whip the egg white to a snow, trickling in the sugar, and when this has fully dissolved fold the egg white carefully into the fruit purée and freeze all to a creamy consistency. Partner the sorbet with a sauce of wild strawberries and decorate each portion with a slice of lime.
Serves 4 to 6.

Tamarind Sorbet

Sorbet aux tamarindes

An incomparable aroma is created through the combination of tamarinds with well-ripened mangoes.

150 g/5 oz tamarind pods (to yield
50 g/2 oz fruit flesh)
100 ml/4 fl oz hot water · 100 g/4 oz sugar
1 well-ripened mango (about 400 g/14 oz)
250 ml/8 fl oz mineral water
chocolate straws and icing sugar
for decoration

Peel the tamarinds and separate the flesh from the seeds. Put it into an earthenware bowl, cover with the hot water and leave to soak for some hours, preferably overnight. Afterwards add the sugar, bring it to the boil, reduce the heat and continue cooking for 3 to 4 minutes. Push the mixture through a fine sieve and leave it to get cold. Peel the mango, remove the stone and purée the flesh (you should get some 250 ml/8 fl oz). Mix the purée with the cold tamarind syrup, stir in the mineral water and freeze it all to a creamy consistency. Pipe the sorbet into individual glasses through a piping bag fitted with a round nozzle. Decorate each portion with chocolate straws and a little icing sugar. Serves about 6.

Melon Sorbet

Sorbet au melon

50 g/2 oz sugar
2 tablespoons honey
1 tablespoon lemon juice
200 ml/7 fl oz water
1 cantaloup melon (about
575 g/1½ lb)
2 tablespoons brandy
fresh peppermint leaves

Cook the sugar, honey and lemon juice together with the water until the sugar has dissolved. Leave this syrup to get cold. Halve the melon, remove the seeds and cut out 18 melon balls with a melon or potato scoop, or the flesh may be diced. Put the melon balls or cubes into a bowl, sprinkle them with the brandy, cover them and put them in the refrigerator. Purée the rest of the melon (about 300 g/11 oz), mix it well with the syrup, and freeze it to a creamy consistency in an ice cream machine. Serve portions with a spoon into each glass, add 3 cubes or balls of melon and a few peppermint leaves and top the arrangement with a further spoonful of sorbet.
Serves about 6. For a very successful, though more liquid, variation pour some dry champagne or sparkling white wine over the sorbet.

Redcurrant Sorbet

Sorbet Aux Groseilles

450 g/1 lb redcurrants
scant 150 ml/¼ pint sauternes
2 egg whites
100 g/4 oz sugar
6 to 8 tinned peach halves
crème de cassis liqueur

Purée the redcurrants, add the wine and sieve this. Whip the egg whites to a snow, letting the sugar trickle in slowly. Fold it into the redcurrant purée with a balloon whisk and freeze till creamy. Place half a peach, cut side upwards, on each plate, sprinkle it with crème de cassis and pipe the sorbet onto it. Serves 6 to 8.

Coconut Sorbet

Sorbet à la noix de coco

250 ml/8 fl oz tinned coconut juice
scant 150 ml/¼ pint mineral water
2 tablespoons dark rum
2 egg whites
100 g/4 oz sugar
2 bananas
chocolate sauce

Mix the coconut juice with the mineral water and the rum. Whip the egg whites to a snow, letting the sugar trickle in slowly. Stir the egg snow into the coconut mixture with a balloon whisk, and freeze till creamy. Arrange on plates with sliced banana and chocolate sauce. Serves about 6.

Apple Sorbet with Mango Sauce

Sorbet aux pommes à la sauce de mangue

450 g/1 lb tart apples
scant 150 ml/¼ pint Beaujolais
scant 150 ml/¼ pint dry cider
juice of 1 lemon
100 g/4 oz sugar
a piece of cinnamon stick
2 mangoes (about 350 g/12 oz flesh)

Peel and cut up the apples. Cook them with the Beaujolais, cider, lemon juice, sugar and cinnamon for 2 to 3 minutes. Remove the piece of cinnamon stick and purée the mixture. Let it get cold and then freeze to a creamy consistency. To make the sauce, peel the ripe mangoes and remove from the stones. Purée the flesh in the blender and chill well. Serves about 6.

Spooms

These are the frothiest and sweetest kind of sorbet. Meringue is incorporated into the frozen sorbet, generally made of wine or champagne, and the mixture served in glasses.

Pink Champagne Spoom

Spoom au champagne rosé

300 g/9 oz sugar · 300 ml/½ pint water
1 teaspoon ginger syrup
juice of 1 lemon and 1 orange
500 ml/17 fl oz pink champagne or
red Sekt
3 egg whites · 5 tinned peach halves

Bring 150 g/5 oz of the sugar, the water, ginger syrup and lemon and orange juices to the boil. Cool, and mix with the champagne or Sekt. Freeze it firmer than a normal sorbet, then fold in the meringue (made from the remaining sugar and the egg whites beaten to a stiff snow) into the sorbet. Serve in glasses with slices of tinned peach.
Serves 10.

Sauternes Spoom

Spoom au vin de Sauternes

250 g/9 oz sugar
300 ml/½ pint water
juice of 2 limes
2 fresh peppermint leaves
600 ml/1 pint sauternes
3 egg whites
cherry brandy

Bring 100 g/4 oz of the sugar, the water, lime juice and peppermint leaves to the boil. Leave it to cool then strain into the Sauternes. Freeze the sorbet, and incorporate the meringue, made with the egg whites and remaining sugar beaten to a stiff snow. Serve it in glasses with a spoon or a piping bag, and add to each a tablespoon of cherry brandy, poured over the top or down the side.
Serves about 10.

Fold in the meringue. Italian meringue is the name given to sweetened, beaten egg whites. Preferably use a chilled wooden spoon to incorporate it with the frozen sorbet. Although it is quicker with a balloon whisk, the mixture will liquefy more easily.

THE CREAM OF ICE CREAMS

Ice bombes, frozen soufflés and parfaits

When at the end of a splendid dinner the ice bombe makes its appearance it is not just a question of its merely being served: it assumes the centre of the stage. The star of the show often used to materialise out of total darkness – and sometimes still does – so that the amazing achievement of the ice sculptor's art would appear the more dazzling and impressive. All the lights in the dining room were extinguished and the waiters filed in, every available one, each holding aloft a block of ice with a pink or blue or green light inside it, on which sat enthroned a glittering creation that was met with a universal gasp of delight: the ice bombe, the very perfection of culinary artistry. Today it is made of ice cream cunningly composed in several layers: a very firm one enfolding and supporting another one of a rather softer texture, and right in the middle a surprise, perhaps something dry and crisp, or maybe fruit or some melting sweetmeat.

The special ices – the parfaits, iced cakes and bombes – are also naturally the most difficult to make and, as more frozen iced desserts come on the market, a host or hostess is inclined to pack away a collection of such ready-made products in the freezer, breathe a sigh of relief and say: 'There, I've got it in stock; I'm all right whatever happens. Let them all come, even without warning, I'm ready for them – I only have to get the bombe out of the freezer and put it on the table.' For party-givers a first-class iced dessert has the further great advantage that, like a cream or a fresh fruit salad, it can be prepared at a convenient moment and is thus a ready-to-serve item on the menu that needs no further attention while the meal is being prepared. This gives the cook a certain amount of peace and quiet, and more time to be with his or her guests. Both these advantages apply as much to the bought as to the home-made article, but those who like to honour their guests with original dishes, or who are quite simply so fond of cooking that they lose no opportunity for creative experiment, will make their own bombe. But if they wish to take one or two short cuts or if, as is very likely, no large or expensive ice cream maker is at hand, so that even the preparation of the various foundation ice creams presents a problem, the use of some commercially made ice cream is a perfectly justifiable alternative, for almost all ice cream manufacturers market at least one luxury variety that can be adapted to the recipes on the following pages.

How best to combine the bought with the home-made is often determined by circumstances, but in general it is the basic flavours that are of the highest quality: vanilla, hazelnut or chocolate for example. But the fruit ice creams made from blackcurrants, tropical fruits or wild berries have a stronger and fresher taste when they have been made at home. It is a good thing to build up a reserve of first-rate ingredients, making use of the various fruit seasons as they come around. Your reward will be an iced dessert which can be brought to the table with as much ceremony, and eaten with as much pleasure, as that from the grandest restaurant.

The grandest frozen desserts are the parfaits, the moulded iced soufflés and the soaring ice bombes. Their creation requires a sure instinct for combining flavours and a feeling and imaginative flair for creative design. The recipes on pages 183 and 185 will give more information about these.

Neapolitan Ice Cream Cake

Crème glacée Neapolitan

550 ml/18 fl oz double or whipping cream
100 g/4 oz caster sugar
plus 1 tablespoon
50 g/2 oz plain chocolate
seeds of $\frac{1}{2}$ vanilla pod
75 g/3 oz puréed fresh strawberries
a 1-litre/1$\frac{3}{4}$-pint rectangular mould

Stiffly whip 450 ml/$\frac{3}{4}$ pint of the cream with the 100 g/4 oz sugar and divide equally between 3 chilled bowls. For the first layer stir in the chocolate, previously melted in a double boiler, into one portion of cream. Spread this chocolate cream mixture into the mould and freeze it for about 10 minutes. Meanwhile stir the vanilla seeds into the second bowl of whipped cream. Spread this over the chocolate layer and

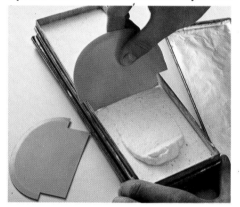

1 **Individual layers** can be levelled off accurately by a simple device. Cut two dough scrapers to the correct size for fitting in the rectangular mould down to the desired level. Line the bottom and the lid of the mould with kitchen foil to avoid difficulty in opening the mould after freezing.

2 **Neapolitan slices** are typical of the ice creams in the 'lightly frozen' category. They consist of whipped cream with the traditional flavourings: chocolate, vanilla and strawberry. Ice creams may be frozen in any form you wish, but with the brick-shaped mould serving out portions is no problem.

freeze for 25 minutes. Blend the third bowl of cream with the tablespoon of sugar and the strawberry purée, and fill up the mould. Freeze for at least 3 to 4 hours. Cut into 8 blocks and decorate each with the remaining whipped cream and a quarter strawberry. Serves 8.

Iced Orange Soufflé

Soufflé glacé a l'orange

8 egg yolks · 275 g/10 oz sugar
3 leaves gelatine or 15 g/$\frac{1}{2}$ oz
powdered gelatine
300 ml/$\frac{1}{2}$ pint fresh orange juice
2 tablespoons Cointreau
4 egg whites
350 ml/12 fl oz double or whipping cream
2 tablespoons cocoa powder for dusting
1.25-litre/2$\frac{1}{4}$-pint freezerproof soufflé dish

Cream the egg yolks with 125 g/4$\frac{1}{2}$ oz of the sugar. Put in the softened and well squeezed out gelatine leaves or the powdered gelatine and warm the mixture in a double boiler stirring constantly, until the mixture is thick enough to coat a spoon lightly. Remove from the heat and stir in the strained orange juice and the Cointreau. Transfer to a large mixing bowl and chill for about 30 minutes in the refrigerator until the mixture becomes syrupy. Stiffly whip the egg whites, trickling in all but 2 tablespoons of the remaining sugar by degrees.

Fold this into the chilled orange mixture with a balloon whisk. Stiffly whip the cream with the remaining sugar and fold it in carefully with a wooden spoon. Fix a paper collar around the soufflé dish, pour in the mixture and freeze.

Serves 10 to 12.

1 **Beaten egg whites and whipped cream** make this a particularly light soufflé. First the stiff egg snow is folded with a balloon whisk into the cold egg yolk mixture which with the added gelatine is now very creamy. Only then fold in the whipped cream carefully with a wooden spoon.

2 **Pour in the soufflé mixture.** Make a collar of kitchen parchment, folded double for extra strength, and cut it so that it rises 4 to 5 cm about 2 in above the rim of the soufflé dish. Wrap it around and secure it with two strips of tape. Chill the prepared soufflé dish before filling it.

3 **At least 4 hours' freezing time** will be needed to set the soufflé right through. Do not take off the paper collar before this. Finally, sift cocoa powder over the top, or you can decorate the soufflé with whipped cream and in that case sprinkle it with some finely chopped candied orange peel.

4 **The iced orange soufflé** with its top dressing of cocoa powder does not merely look like its namesake that is served hot, it is also extraordinarily light. Equal portions can be cut with a knife, or it may be served with a spoon. Chocolate sauce is an excellent partner.

'Bénédictine' Iced Soufflé

Soufflé glacé 'Bénédictine'

20 sponge fingers
4 tablespoons Bénédictine
7 egg yolks
grated rind of 1 orange and 1 lime
250 g/9 oz sugar
600 ml/1 pint double or whipping cream
1.5-litre/2¾-pint freezerproof
soufflé dish

For decoration:
cocoa powder, whipped cream, a
chocolate flower and a
glacé cherry.

Trim the sponge fingers to a point as illustrated for the final decoration of the soufflé. Lay the trimmings in the soufflé dish already prepared with a parchment collar and sprinkle them with 1½ tablespoons of the Bénédictine. Beat the egg yolks with an electric mixer. Bring the grated orange and lime rind to the boil in a saucepan with the sugar and 4 tablespoons water and reduce for about 4 minutes. Then add this hot syrup in a thin stream, stirring continuously, to the beaten egg yolks and beat them for a further 10 minutes before adding the rest of the liqueur. Stiffly whip the cream and with a wooden spoon fold it into the egg yolk mixture. Pour it into the previously chilled soufflé dish, cover with the sponge fingers in flower-petal formation and freeze for at least 4 hours. Sift some cocoa powder over and decorate with a rosette of whipped cream, the chocolate flower and the cherry. Serves about 12.

Vanilla Parfait

Parfait à la vanille

As with creams and sauces, the vanilla version of the parfait is the basic recipe on which the variations are constructed.

6 egg yolks · 200 g/7 oz sugar
250 ml/8 fl oz milk · 1 vanilla pod
350 ml/12 fl oz double or
whipping cream
1.5-litre/2¾-pint freezerproof mould

Prepare the egg custard in the same way as the English custard on page 54. Beat the egg yolks with the sugar, add the hot, vanilla-flavoured milk and cook the custard till it coats the spoon lightly. Transfer it to a mixing bowl and beat it till cold, then fold in the stiffly whipped cream.

The basic recipe for 'Bénédictine' iced soufflé can with a few alterations be turned into a 'Grand Marnier' or 'Cointreau' iced soufflé. Only the specific liqueur need be changed, since all three are wholly compatible with orange and lime flavours. A soufflé may also be built up in differently flavoured layers. For example: prepare the recipe for iced orange soufflé on the opposite page, substituting rum for the Cointreau, and put the finished mixture into two bowls. Stir 100 g/4 oz melted chocolate into one half, pour it into the soufflé dish and top with the orange mixture.

1 **Beat the English custard** with the electric mixer at medium speed for about 15 minutes until cool. It should have a good airy and creamy texture. Let it get quite cold in the refrigerator: the temperature of the custard and the whipped cream must be the same. Chill the mould in the freezer.

2 **Fold the whipped cream into the custard.** This should be done with a wooden spoon and the stiffly whipped cream incorporated into the vanilla custard very carefully a little at a time so that it loses as little volume as possible. Then pour the mixture into the mould and freeze for at least 3 hours.

Brandy parfait/Parfait à *l'eau-de-vle de vin*. Beat 6 egg yolks with 200 g/7 oz sugar. Bring 250 ml/8 fl oz milk to the boil with a vanilla pod and stir it by degrees into the beaten egg yolks and sugar. As with the basic custard, heat the mixture till it thickens sufficiently to coat the spoon, then beat it till cool and add 4 tablespoons brandy. Chill thoroughly: the temperature of the custard must be the same as that of stiffly-whipped cream which now has to be folded into it with a wooden spoon. Freeze in a 1.5-litre/2¾-pint rectangular freezerproof mould and serve it sliced with a fresh fig sauce sprinkled with coarsely ground pink pepper corns. Serves 12 to 15.

Chestnut parfait/Parfait aux marrons. Make a basic parfait base from 4 egg yolks, 150 g/5 oz sugar, a scant 150 ml/¼ pint milk and 1 vanilla pod. Stir in 200 g/7 oz unsweetened chestnut purée and 2 tablespoons dark rum while the mixture is still lukewarm. Chill well. Whip 2 egg whites with 50 g/2 oz sugar to a very stiff snow, and stiffly whip 500 ml/17 fl oz cream also. With a balloon whisk first fold the beaten egg white into the chestnut custard and then carefully fold in the whipped cream. Pour it into a 1.5-litre/2¾-pint bombe mould and freeze for at least 3 to 4 hours. For the decoration shape miniature chestnuts out of sweetened chestnut purée and dip them in melted chocolate. Make a cranberry sauce to go with it. Serves about 12.

Walnut parfait/Parfait aux noix. Melt 75 g/3 oz sugar in a saucepan. Add 100 g/4 oz coarsely chopped walnuts and as soon as the nuts are caramellised let the brittle cool on a very lightly oiled baking sheet and break it up roughly. Make a simple parfait base (see the recipe for vanilla parfait on page 181) from 4 egg yolks, 50 g/2 oz honey, 75 g/3 oz sugar, 200 ml/7 fl oz and ½ vanilla pod, chill and stir in 2 tablespoons fresh lime juice. Stiffly whip 300 ml/½ pint cream and together with the chopped nut brittle stir it into the custard. Freeze in a 1-litre/1¾-pint rectangular freezerproof mould and serve with chocolate sauce. Serves 12.

Ceylon tea parfait/Parfait au thé de Ceylon. Pour 250 ml/8 fl oz boiling water over 40 g/1½ oz Ceylon tea, let it infuse for 4 to 5 minutes, squeeze through a cloth and bring to the boil with 100 ml/4 fl oz milk. Make a basic parfait mixture from 4 egg yolks with 150 g/5 oz soft brown sugar and the milky tea. Stir in 2 tablespoons dark rum. Stiffly whip 300 ml/½ pint cream and stir it into the parfait mixture when well chilled. Pour it into a 1-litre/1¾-pint rectangular freezerproof mould lined with kitchen parchment and freeze for at least 3 and preferably 4 to 5 hours. Turn out and slice the parfait. Serve with fresh mango sauce. Serves 12.

Poppy Seed or Hazelnut Parfait

Parfait pavot aux noisettes

Only fresh poppy seeds should be used.

100 g/4 oz poppy seeds or
ground toasted hazelnuts
1 vanilla pod
250 ml/8 fl oz milk
4 egg yolks
100 g/4 oz sugar
1 tablespoon honey
400 ml/14 fl oz double or
whipping cream
1 sponge cake base
a 1.25-litre/2¼-pint ring mould

For decoration:

25 g/1 oz toasted, flaked almonds
250 ml/8 fl oz double or
whipping cream
2 tablespoons caster sugar
1 tablespoon kirsch
a little cocoa powder
12 tinned sour cherries

Cook the poppy seeds or ground hazelnuts together with the vanilla pod in half the milk for about 8 to 10 minutes. Take out the vanilla pod and scrape the seeds back into the milk. Beat the egg yolks with the sugar, bring the rest of the milk to the boil with the honey and then gradually stir it into the egg yolks and sugar mixture. As with an English custard, cook the mixture until it begins to thicken.

Let it cool, stir in the poppy seed or hazelnut mixture and then chill it well. Stiffly whip the cream with the caster sugar and fold it into the poppy seed mixture with a wooden spoon. Pour it into the ring mould and freeze for at least 3 to 4 hours.

Turn the parfait out onto the spongecake base, trimming off any surplus from around the outside and the middle of the sponge cake. Press the almonds around the base of the parfait. Stiffly whip the cream with the sugar and kirsch. Pipe 12 rosettes round the top with a piping bag and star nozzle, sift a little cocoa powder onto each and top with a cherry.

Serves 12.

As for all turned-out desserts, a parfait mould should preferably be made of thin metal so that it need only be dipped in hot water for a moment in order to loosen the dessert. With thick earthenware moulds it is impossible to tell exactly how long this might take. Rectangular moulds can be lined with kitchen parchment or aluminium foil before use, and the ice will then almost drop out by itself or a hot kitchen cloth laid over the mould for a moment or two will suffice.

Mocha Parfait

Parfait au mocca

(Illustrated on page 178)

6 egg yolks
225 g/8 oz sugar
25 g/1 oz ground coffee
scant 150 ml/¼ pint double or
whipping cream
2 tablespoons brandy
6 kiwi fruit
350 ml/12 fl oz whipped cream
1.5-litre/2¾-pint rectangular
freezerproof mould

Beat the egg yolks with the sugar, brew the coffee with a scant 150 ml/¼ pint boiling water and add, with the cream, to the egg yolk mixture. Continue to cook it like an English custard. Add the brandy and chill thoroughly. Fold in the stiffly whipped cream with a wooden spoon, pour the mixture into a mould and freeze it. Serve with sliced fresh kiwi fruit and whipped cream.
Serves 12.

Bombes

When an ice cream is served with a scoop or, as in the case of a parfait or ice bombe, cut into slices it is necessary to work rapidly and in the coolest possible conditions. But there is an art in the making of ice bombes, where ice creams of varying consistencies are used together, and it really demands a professional approach: it is the technique that is different, not the materials. The essence of a bombe is the building up of its several layers from the shell to the centre. The outside shell is a custard ice cream which makes a good lining for the mould. This can, or should, be followed by a second layer, and the centre must then be an ice cream or a parfait. The problem for us is that a mould holding 1 litre/1¾ pints needs about 350 g/12 oz custard ice cream for the outer layer. That, for the professional, is quite

simple – he can draw on his stock of ice cream varieties. But at home it is hardly practical to make such a small quantity for just one layer. One solution is to use bought ice cream which, however, does not process so well.

Also, there must be long periods of waiting while the bombe is in the freezer between each stage of the operation. The ideal answer is to use a small electric ice cream machine like the one pictured on page 171. With this gadget lovers of ice bombes need fret no longer because it will produce fresh ice cream in any desired amount.

1 **The first layer,** or outside coat, always consists of custard ice cream, since this is the only kind that is sufficiently dense to cling successfully to the chilled mould. Put the mould in a bowl of ice cubes and spread the custard ice cream into it evenly with a spoon. There should be no gaps between the mould and the ice cream.

2 **Another kind of custard ice** cream is spread in, after the first has been left to freeze for 30 minutes. Trim off surplus ice cream from the first layer and spread in the second evenly. Briefly freeze and trim this also, then fill up the mould with the parfait. Let it harden again in the freezer.

3 **Seal the bombe with a layer of the custard ice cream** used for the outside coat or, alternatively, a thin layer of sponge cake. The filling will have shrunk somewhat and so made room for it. Finally cover it with a round of greaseproof paper cut to size, and put on the lid.

4 **Pull off the paper** when the ice bombe is quite firmly frozen. It should then be briefly dipped in hot water to loosen it slightly. It is important that the water should reach the top of the rim, otherwise the bombe will still cling fast around the rim and become too soft lower down.

5 **Hold the bombe with one hand,** and revolve the mould with the other. This can only be done with a hemispherical mould. More complicated ones must be tapped on the table till the ice cream loosens. Run some cold water over the turned-out bombe. It freezes and makes a smooth surface.

6 **The decoration must not be too elaborate.** If it is, the bombe will begin to melt. So stand it for a moment in the freezer and have the whipped cream and other decorations all ready. Any of the ingredients in the bombe itself would be suitable, or decorations made from chocolate, meringue or wafer pastry.

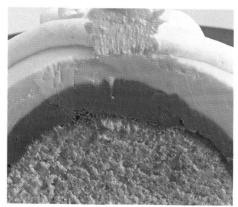

7 **The first cut will show how carefully the work has been done.** First and foremost, of course, the composition must be a harmony of flavours. But the eye should be able to feast too and so the individual layers should also be built of happy combinations of colours.

Which Shape for an Ice Bombe?

Old ice bombe moulds have a well-fitting lid and often a handle too. This was necessary since the bombes were frozen in block ice with salt. The best ones were made of copper, a good conducter of heat and cold which helps the bombe to freeze quickly. Even today, the mould should be made of the thinnest possible metal so that a quick dip in hot water will loosen the bombe, if it is to be turned out. Alternatively the filled mould can be placed upside-down on a chilled plate, a hot towel laid over it and the mould itself lifted off.

Pistachio Ice Bombe

Bombe glacée aux pistaches

(Illustrated opposite)

450 ml/15 fl oz vanilla custard ice
cream, unfrozen
250 ml/8 fl oz chocolate custard
ice cream, unfrozen
scant 150 ml/¼ pint milk
50 g/2 oz finely chopped pistachio nuts
2 egg yolks
100 g/4 oz sugar
2 tablespoons maraschino liqueur
150 ml/¼ pint double or whipping cream
1-litre/1¾-pint ice bombe mould

For decoration:
250 ml/8 fl oz cream · 25 g/1 oz sugar
1 tablespoon maraschino liqueur
1 tablespoon chopped pistachio nuts,
meringue flowers and chocolate leaves

Freeze the freshly made vanilla custard ice cream then spread three-quarters of this around the inner surface of the chilled mould. A freshly made custard makes an ice cream which is especially creamy and easy to spread. Keep the rest of it in the freezer to use for the base. While the vanilla layer is freezing hard, freeze the chocolate custard ice cream. Then after about 30 minutes spread it also into the mould as a second layer. Leave it again for 30 minutes to set in the freezer and meanwhile prepare the pistachio parfait. Bring the milk to the boil with the pistachio nuts. Beat the egg yolks with the sugar and maraschino over hot water until the mixture is hot and creamy. Pour on the warm pistachio nut milk and stir till cold.

Stiffly whip the cream and fold it into the pistachio nut custard. Fill up the mould with the parfait mixture then put it back into the freezer. It will be firm enough after 2 hours for the rest of the vanilla ice cream to

be spread on top. Cover the mould with paper and the lid and finish freezing. Serves about 8.

Cherry Ice Bombe

Bombe glacée aux cerises

(Illustrated on page 178)

300 ml/½ pint chocolate custard
ice cream, unfrozen
300 ml/½ pint mocha custard ice
cream, unfrozen
100 g/4 oz glacé cherries
2 tablespoons kirsch
250 ml/8 fl oz double or whipping cream
50 g/2 oz icing sugar
generous pinch vanilla seeds
a sponge base, about 1.5 cm/½ in
thick, to fit the mould
1-litre/1¾-pint ice bombe mould

For decoration:
250 ml ¾ pint whipping cream
25 g/1 oz sugar
cocoa powder for dusting
1 meringue bee

Freeze the freshly made chocolate custard ice cream, spread it over the inside of the chilled mould and put it into the freezer. Prepare the mocha ice cream and after 30 minutes in the freezer make the second layer in the mould with it. Freeze again. Coarsely chop the glacé cherries and macerate them in the kirsch in a covered container. Stiffly whip the cream with the sugar and vanilla, combine it with the cherries and their liquid and fill up the ice bombe with the mixture. Leave it in the freezer for 3 hours, then turn it out onto the sponge cake layer and decorate with vanilla-flavoured and sweetened whipped cream piped through a piping bag, using a round nozzle. Pipe the entire surface with whipped cream, as shown on page 178, then dust with cocoa powder and place the meringue bee on top. Serves 8.

Strawberry Ice Roll

Roulade glacée aux fraises

(Illustrated on page 178)

Swiss roll batter (half the recipe on
page 62)
450 g/1 lb ripe strawberries
175 g/6 oz icing sugar
juice of 1 lemon · 350 ml/12 fl oz cream
icing sugar for dusting

Spread the Swiss roll into a baking sheet to form a rectangle some 25 × 35 cm/

10 × 13 in. Bake and cool it thoroughly, covered with a damp cloth. Purée the strawberries and mix them with the sugar and lemon juice.

Lightly whip the cream and stir it into the purée. Freeze the mixture until creamy, then spread it on to the sponge. Roll this up at once, wrap it in aluminium foil and let it get firm in the freezer for about 1 hour. Sift icing sugar over the roll and serve it with whipped cream and fresh strawberries.

Serves 10 to 12.

Baked Apricot Ice Roll

Roulade glacée aux abricots au gratin

(Illustrated on page 178)

Swiss roll batter (half the recipe
on page 62)
500 g/18 oz fresh, well-ripened
apricots (to yield about
350 ml/12 fl oz purée)
300 g/11 oz sugar
75 cl/2½ fl oz water
2 bitter almonds
2 tablespoons apricot brandy
60 g/2½ oz almond paste
375 ml/12 fl oz double cream
4 egg whites
seeds from 1 vanilla pod
half an apricot
and 2 chocolate leaves
for decoration

Spread the Swiss roll batter into a greased rectangular Swiss roll tin some 25 × 35 cm/10 × 13 in. Bake then cool it thoroughly, covered with a damp cloth. Blanch the apricots, peel, stone and purée them. Bring the 200 g/7 oz sugar, water and coarsely chopped almonds just to the boil, add the brandy and strain. Knead the almond paste with 1 to 2 tablespoons of this sugar syrup, then with an electric beater little by little blend in the remaining syrup and the apricot purée. Cool in the refrigerator and then fold in the lightly whipped cream. Freeze the mixture to a creamy consistency and spread it over the well-chilled sponge cake. Roll it up at once from one of the short sides, wrap it in aluminium foil and leave it to get firm in the freezer for 1 hour. Whip the egg whites and the remaining sugar to a stiff meringue, then add the vanilla seeds. Use a piping bag and star nozzle to pipe the roll in stripes set closely together and spread the rest of the meringue over the ends. Cook under the grill, until the meringue is edged with brown. Decorate with half an apricot and 2 chocolate leaves.

Serves 10.

Moulds and other Utensils

Basically it may be assumed that almost all desserts can be made with the normal range of utensils found in a well-equipped home kitchen. But others in use among professional cooks have proved their worth in a thousand ways, and everyone interested in fine dessert-making will find certain moulds and other special tools very useful. The former in particular can be bought quite cheaply.

The choice of utensils available, especially where moulds are concerned, is so wide that only a small selection can be shown here. But equipment necessary for particular recipes is shown in the step-by-step pictures.

1 **Electric mixer.** These domestic machines operate on the same principle as the large machines used by professional pastry cooks. They do an excellent job and are to be preferred to any hand-operated mixer. Ideal for cake batters, meringue, yeast dough and choux paste.

2 **Stainless steel balloon whisk and wooden spatula.**

3 **Greaseproof paper** for lining baking sheets.

4 **Wood-framed sieve** for confectioner's custard or fruit purée.

5 **Wire cake rack and tin,** ideal for draining glazed desserts.

6 **Individual savarin or rum baba moulds.**

7 **Ring mould,** fluted or straight-sided.

8 **Round and boat-shaped tartlet tins.**

9 **Brioche tins** of various sizes.

10 **Petits fours moulds,** for lining with pastry.

11 **Pastry cutters:** a fairly wide selection saves extra work.

12 **Piping bag and nozzles:** it is important to have various sizes of both.

13 **Straight-edged palette knife,** helps to smooth pastry surfaces evenly.

14 **Palette knives or spatulas** in varying sizes, for spreading whipped cream etc.

15 **Long-bladed knife,** for trimming sponge cake or pastry.

16 **Metal spatula,** for making chocolate straws and cleaning baking sheets.

17 **Fruit/vegetable knife,** useful for shaping very small decorations.

18 **Potato or melon ballers,** circular and oval, for shaping pieces of fruit.

19 **Cannelle knife for citrus fruit** will take off strips of rind of equal width.

20 **Dough scraper and decorating comb,** made of plastic or rubber.

21 **Natural bristle pastry brush,** for applying fruit glazes.

22 **Individual moulds** for cream caramel and custards.

23 **Ice bombe moulds,** with and without lids.

24 **Measuring jug** in clear plastic.

25 **Spring action** ice cream scoop.

26 **Sugar thermometer.**

27 **Saccharometer,** for measuring the sugar density of syrups for fruit ices.

INDEX